FUN & UNBELIEVABLE BASEBALL FACTS FOR KIDS

A Collection of Fascinating Trivia, Jaw-Dropping Home Runs, and Quirky Rituals to Live the Magic of America's Favorite Sport, Together!

W. Bo Cricklewood

INTRODUCTION

Baseball isn't just a game. Nope, it's a whole universe packed with more incredible tales than there are stitches on a regulation ball (that's 108, by the way—but we'll get to that later!). We're talking about a sport where every crack of the bat, every slide into home, and every "Hey batta batta!" from the stands is part of a story that's been unfolding for over 150 years.

"Why should I care about baseball facts?"

Let me put it this way: Imagine you're at a game with your grandpa. The batter steps up to the plate, and suddenly, your grandpa leans over and whispers, "Did you know that guy once hit a home run so far, it knocked a hot dog out of a fan's hand in the upper deck?" Cowabunga! Suddenly, you're not just watching a game—you're part of a secret club, sharing in the magic that makes baseball more than just nine innings of throwing and hitting. That's the power of baseball trivia. It's like a secret handshake that connects fans across generations. It's the reason why a 10-year-old kid can have an awesome conversation with an 80-year-old superfan. Because in baseball, the stories never get old—they just get better, like a well-oiled glove.

Think about it: Where else can you find a guy nicknamed "The Babe" who is just as famous today as he was 100 years ago? Or where a curse involving a goat can keep an entire city on edge for decades? This stuff isn't just trivia—it's the stuff pumping through the veins of every true fan. Baseball is like a time machine. When you learn about a record set in 1920, you're not just learning about a guy swinging a bat—you're peeking into a totally different world. And, suddenly, history class gets a whole lot more interesting, right?

Now, let's talk about why baseball is the ultimate playground for fact lovers and number crunchers. See, baseball has this awesome thing going for it—it's built on numbers that make sense no matter when or where the game is played. Three strikes and you're out? That's been true since your great-great-grandpa was swinging a stick at a rock. Nine innings? Yep, same deal. This means that when someone tells you that a player today hit .300, you can compare that to a player from 50 years ago who also hit

.300. It's like they're playing catch across time! And don't even get me started on the stats. Yup, baseball has more numbers than a math textbook, and each one tells a story. Ever heard of a player's WAR? No, it's not about fighting—it stands for Wins Above Replacement. It's a super cool way to measure how valuable a player is to their team. See? You're learning already!

But baseball facts aren't just about numbers. They're about the heart and soul of the game. They're about the time a pitcher threw a no-hitter while tripping on LSD (yeah, that actually happened), or the day a 3-foot-7-inch player drew a walk because his strike zone was smaller than a postage stamp. These are the stories that make baseball more than a game—they make it a legend.

Knowing these nuggets of baseball gold?

It's like having superpowers at the ballpark. Imagine sitting there, munching on your hot dog, when suddenly the guy next to you says, "Man, I wish something exciting would happen." That's your cue to lean over and say, "Did you know that in 2001, Randy Johnson threw a fastball that exploded a bird in mid-air?" Bam! You're not just watching the game—you're the master of the show! Every fact you learn is like a key that unlocks a whole new part of the game. Learn about how the spitball was banned in 1920, and suddenly you're wondering about all the other crazy pitches players have invented over the years. Hear about the time a player stole first base (yep, you read that right), and you're diving into the rulebook to see what other loopholes might be hiding in there.

That's the beauty of baseball—it rewards the curious. The more you know, the more you want to know. It's like a never-ending scavenger hunt where every clue leads to another adventure. Trust me, once you start down this path, you'll never watch a game the same way again. Every pitch, every play, every random squirrel running across the field becomes a potential piece of baseball history in the making.

This book?

It's your ticket to the wildest, weirdest, most wonderful world of baseball facts out there. We're going to cover everything from record-breaking feats that'll make your jaw drop, to superstitions so bizarre you'll wonder if these players are from another planet. We'll dig into legendary home runs that defied gravity, plays so unbelievable you'd swear they were CGI if you didn't see them with your own eyes, and stories so strange you couldn't make them up if you tried. But this is just the beginning. Think of each fact in this book as a first pitch—it's up to you to swing for the fences and see where it takes you. Maybe you'll read about a player's quirky pre-game ritual and decide to dive deeper into the psychology of sports. Or perhaps a crazy coincidence will spark your interest in the mathematical probabilities in baseball. The possibilities are as endless as a game with no time limit (which, by the way, is another cool thing about baseball).

Just like in baseball, the most important thing is to keep your eye on the ball. In this case, the "ball" is your curiosity. Follow it wherever it leads you and you'll discover a whole new level of love for this amazing game. Every great baseball fan started by learning their first fascinating fact. Maybe it was the number of stitches on a baseball, or the reason why players wear stirrups, or blood of the friendly people to whom Norway would necessarily look for assistance in time of need, and on whom she depends, not only for the continuance of her present prosperity and independence, but for her existence as one of the foremost seafaring nations of the world.[2]

Ihlen replied a few days later, claiming the right of neutral states to trade with both sides in wartime. But he gave in nonetheless, signing a 'Copper Agreement' on 30 August which stopped the export of copper to Germany.

Through these two compacts Britain gained a significant degree of control over Norway's economy and trade; but the amity was not to last. On 18 December Britain accused the Norwegians of not adhering to either agreement. Retribution was not long in coming. On the 22nd Britain imposed a coal embargo on Norway. This was nearly a disaster. The winter of 1916/17 was one of the worst in recent history and bitter cold. Not only industry but the population too suffered, just as they had in the Napoleonic Wars 100 years earlier. Schools closed, locomotives were fired by wood, restaurants and shops reduced their hours, people shivered and froze. Both economic and population survival were at stake. The embargo did not end until mid-February 1917, when Norway informed the British government that they were willing to cease all pyrites exports to Germany. Might is right.

Coal as a Weapon

The nineteenth century was built on coal. As late as 1850 Britain was producing more than twice the amount of coal as the rest of the world put together, and it was the need to pump water out of the coal mines which had driven the development of the 'prime mover' of Britain's Industrial Revolution, the steam engine.

The war of 1914–18 was powered by coal. Men, mills and machines required high-quality coal, as did steamships, navies and countless industrial and domestic activities, and the best coal came from Britain. In the South Wales coalfields Britain had the optimal coal for naval and industrial purposes; Welsh steam coal. South Wales also had a highly-developed infrastructure for extracting and transporting the coal to the coast, from where the world's largest collier fleet could move it to any of the global network of British coaling stations; or to Britain's favoured allies and neutrals.

Before the war, France's imports of coal had been around a half to a third of its domestic consumption. But France had become utterly dependant on British coal from August 1914 onwards. The German invasion cost France fourteen per cent of its total industrial output. Before the war the areas now occupied by the German army and the trenches had produced seventy-five per cent of all French coal output, eighty-one per cent of its iron and sixty-three per cent of its steel. Only coal from the United Kingdom kept French industry alive. The *Bureau National des Charbons* centralised the import requirements and sent them to a British Coal Controller, based at the Board of Trade, who arranged the delivery of the necessary tonnages through liaison with the colliery and collier owners. The coal carriers were also instructed by the Board as to which port they should load and unload their shipments.

Germany gained an extra supply of coal from the takeover of the Belgian mines, which gave her some additional 23 million tons,[3] but had already been largely self-sufficient, producing nearly three times as much coal as France pre-war, at 114 million tons. Britain by contrast produced 290 million tons in 1913. When Italy joined the Allies in 1915, part of the 'deal' offered to her was access to coal, for she was almost entirely dependent on imports.

None of the Scandinavian states was self-sufficient in coal. In 1913 they imported 10.3 million tons of coal, ninety-five per cent of which came from Britain.[4] They depended on Britain for supplies; and this gave the Allies a weapon. The Admiralty had taken the lead in using coal as a tool of war by refusing bunker coal for ships in the iron ore trade from Narvik, and in July 1915 had extended the system for all ships carrying goods of enemy destination or origin. There would be no coal available to such vessels once they had left their home port.

Furthermore, Norway's merchant marine had become rather a specialist in the coal trade between Britain and France. This proved very profitable for the Norwegian shipowners as, for the reasons given above, this trade boomed during the early years of the war, and freight rates blossomed with it. The cost of transporting a ton of coal from Cardiff to the French Channel ports rose from 4s 3d in July 1914 to 23s in July 1916.[5]

But in May 1916 the British and French authorities announced that they had reached an agreement imposing maximum rates on the coal trade. In addition, neutrals had to accept these terms if they wanted bunker coal. After threatening to stop sailing, the Norwegian ship owners negotiated somewhat better conditions and complied.

Norway had again felt the weight of this weapon at the end of 1916; they would not be the last country to so suffer. Coal was important everywhere, and Britain had it.

America and the Declaration of London

America continued to insist on the rights of the sea and the obligations of the London agreements. On 26 May she sent a diplomatic note to the British Government, protesting against the searching of mails. It made little difference. On 7 July 1916 Britain issued an Order in Council rescinding Declaration of London of 1909 and reassumed her traditional maritime rights. The French Government followed suit.

On 28 July the United States Government formally protested to the British Government against the 'Black List' policy. This too had little effect. Britain was in a war to the knife at last.

President Wilson was enraged by Britain's abrogation of the Declaration of London and by the 'Black List'. He asked Congress for powers to deny Allied shipping access to American ports in retaliation. But by the time such powers were granted, in September 1916, it could be seen that such an action would jeopardise the very considerable profits that US companies were making out of the European war.

In any event, the hackles of US shippers and manufacturers had been to some extent smoothed by the introduction of 'navicerts', which removed some of the risk and more onerous conditions imposed by the Royal Navy's blockade. Navicerts were a system whereby the British Embassy at Washington received applications from any intending shippers from the United States who wished to know whether a particular consignment proposed to be sent by them to a neutral country was likely to meet with difficulties in getting through Royal Navy patrols. Before responding to the request the Embassy staff contacted the new Ministry of Blockade, which would telegraph by return a response as to whether the goods were considered undesirable or not. The classical education of the British civil servant now came to the fore. If the shipment was considered unwanted, the reply was *'nolo'* (Latin for 'I do not want'). If acceptable, *'accipe'* (take) was the response; and if further investigation was required *'pendens'* (hanging). In this way the bureaucrats thought to keep the system from the prying eyes of the assumedly less classically-educated Americans and Germans. Once a certificate had been granted, the ship could sail knowing that possession of it would spare any problems with interception and investigation.

On Patrol

While the diplomats argued, the work of patrolling the seaways and hunting for U-boats went on. A swept channel some 540 miles long, from Dover to the Firth of Forth, and a mile wide had to be maintained and kept free of mines and U-boats had to be deterred from entering the area. Much of this work on the eastern coast of Britain was conducted by auxiliary vessels, trawlers, drifters and sometimes luxury yachts.

One such yacht was the 1894-built, 270-ton *Evening Star* belonging to Lady Alexander Paget, the widowed daughter-in-law of Henry Paget, 2nd Marquess of Anglesey. At the outbreak of war her husband's cousin, Admiral Alfred Wyndham Paget, sixty-two years old and who had retired from the navy in 1911, volunteered the yacht, and himself to command it, for naval service. The brother of the MP Almeric Hugh Paget, 1st and only Baron Queenborough, the admiral had last served afloat in 1906, but this did not stop him answering his country's call. The Admiralty accepted both the yacht and the admiral, giving him the rank of commander in the RNR, and sent them to the Humber to serve on anti-submarine duties in the swept coastal channel.

Paget chronicled his adventures in letters to his wife Viti, who was serving in France as a volunteer nurse in the Hospital Anglais, Nevers. It would appear that the yacht was a poor sailer in the conditions of the North Sea. 'Steamed well, but under heavy seas sweeping along deck seas poured down [into the cabins].'[6] After two days on patrol he was moved to report: 'I don't think I can possibly stay out more than three days as navigating is anxious to work in the offing, honeycombed with shallows and all shore lights put out'.[7] Four days later he added: 'she is a devil to steer and going into the long lock [at Immingham] crowded with destroyers with a swishing tide race outside is a hard trial.'[8]

Of course, what he really wanted was to bag a U-boat. 'I am longing to spot a German submarine. Still there is always something exciting ... I feel that I am just doing something for the country.'[9] Quite how his two ancient 6pdr guns would have fared against a U-boat's deck gun and torpedoes is open to question. But the effrontery of the Germans amused him. 'German U-boats have recently surfaced alongside trawlers to ask for fish', he noted.[10] But he was fairly happy with his lot. 'I would love a faster and bigger yacht but I love all my officers', he told his wife.[11] His wish came true the following April, when he took command of the Immingham-based yacht *Eileen*, originally built in Glasgow for Solomon B Joel*, 910grt and requisitioned in November 1914 to be fitted with two 12pdr guns.**

Jellicoe certainly appreciated the efforts of the old admiral and his ilk, writing: 'Sir Alfred, in common with many other officers who took up this work, was over sixty but age did not discourage these gallant seamen from facing the hardship and discomfort of service in the North Sea.'[12]

Another of these unlikely warships was the yacht *Mekong*, based at Immingham and acting as a sort of flagship for the random collection of small boats which worked from the port. She had a colourful history. Built as the *Maund* in 1906 by Ramage & Ferguson of Leith, she was 199ft long and of around 900 tons, with two boilers and a single screw. Her first owner was Adam Mortimer Singer, son of the founder of the Singer Sewing Machine empire and a British citizen since 1900. For her first voyage Singer sailed her to Stockholm, where King Oscar II paid a visit to the vessel. She then passed through several hands before becoming the property of Ferdinand d'Orléans, Duc de Montpensier, younger brother of the Orléanist claimant to the throne of France.

In April 1915 the Admiralty found her docked at Southampton and promptly requisitioned her under wartime emergency powers. She was commissioned into the Royal Navy as HM Yacht *Mekong*, fitted with two 3in guns and put under the command of retired Admiral Frank Finnis with a crew of forty-nine. Finnis, who had retired from the navy in February 1909, returned to the sea as a captain RNR in April 1915 and became *Mekong*'s first (and only) naval commander at the age of sixty-four. Now based on the

---

* A South African-based millionaire financier. The yacht was originally named *Doris* after his daughter, and when requisitioned became *Eileen* after another of his children.

** Paget was to die before the war ended, in June 1918.

Humber, armed and with a relatively powerful wireless as befitted her command position, she and her consorts maintained a patrol of the Yorkshire coast between Humber and Berwick, looking for U-boats.

The Germans were not the only enemy. As through the ages, the weather was sometimes a much worse foe. On 9 March Finnis had sailed to his patrol area. The weather was poor, but by the 11th it had deteriorated significantly, with a strong north-easterly gale driving heavy rain before it. Just after midnight a particularly heavy sea struck the vessel and water entered via the ventilators, filling the cabins below. Finnis decided to make for shelter between Flamborough Head and Filey Brigg, but at 0430 *Mekong* ran on to rocks with heavy seas now breaking over her. Cliffs could be seen about 150 yards away, and signals were made by Very light and gunfire. At 0520 a boat was lowered with five men in it, but it was immediately swept from sight, although the men did struggle to the shore.

There now followed three of those sporadic acts of bravery that seem, in retrospect, to deserve more attention than they attracted at the time. Thirty-one-year-old William Chaplow, a fireman MMR (Mercantile Marine Reserve), attempted to swim ashore with a line but was instead washed against the rocks and drowned. Undeterred, Able Seaman Roger Piper MMR, twenty-one years old, attempted the same thing and suffered the same fate. Finally another engine-room man, Ernest Thorn, succeeded in getting ashore and raising the alarm, an act of courage that was rendered nugatory by the arrival of the Filey Rocket Brigade, a coastguard rescue unit. As the waves continued to drive the boat ashore at a spot known as the Chimney Hole, they manged to get a line out to the stricken boat and set up a breeches buoy to haul the crew up to safety on the shore. Even now disaster was lurking, and Able Seaman John Davies MMR fell from the line to his death. Because of his age, Finnis was spared the traditional requirement that the captain is the last man to abandon his ship, his first lieutenant taking that role.

The subsequent court of enquiry decided that no one was at fault, a verdict with which the Admiralty disagreed. They thought that faulty navigation by Lieutenant George Parker RNR was to blame and that 'the mistake indicated ignorance rather than negligence'.[13] Parker's commission was cancelled and he was discharged from the navy. As for Fireman Chaplow, Finnis wrote to his wife of just eight months, Gertrude: 'His gallant efforts to get onshore to render us assistance will never be forgotten, and you may rest assured that his death was as noble as if he had been killed in action.'[14]

A 'Neutral with Reservations'

By 1916 the British blockade was being felt severely in Sweden. Unemployment and serious food shortages were beginning to bite. Swedish ships were kept in British harbours and prevented from returning home. Under the 'Black List' orders of 23 December 1915, Britain had blacklisted Swedish firms and businessmen who were assumed to be trading with Germany. Their goods were stopped from passing the Northern Blockade without proofs that they would not be re-exported from Sweden to the enemy. As noted in Chapter 6, Swedish Prime Minister Hammarskjöld refused to accept these strictures regarding non-re-export guarantees, and this further ramped up the tension.

Germany had been consistently 'leaning on' Sweden to close the entrance to the Baltic completely. For Germany the Baltic Sea was a key pressure point. Sweden and Denmark between them controlled the access to the Baltic Sea. This was a source of historic great concern to Germany, as it also meant that these two countries commanded the approach to much of Germany's coastline and to the important port and naval base of Kiel, one of two *Reichskriegshäfen* (Imperial War Harbours).

As early as 1906, Fisher had exploited this concern by sending the Channel Fleet into the Baltic during the Algeciras Conference, putting pressure on the Germans with muttered asides of 'Copenhagening' their Baltic fleet. When war came Fisher was insistent the Baltic was a decisive area of operation and 'emphasised that blockade was the one instrument that could make naval power effective on land. He agreed ... that a commercial blockade of a vital trade route would ultimately force the enemy fleet to sea. This would require the Royal Navy to threaten Germany's only vital maritime route; the iron ore traffic across the Baltic.'[15]

Just before Britain entered the war, First Lord Winston Churchill asked the War Office to study plans for amphibious landings at Ekersund (Norway), Laeso Channel (Denmark) and Kungsbacka Fjord (Sweden); all neutral territory. By December 1914 Churchill was pressing a Baltic operation on Prime Minister Asquith, which the latter declined on the basis that it would violate Danish territorial waters. Churchill followed this up with a memo to the War Council of 25 January 1915 stating that 'the ultimate object of the navy was to obtain access to the Baltic ... this operation was of great importance as Germany was, and always had been, very nervous of an attack from the Baltic'.[16]

Churchill had set May 1915 as the target date for securing control of the Baltic. The Danes got wind of what might be planned and regarded the consequences for their country as extremely dangerous, as it would undoubtedly bring about a German invasion. 'There were reportedly sighs of relief when ... Churchill left office in 1915.'[17] This relief was shared by the British Foreign Office.

There were other reasons for this focus on Baltic operations too, not least the fact that since the start of the war some ninety-two British and Allied merchant vessels had been trapped in the Baltic, in Swedish and Russian ports, unable to get out because of mines and submarines, and the ever-present German naval threat. By mid-1915 the demands on shipping were such that their putative availability could no longer be ignored. An Anglo-Swedish syndicate was formed to extract them, and some of the ships began to make the perilous passage through the Sound, Katttegat and Skaggerak by hugging the Swedish and Norwegian coast and staying in their territorial waters. Individual Swedish naval officers behaved with bravery on occasion to protect these transiting vessels, as for instance on 16 November, when the Swedish torpedo boat *Pollux* (two 6pdr, two 3pdr guns, two torpedo tubes) cleared for action when a German torpedo boat threatened the steamer SS *Thelma* in Swedish waters north of Malmo. And on 23 January 1916 the Swedish torpedo boat *Castor* (similarly armed to *Pollux*), with Prince Wilhelm of Sweden* on the bridge, saw off a pair of German destroyers which were trying to capture the *F D Lambert*. Wilhelm also saved the *Dunrobin* in the June. A total of twenty-nine ships made their escape, but the Germans knew that blocking the channel would make it a certainty that the remainder could not leave.

On 28 July the Swedes finally gave in to German pressure, their decision no doubt influenced by the ongoing dispute with Britain, including blockade and bunker restrictions. They mined the Kogrundsrännan channel running through the Øresund Straits and

---

* Prince Wilhelm, Duke of Södermanland, second son of King Gustav V.

announced it was closed to all but Swedish ships, which would be led through the minefields by pilots. This shut Germany's enemies out of, or in, the Baltic Sea for the duration. It also meant that British ships could no longer hug Falsterbo to exit the Baltic, but had to leave Swedish waters, and make for the Drogden Channel, where they were bound to be captured by German patrols. The Allies were, unsurprisingly, critical, describing Sweden as 'neutral with reservations' at a meeting on 8 August.[18]

But all was not considered lost. On 4 August the British Consuls at Kristiania and Gothenburg were directed to send as many as possible of all the trapped vessels that wished to reach the United Kingdom into Stavanger, there to await further orders. Eleven such vessels were eventually collected. Jellicoe was on leave from the Grand Fleet, with Admiral Cecil Burney standing in for him, and Burney arranged to send eight destroyers to meet these merchant ships off Utsire at 0500 on the 12th and escort them across the North Sea until darkness, when they would be met by the Peterhead Patrol. However, a dense fog prevented the escort from sailing and the rendezvous was delayed by 24 hours. The convoy finally sailed on the 13th.

The delay had favoured the Germans, who became aware of the gathering and directed U-boats to the coast, but the convoy was well marshalled and put to sea at 9 knots. At 1400, seven of the steamers with four destroyers went on at 11 knots, and arrived safely off Peterhead at about 1600 on the 14th, followed by the slow division some eight hours later. There were no losses. It is probable that the foggy weather aided the passage, for many had been doubtful whether the crossing could be made without suffering a U-boat attack. Eleven merchant ships had enjoyed an escort of twelve warships in total (eight destroyers plus the Peterhead vessels), a never-to-be-repeated ratio. But in this crossing was laid the germ of an idea which would come of age at the beginning of the following year; convoy.

The merchant ships which still remained trapped were a constant source of irritation. On one occasion a Swedish businessman, Ivan Lignell, offered to purchase the ships and try and pass them through under a Swedish flag, but his offer was rejected by the Admiralty on the grounds that, using the Treaty of London as their justification, the Germans would repudiate the validity of the transfer in time of war.

Hunting for Contraband

The 10th Cruiser Squadron, manning the Northern Patrol, was tasked with intercepting ships and contraband trying to enter the North Sea by blocking the Norway–Shetland–Iceland gap. But there was still traffic which escaped their attentions and other ships whose voyages originated inside the North Sea in Norwegian, Swedish and Danish ports and which might carry contraband goods. Occasional patrols were sent out from Scapa Flow to look for them, and it was a duty not much sought after. Lieutenant Stephen King-Hall was an officer in the light cruiser HMS *Southampton,* and his ship was sent on such a mission in September 1916. The biggest problem was the weather. In his diary King-Hall wrote:

> We picked up a gale almost at once and during the first watch at about 2300. A very heavy sea landed on the bridge, smashed up a searchlight, carried away the bridge ladder, bust in the bridge opposite the wheel, and did other damage. The Gunner (T), Morgans, had his head cut open. When I came on watch at Midnight we had eased to 15; it was blowing and raining very hard. I was feeling very seasick. At 0300 I had a cup of cocoa, which I held on to until 0330, when I was very sea-sick until 0400.

He continued:

> During the forenoon we went to control drill, and at 1300, being in the vicinity of the Little Fisher Bank [off the Danish coast] … we went to action stations. We remained thus until 0400, when we turned West. I managed to snatch a couple of hours' sleep on a gun cover, stretched on the floor of the after control. It was not very nice, being extremely draughty and wet. Booth eventually came and lay down with me, and we got a little mutual warmth.[19]

On another occasion it was the severe cold that made the patrol almost unbearable.

> We swept up from the Naze to about 60° N. It was a lovely day, but bitterly cold, and … was extraordinarily unpleasant. In fact, I was chilled to the bone in the foretop, and was laid up

for twenty-four hours on arrival in harbour. The Norwegian coast was covered with snow, and had not the cold been acute I should have appreciated the magnificent panorama of rocky coastline and distant mountains which unrolled itself along our starboard hand as we steamed north.[20]

In August 1916 two such patrols were carried out, as usual by light cruisers, between 31 July–3 August and 8–10 August. Neither sortie produced any results other than tired and cold crews. For the third attempt that month a different strategy was devised.

Dundee and *King Orry* were armed boarding steamers, civilian vessels until wartime and now used, owing to their size and comparative (to a larger warship) agility, to stop and search vessels suspected of carrying contraband. *Dundee* had been built by Caledon Shipbuilders at its Dundee yards and was launched on 24 August 1911. In November of that year she entered service with the Dundee, Perth & London Shipping Company as a small cargo/passenger carrier, and sailed for them until the outbreak of the war. Of 2,187grt and capable of 15 knots, fast enough to catch most merchant ships she would encounter, she was lightly armed with two 4in guns and two 3pdrs, and was, of course, completely unarmoured. *King Orry* was built by Cammell Laird at Birkenhead in 1913 for the Isle of Man Steam Packet Company. Of 1,877grt, she could reach 21 knots and was taken up by the navy in November 1914. Both were based at the Shetland Islands for operations with the Northern Patrol.

One problem for the light cruisers was that they were very obviously warships and could be sighted at a distance, allowing their intended prey to escape. This was not the case with the two steamers; with very little work they could be made to resemble the harmless merchant ships that they once were. It was in this guise that they were deployed into the North Sea on 15 August (the *King Orry* now temporarily named the *Viking Orry*), supported at a safe distance and well to seaward by two destroyers and the brand-new (January 1916) 'C'-class light cruiser HMS *Constance*. The *Dundee* was stationed between Utsire and Lister, and the *King Orry* off Stadlandet. Their orders laid down that no vessels were to be boarded or molested inside the four miles limit off the Norwegian coast.

The plan soon met with success. On the 17th the Norwegian SS *Britannic*, carrying 3,200 tons of magnetic iron ore from Kerkeness to Rotterdam, was intercepted by the *King Orry* eight miles off Utvaer and sent into Kirkwall under an armed guard. It was a major capture of a valuable resource, clearly intended for Germany. So far as the rest of the little force could tell, no other German nor neutral steamers ventured outside territorial waters, but hugged the coast line to avoid detention. For the rest of the year *King Orry* remained on the station, enduring continuous foul weather, until sent for a much-needed refit in Liverpool. The light cruiser crews did not miss being on such duty.

Wilson Lines

While this generally fruitless patrolling was taking place, shipping businesses whose traditional source of income came from trade across the North Sea were being hit particularly hard by the war; none more so than Wilson Line of Hull. Founded in 1841 as Thomas Wilson and Co, and with the core of their operations involving trade (initially iron ore) with, and passengers from (particularly emigrants *en route* to the New World), Norway and Sweden, Wilson's entered the steam shipping business in the early 1850s and experienced rapid growth through the 1860s, 1870s and 1880s. At the opening of the twentieth century it was described by no less than *The Times* as the largest privately-owned shipping line in the world. With regard to Hull, from the early 1890s down to the war the Wilson Line owned at least half of the tonnage registered in the port. Resplendent in the house livery of red, black-topped funnels, brown derricks, white upper works and green hulls, their ships were known to the locals as 'Wilson's Parrots'. Chaired by Lord Nunburnholme (already met in the previous chapter), the beginning of the war saw them highly profitable and operating eighty-four ships of various types.

But the war treated the firm badly. From the start they suffered heavy losses (in the course of the war the company was to lose forty vessels, all but four to German torpedoes or mines). And three weeks in 1916 broke the heart of the shareholders and their resolve that they could remain profitable, for they lost three of their most prestigious and largest vessels to enemy action.

The SS *Calypso* (2,876grt) had been taken up by the Admiralty at the start of the war (as HMS *Calyx*) for use as an AMC and armed with eight 4.7in guns. However, she proved unsatisfactory in the role and was returned to Wilson's in June 1915. On 10 July 1916 she was sailing from London to Kristiania with general cargo when she was torpedoed and sunk by *U-53* (Hans Rose) fifteen miles west of Listafjord, Norway. All thirty crewmen on board lost their lives, including the Master, C C Smith.

The SS *Eskimo* (3,326grt) had also been taken up by the Admiralty and returned as unsuitable. On 26 July she was captured as a prize by the German auxiliary cruiser *Moewe* (sailing as the *Vineta*), under her famous commander *Korvettenkapitän* Nikolaus Burggraf und Graf zu Dohna-Schlodien, at Risor in Norway, the only success of *Moewe*'s second cruise.[*]

Then, on 1 August, the SS *Aaro* (2,603grt) was on her way from Hull to Kristiania. She was twenty-five miles off Stavanger when she was torpedoed by *U-20* (Walther Schwieger). Three crewmen died, including sixty-six-year-old mess steward Edward Proctor of Hawthorn Avenue, Hull.

This situation was now of great concern to the Wilson family, and the decision was taken to sell the company to Sir John Ellerman, reputedly the richest man in Britain and owner of the Ellerman Line, for £4.3 million. The Wilson Line was never the same force again.

---

[*] For the full story of the *Moewe*, see Dunn S R, *Blockade*, Seaforth Publishing (Barnsley, 2016).

CHAPTER 8

A Mounting Crisis, 1916–1917

The U-boats were out in force. On one day alone, 21 October 1916, the Scandinavian neutrals lost thirteen vessels. The *UB-18* sank three, *UB-22* and *UB-39* claimed two each, and *UB-35*, *U-71*, *UB-23*, *UB-29*, *UB-30* and *UB-21* one apiece.

Up to August 1916 the greatest number of Norwegian ships sunk in a month was thirteen, but in September and October the losses rose to twenty-nine and fifty-six respectively. Those of the Swedes rose from a monthly rate of nine to twenty in October.[1]

The losses of ships engaged in the Scandinavian trade to U-boats and mines had become too much for Norway to bear. As Jellicoe himself noted, in October 1916: 'The losses to Norwegian and Swedish ships was three times as great as the previous highest month.'[2] In the final quarter of 1916, 160,000 tons of Norwegian shipping was sunk. The Norwegian Bureau of War Insurance refused to insure certain types of voyage, and there were rumours that freight and ship insurance premiums were going to increase and that the Anglo-French coal trade, which was dominated by Norwegian merchant ships, was in jeopardy.

Losses in the North Sea were not the only problem that Norway's merchant marine faced. In the autumn of 1916 German submarines made their way to the Arctic Sea. At the end of September they started to sink ships engaged in traffic with Russia through Archangel, a completely new development. Norwegian public opinion was incensed. Newspapers ran headlines such as '*De døde kalder*' (the dead are calling),[3] and the press demanded that the government take action. On 13 October the Norwegian state issued a Royal Decree stating that 'submarines equipped for warfare and belonging to a belligerent Power, must not navigate or stay in

Norwegian maritime territory. If they violate this prohibition, they risk being attacked by armed forces without warning',[4] although the edict did not come into effect until January 1917.

Germany was much angered and threatened retribution, but did not in the end press her protest to an ultimatum, perhaps being more occupied by a proposal from Imperial Chancellor Bethmann-Hollweg that President Wilson of the United States arbitrate between the warring powers to achieve a negotiated peace. Germany considered that it was in a position of strength to dictate terms.

But while this contretemps took place there was serious talk of Norway entering the war on the Allied side. At the Foreign Office, Eyre Crowe suggested that Britain's interests might be best served if Norway entered the war on the allied side, for 'If the only way for Norway to avoid capitulation [to German threats] is to resist even at the cost of rupture with Germany, then, from a blockade point of view, it is to the advantage of the Allied cause that Norway should enter the war'.[5]

Thus the British Foreign Office asked the Admiralty and Jellicoe at Scapa to devise a plan to support Norway in the event of a German invasion, demonstrating what a naval writer later described rather tartly as 'an exaggerated idea of the potency of the Grand Fleet, and assumed that British naval power could ensure Norwegian territory from invasion'.[6] Actually, Jellicoe and his staff believed that there was little that they could do. The Admiralty could not afford to send a force of any strength to Norwegian waters, and there was no base in southern Norway capable of accommodating a fleet superior to the High Seas Fleet. Jellicoe could only promise to base the 2nd Cruiser Squadron (five armoured cruisers, a type that he had come to distrust), with nine submarines and sixteen destroyers at Kristiansand if necessary.

Meanwhile, on 23 September, the Norwegian government made a formal request through the British Board of Trade for their ships to be given protection by the Royal Navy, her own naval forces being inadequate in number and design. Norwegian shipowners had been prompted to ask for this request by their insurers, and the Board of Trade supported the entreaty.

This caused alarm in many government quarters, as it was thought that the Scandinavians might hold up sailings, disrupting vital supplies of materials such as ores, wood and nitrates to the war industry, should their request not be granted. Certainly this was a clear and present danger, for in November Norwegian crews threatened to refuse to sail without more effective protection.* What could be done?

Protected Sailing

The Norwegian request was not received with much enthusiasm at the Admiralty. The Trade Division, under Captain Richard Webb RN, was 'stoutly opposed to convoy'[7] and proposed a patrolled route between Shetland and Norway. This was rubbished by Vice Admiral Sir Henry Oliver, Chief of the War Staff, who with his usual acuity pointed out that this would require at least ten ships stationed twenty miles apart and always at sea (which meant more like twenty in total); vessels which neither he nor anyone else could spare. Oliver suggested instead a system of controlled sailings on the same lines as was provided for the protection of the Dutch traffic, with merchantmen assembling and crossing on prearranged days, while grumpily complaining that 'it had never been contemplated that we should have a big enough navy to protect the whole of the world's commerce'.[8]

This proposal was given to Jellicoe at Scapa to implement, and he passed it to Vice Admiral Sir Frederic Brock, commanding Orkney and Shetland, whose armed trawlers would be an important part of any escort provided. But the wheels of change grind slow, and it was not until 15 December that the Admiralty authorised Brock's plans, and the first 'protected sailings' took place between Shetland and Norway only on 29 January and 10 February 1917.

While the wheels had ground around, and rather less than helpfully, the Norwegian Legation was presented with some very general advice for Norwegian masters, 'including the somewhat comfortless recommendation that they should study closely the positions and times of sinkings of other Norwegian vessels'.[9] And although no Norwegian vessels were lost to U-boats in the North Sea during November, ten were sunk in December, by eight different assailants.

Brock's approved plan fixed a number of alternative routes between Norway and Shetland which were to be used by all vessels trading between Scandinavia and the Allied countries. The main part of the passage was intended to be made by night. The route in

---

* In fact, Norwegian ships did not sail for eighteen days at the end of 1916.

use at any particular time terminated at the western end with a daybreak rendezvous point which was patrolled by local forces from the Orkneys and Shetland Islands, assisted when possible by small craft from the Grand Fleet. These vessels also provided the initial escort for fifty miles of the eastern passage. The Senior Naval Officer, Lerwick, was in charge of the detailed arrangements.

It was intended that ships would sail alone through these protected sea lanes, but at first individual ships were escorted through the east-bound 'daylight leg'. On 24 February the initial group sailing took place, a sort of proto-convoy of eight Norwegian ships and one British merchant vessel. They were escorted by a destroyer, a whaler and two armed trawlers for the first fifty miles east of Lerwick harbour. Subsequent sailings were usually of merchant ships in pairs.

For the return trip, vessels were supposed to cross from Bergen at night and be met by armed trawlers fifty miles from Lerwick. This rarely worked out in practice, navigating and dead reckoning at night being rather challenging for many merchant masters and RN captains alike.

Generally, convoying remained a temporary measure, and throughout February and March it was more usual for vessels to be escorted singly or in pairs.

Change at the Top

One reason that it had taken so long for the proposals regarding protected sailing to be approved was the decision to change the top echelons of the Admiralty in the search for a more dynamic approach to the war. On 11 December 1916 Sir Edward Carson became First Lord; a week earlier Admiral Jellicoe had been offered and had accepted (not without reservations) the post of First Sea Lord.

Jellicoe had commanded the Grand Fleet since the outbreak of war, groomed for the role by Fisher over many years. He had been appointed by Churchill as war was declared, replacing the incumbent CinC, Admiral Sir George Callaghan. Jellicoe protested so much against taking the role in this manner that it almost verged on insubordination. Now he had another role that he appeared not to relish, telling a small group of officers that he expected to last only six months in the post. That he 'was a very tired man when he came to Whitehall … after twenty-seven months in the most exacting and responsible of sea-going commands', and the fact that he 'had always shown a reluctance to delegate',[10] would tell against him.

Carson was the leader of the Unionist cause, a strong advocate for Ulster and Northern Ireland. He had made his reputation as a formidable barrister, not least when he represented the Marquess of Queensbury in the case that destroyed Oscar Wilde, and had served as Attorney General when the coalition government was formed in May 1915. Prime Minster Asquith felt he was rather pushed into appointing Carson, whom he did not hold in high regard, calling him 'ambitious, at the same time histrionic and arrogant on the surface and vacillating and infirm of purpose down below'.[11] Carson resigned from the coalition ministry on 19 October 1915, thus becoming the *de facto* leader of those Unionists who were not members of the government, effectively Leader of the Opposition in the Commons. When Lloyd George defenestrated Asquith (*vide infra*) and became prime minister he appointed Carson to the Admiralty, as Carson had supported his putsch and to keep the Unionists 'on side'. Carson 'always went along with the naval members of the [Admiralty] Board very readily',[12] but this lack of challenge ensured that the same old nostrums were trotted out and little new thinking developed.

Jellicoe's replacement as CinC Grand Fleet at Scapa was David Beatty. Had he not been a senior and decorated officer in the Royal Navy, Vice Admiral David Richard Beatty might have been considered a bit of a cad. Even with his status guaranteed there were always 'elements of a bounder'[13] about him. Appointed the youngest commander in the Royal Navy in November 1898 at the age of twenty-seven years and ten months, and captain just two years later, he had been advanced to flag rank in January 1910 by order in council, as he had not completed the necessary time at sea as a captain. He then committed himself to the wilderness of half pay by turning down the appointment of second-in-command of the Atlantic Fleet, preferring to remain at home.

One reason for this preference was that he had pursued the heiress of the Marshall Field's department store, the extraordinarily wealthy Ethel Tree, a married woman who Beatty, a reckless and fanatical huntsman, had met and fallen for on the hunting field. After some 'will they/won't they', Ethel obtained a divorce and she and Beatty married in 1901, which made him wealthy and independent. It also meant that Beatty was an object of suspicion in certain society circles; marrying a divorcee in such circumstances was considered rather *infra dig.*

In 1911 he attended the Royal Naval War College, where his instructors found him 'smart & able; apt to be rash in conclusion'.[14] Overall he was placed fifth in order of merit out of eight flag officers on the course.

Nonetheless, in 1913 Beatty obtained the command of the 1st Battlecruiser Squadron, a prime plum for a dashing officer and largely granted as a result of Churchill's influence. (Later, on 8 February 1915, he would command all the battlecruisers, which were given the designation 'Battlecruiser Fleet'.)

With his non-regulation three-button monkey jacket and his cap worn at a rakish angle he was manna to the press and an instant public darling. From August 1914 he served directly under Jellicoe. His performance in this role, and especially at Jutland, has divided historians ever since, but it is fair to say that he probably could have done better. His actions as First Sea Lord after the war, to rewrite history in a light more favourable to him and sometimes at considerable variance with the truth, did him little credit.

With Jellicoe's sublimation to the post of First Sea Lord, Beatty took his place as CinC Grand Fleet, based at Scapa Flow, on 4 December. By now he was involved in another love affair with a married woman, Eugénie Godfrey-Faussett, the wife of a fellow officer (and naval aide-de-camp to the King from 1915 until 1918). Eugénie remained his mistress for a decade.

Jellicoe had been a centraliser and recognised as a good administrator. Beatty was unproven in this regard; indeed, just before these changes happened, Prime Minister Asquith (with days left to serve, had he but known it) wrote to First Lord Arthur Balfour (who was likewise unaware of his own demise): 'I quite realise the difficulty of taking him [Jellicoe] at this moment from the Grand Fleet, especially as his only possible successor in the command (I am sure you would agree) from the combatant point of view is Beatty, who, with all his fine fighting qualities, is yet comparatively untried in the domain of fleet administration on a large scale.'[15]

However, Beatty quickly surrounded himself with a by-and-large highly competent staff. They and he would now be responsible for the control and direction of the protection of the Scandinavian convoy system.

The French Coal Trade

The importance of Norwegian ships to the French coal trade has already been noted; and Norway was bleeding ships and men not just in the North Sea but also in the English Channel. The French needed to import at least one-and-a-half-million tons of coal from Britain per month. This utilised around 800 colliers, some fifty per cent of which were Norwegian. During the last quarter of 1916 U-boats achieved considerable success against this trade, which badly effected supply. Ships loaded with coal were held over in ports (some thirty to forty per cent of planned sailings in November and December), and in the last month of the year French factories were forced to shut down owing to lack of coal. As a result, on 30 December the French authorities sent one Commandant Pierre Vandier* to London to explain their parlous position and suggest that daily convoys might be a more practical and safe solution.

The Admiralty agreed to consider his request and assigned three officers to work with Vandier. On 3 January 1917 this small team presented its findings at a conference. Their plan called for four daily crossings for all steam vessels engaged in the French coal trade. They were described as 'controlled sailings', rather than convoys, as there were complicated questions of insurance related to the neutral vessels, as it might have been assumed that the term 'convoy' connoted 'protection'.

The new system was actuated on 6 February 1917, and had immediate effect. In the next three months to the end of April, U-boats sank only five colliers in over 2,500 vessel sailings.

Thus, from opposite ends of the British Isles, naval minds began slowly to reach towards an old solution to the problem of protecting merchant ships in time of war – convoy. But not yet.

Futility

The frustrating business of trying to intercept contraband-carrying ships continued to tax the resources and patience of the Royal Navy. In January 1917 the Grand Fleet was at sea, testing out an exercise in concentration, when Beatty received intelligence that two German ships carrying iron ore were expected to be off Cape Lindesnaes and outside Norwegian territorial waters around 15

---

* Vandier had previously helped organise the evacuation of the Serbian army from Albania in November 1915.

January. These were the *Aeolus* and *Mercure*, sailing down the Norwegian coast from Narvik. Beatty immediately ordered away *Inconstant* and *Cordelia*, from the 1st Light Cruiser Squadron, with accompanying destroyers, to intercept. They arrived off the Norwegian coast near Feisten, where they commenced a sweep for shipping.

At 0955 on the 16th the destroyer HMS *Onslow* reported a steamer close inshore, which on investigation was seen to be the *Aeolus*. When sighted, she hoisted German colours and anchored off Egersund, one of the best natural harbours in Norway, being careful to remain in Norwegian territorial waters. The British ships swept northward and south again, but *Aeolus* did not venture out. The tableau was acted out in front of a Norwegian destroyer, which had arrived shortly after the British vessels and was keeping a close watch on the RN ships as they steamed up and down in international waters. Patience is an unlimited virtue but fuel supplies are finite and, as the destroyers were beginning to run out of the latter, the British force had to retire without having any impact or effect.

Deciding to try a different tactic, Beatty sent the brand-new, enormous steam-powered submarine *K-3* to patrol submerged outside territorial waters off Stadlandet, a peninsula considered to be the dividing point between the Norwegian Sea to the north and the North Sea to the south, with orders to intercept and sink any German merchant vessels emerging from the inner lead, and to attack any enemy submarines. She had only just recovered from an uncontrollable dive with the future King George VI aboard the previous December, and on 9 January had suffered a flooded boiler room while on patrol in the North Sea.

The *K-3* patrolled there for four days, 19–22 January, which, given her previous mishaps, must have taxed the morale of her company. In that time only one merchant vessel, of unknown nationality, was sighted going north in territorial waters. Beatty also despatched the C-class light cruisers *Constance* and *Cambrian* to the south of *K-3*'s position, where between the 21st and 24th they swept off Utsire. The weather was unusually clear and fine but they sighted only two vessels, one of which was boarded and proved to be a Danish steamer bound from Dartmouth to Esbjerg. The other was inside Utsire Island, and thus in territorial waters, and was allowed to pass. It had been another exercise in futility.

Sweden Suffers

The effect of the Royal Navy's blockade, a poor harvest in 1916, the refusal of Prime Minister Hammarskjöld to soften his German-leaning stance and his continued antipathy to British demands for the cessation of exports to Germany all meant that from a profitable and wealth-creating neutrality of 1915, Sweden at the end of 1916 and early in 1917 found itself rapidly becoming ragged at the edges. Food was scarce and expensive, a problem not unaffected by the Hammarskjöld government's pricing and monetary policies. Official maximum prices were consistently set too low, and, instead of selling their meat, farmers withheld their goods or were tempted to sell them illegally. Some people made huge profits on the black market, and the *arriviste* merchants in the cities were soon referred to as the 'goulash barons', copying the earlier Danish usage.

Rationing was introduced. Firstly sugar and bread, followed by meat, eggs, milk and butter. But the real problem was that there was not enough food to buy. People had to change their diet, meat and potatoes being replaced by herring and turnips. Annual meat consumption *per capita* fell from 126 kilos in 1907 to 26 kilos in 1917.

Social unrest was not slow to follow. In the spring of 1917 people gathered all over the country in protest meetings. Strikes broke out, many initiated by women demanding food to feed their children. Trade unions joined the protests with hunger marches and petitions. There were rumours of revolution in the air.

Despite these problems, Hammarskjöld continued to resist an agreement that might loosen the blockade in return for reducing exports to Germany. Amongst his concerns was a fear of angering the Germans and being seen as favouring the Allies. But the domestic situation was such that he agreed to send a delegation to London to negotiate a trade agreement in December 1916. This coincided with a change in political leadership in Britain.

Many parliamentarians, and others who had power without responsibility, such as the press baron Lord Northcliffe, had become disenchanted by what they saw as Asquith's 'half-hearted' prosecution of the war. Led by Lloyd George they began to conspire for his removal, a putsch which was completed on 7 December 1916 when Lloyd George kissed hands as the new prime minister. Asquith left 10 Downing Street on the 9th, and Sir Edward Grey followed him out of office the next day. The new Foreign Secretary was Arthur Balfour, like Robert Cecil another scion of the Salisbury family (on his mother's side) and previously First Lord of the Admiralty.

But if the Scandinavian neutrals thought that the ratcheting of the screw might be lessened they were mistaken. Cecil continued his pressure and Balfour sought to placate the Americans.

At first, British demands were modest. They did not initially ask for a halt of all the iron ore trade with Germany, but did ask for a prohibition on re-export and for improved transit conditions to Russia. But sensing the growing weakness and desperation of their partners across the table, especially after the detention of all neutral ships in British harbours on 1 February 1917 after the German declaration of unrestricted submarine warfare (see Chapter 9), the eventual terms offered were tough. Britain would not give any guarantees regarding supply of cereals or coal if the Germans cut off their aid to Sweden in response to a trade treaty with Britain. The draft agreement was presented as an ultimatum. Take the whole thing, said blockade minister Cecil, or suffer the consequences.

Hammarskjöld rejected the proposed trade agreement. It had been brokered by Marcus Wallenberg, brother of Sweden's Foreign Minister, Knut Wallenberg, and would have brought some much-needed economic relief to Sweden, despite its harsh terms. The lawyer in the Prime Minister thought that by co-operating with the British in agreeing not to re-export in return for a partial lifting of the Royal Navy's blockade, Sweden would be committing an un-neutral act.

With the obvious conflict between Hammarskjöld and Wallenberg came the end of the road for the former. His coalition allies in parliament rose against him, and Hammarskjöld was forced to resign on 30 March 1917. He was succeeded by Carl Swartz, a conservative member of parliament who served only seven months. In October 1917 Sweden's Social Democratic Party won their first general election, and Nils Edén became prime minister (see also Chapter 11). Sweden had entered an uncertain period of weak and vacillating governance and economic struggle. Of Cecil it was said: 'with those words [the ultimatum] Cecil precipitated a crisis in Sweden's foreign policy that ended only after sixteen months of economic hardship for Sweden and the collapse of two Swedish governments'.[16]

The Crisis Point

As 1917 dawned, the war entered its fourth year. Germany had floated peace proposals at the end of 1916 to placate the USA and which it was sure no one could accept. Sweden, its profitable, German-leaning neutrality gone, faced a difficult and uncertain future. Norway was increasingly dependent on Royal Navy protection, but as 1916 ended was suffering from Britain's coal blockade, the price of its desire to maintain friendly and profitable relations with Germany and its allies.

In Britain itself, by November 1916 casualties had already topped a million men and the war was costing Britain £5 million per day, half of which was being raised in the USA. Additionally, Britain was forced to support its allies financially, especially Russia and France, and its coal maintained France, Italy and the Scandinavian neutrals (the latter at least part of the time). On the 13th of the month the Conservative leader in the Lords and Minister without Portfolio in the government, Henry Petty-FitzMaurice, 5th Marquess of Lansdowne, circulated a paper which asked the Cabinet to consider a negotiated peace. He suggested that Britain's manpower and industrial resources may not be able stand the strain of the war. It was rejected. And Secretary of State for War Lloyd George, soon to be prime minister, wrote a memorandum for the Joint Allied Conference at Chantilly, on 25 November, in which he stated that 'at sea the British allied and neutral shipping on which depends the life of the English people, its food, its munitions and those of its allies, is being destroyed at an alarmingly increasing rate'.[17]

As for the Royal Navy, its blockade was hurting Germany on the home front. Price controls were introduced as early as October 1914 for bread and cereals, followed swiftly by potatoes, sugar and cattle feed. Price supervisory boards were implemented in September 1915, and by May 1916 a 'War Food Office' was called into being. But an absence of co-ordination and lack of food itself brought their efforts to naught. In larger cities so-called 'war kitchens' provided cheap meals to an impoverished local population. By October 1916 there were 1,437 public kitchens operating across Germany, producing nearly two million portions daily. German citizens were eating less and worse than before the war, and diseases of malnutrition were beginning to make an impact.

However, the Royal Navy was terribly stretched. There were not enough smaller units, such as destroyers, and many were kept uselessly tied to the Grand Fleet, swinging around its moorings at Scapa Flow and Rosyth. Sweeps to intercept contraband carriers were time-consuming and ineffective. German U-boats were exacting a heavy toll of merchant shipping despite the navy's best attempts to hunt them down at sea, with 2,327,326grt sunk by submarines in 1916, up more than seventy per cent on the previous year. The crisis point of the war, and of the Scandinavian trade, had been reached.

PART TWO

'Admiral Fisher often wrote that the effect of naval defeat would be starvation.'

(quoted in Friedman, *Fighting the Great War at Sea*, page 51)

CHAPTER 9

Blockade, Unrestricted Submarine Warfare and Food, 1917

The British government's view of the situation at the beginning of 1917 may in part be gained from the newly appointed First Lord of the Admiralty. On the very first day of 1917 Sir Edward Carson hand wrote an appreciation of the 'Present Position of the Blockade'[1] for the January 1917 War Cabinet. It is perhaps more than a little smug in tone and not necessarily reflective of the whole truth, but it nonetheless identifies where the government thought it had got to with regard to limiting goods to Germany through the Scandinavian neutrals.

Carson begins by taking a quick swipe at the French ('we have had a good deal of difficulty with the French'), who were, unbelievably, still exporting wine and spirits to Germany.

With regard to Norway, he notes that 'agreements have been entered into by which the amounts of imports of military value allowed into those countries has been limited by agreement, and where this has been done no difficulty arises'. For Sweden, on the other hand: 'We have only been able to secure agreements in the case of cotton and lubricating oil. With respect to all other articles, we have had to ration Sweden by reference to a figure based on pre-war imports, which we have thought represented her reasonable home requirements, and the same course has been followed in the other neutral countries, where no ration has been agreed.' Imports from America, destined for Germany, however, continued to trouble him.

Negotiations are now pending with the Swedish delegates, the main object of which is to fix by agreement rations for the goods which are more important from a military point of view.

This will involve allowing Sweden to have the right to import larger quantities than she has had in the past year, though probably the lack of tonnage [of shipping] will prevent her from exercising that right. It will also involve certain concessions with regard to black lists and so on, which are not in themselves very desirable. But, in view of the great legal difficulties we are in [with regard to Prize Courts and the American government's insistence of the International Law of the Sea], and also in view of the immense importance of securing increased transit to Russia, which Sweden controls, I think it is well worth while to make an agreement if we can.

Carson then moves on to analyse the trade with Germany of goods which originate in the Scandinavian neutrals. He considers that the principal Swedish exports to Germany are iron ore, wood pulp, bacon, and a certain amount of eggs and butter.

'I see very little prospect of being able to interfere substantially with the iron ore which Sweden digs out of her own soil and carries across the Baltic to Germany, and in some cases down the coast of Denmark and Germany to Rotterdam, under conditions which prevent the fleet from touching it', he dolefully relates. He then notes the advantage that coal gives Britain, but cautiously adds that 'We use a great deal of her iron ore, and some of her other manufactured products, such as ball bearings, which are apparently essential for our munitions. But far more important than even these is the fact that she controls the transit to Russia, and we receive perpetual appeals from the Russian Government not to do anything which may imperil that transit.' The Swedes have means of retribution, in other words.

Returning to Norway, Carson states that she normally exports three articles of great importance to Germany, fish, pyrites, and nickel, 'and we have made great attempts to cut off each of these articles from Germany'. He touches on the 'Fish Agreement' of August 1916, but adds that it 'is unfortunately true that the Norwegians have not fully carried out the agreement, and that a certain amount of fish has been wrongfully exported to Germany'.

Norway was apparently unable to manufacture copper for electrical purposes and consequently had to import a large quantity of copper for its rapidly-developing electrical works. Carson notes that:

By a series of purchases and other transactions in the United States, we have the command of the greater part of the world's supply of such copper, and we have agreed with the Norwegians that they shall not export any of their native copper, or pyrites containing copper, to any belligerent country, except in return for an import from that country of an equal weight of [refined] copper, and we further agreed that since they wanted immediately a large quantity of electrical copper, they should, before they exported any copper to Germany, give us the option of taking in return a very large quantity of pyrites containing some 3,000 tons of copper. The result would have been, if the agreement had been rigidly carried out, to stop altogether the export of pyrites to Germany, at any rate for some considerable time. But, as a matter of fact, we have reason to believe that a certain amount of pyrites, which in the trade is regarded as non-cupreous, containing only half per cent of copper, has been exported to Germany in breach of the agreement.

Bribery had also found its place in the governmental armoury. Carson again: 'With regard to nickel, all that we have been able to do is to arrange with the nickel owners that, in return for a consid-erable payment, they will limit their export of nickel to Germany to a comparatively moderate amount.'*

He adds that: 'We are now putting pressure on the Norwegians by cutting off their coal supply from us, on which they completely depend, to compel them to carry out their agreements to the full. But we certainly have reached a point beyond which it would not be, in my judgment, very safe to go in view of the advice from our military and naval authorities that it is undesirable that Norway should come into the war on either side.'

Finally Carson considers the position of the Danes, with whom

---

* In this Carson was unfortunately misled. Britain and her allies had considerable control of the market for nickel, an important hardening agent for steel, through the Mond Nickel Company in Canada and the great deposits in the French dependency of New Caledonia. Germany obtained much of her requirement from Norway, via the Kristiansand Nikkel Raffineringswerk (KNR), which smelted about sixty tons of nickel per month, nearly all of which went to Germany. Britain signed a deal with KNR to that the latter would limit exports to Germany to eighty tons per month; in return for that guarantee, KNR were paid £1 million. But the British negotiators had been conned; the eighty-ton limit was greater than the company's total output, so Germany continued to import her full quota and Britain was £1 million poorer.

he has a certain sympathy. 'Denmark is, from a military point of view, absolutely at the mercy of Germany which, with a comparatively small force, could easily overrun the whole country and carry off all the livestock and crops, which are of considerable amount.' However, he resents that:

> ... this fact has been made use of to the full by the Danes, and they have contrived out of their military weakness to make very large commercial profits. So long as they were convinced that Germany was going to be victorious it was almost impossible to do anything with them, though the population is overwhelmingly anti-German. Recently, however, their temper has very much changed. Whereas at the beginning of last year and down to June they were exporting much larger quantities of agricultural produce to Germany than they did before the war, and much less to us, they have now, in compliance with repeated remonstrances from us, greatly modified their attitude.

So 1917 opened with the British government seemingly pleased with the some of the progress that had been made in bringing the Scandinavian neutrals to heel. However, it also recognised that there was much still to be done with regard to Scandinavian exports to Britain's enemies. But the Germans were about to change the rules of the game.

Unrestricted Warfare

On 1 February 1917 Germany declared unrestricted submarine warfare. In doing so the Imperial government knew that there was a very strong risk that the USA would be tipped into the war on the Allied side by such an action. Why did they do it? Firstly, the German command group had been convinced by calculations from Department B-1 (the Economic Warfare Plans group) that within five months, if sufficient merchant ships were sunk, Britain could be brought to her knees through lack of food, primarily wheat, as well as through having insufficient vessels to bring in supplies. There was also an issue of national sentiment. The morale of the German people on the home front was at rock bottom. The so called 'Turnip Winter' of 1916/17 had devastated people's faith in their leaders and food rationing was leading to general public unrest and rioting. The ongoing Royal Navy blockade had brought hunger and misery to the home front, and many in Germany cried out to inflict similar pain on Britain and her allies.

It was in this vein that the German Ambassador to the USA, Count Johann Heinrich Andreas Hermann von Bernstorff, wrote an *apologia* to US Secretary of State Lansing in justification of this unrestricted warfare, stating:

> A new situation has thus been created which forces Germany to new decisions. Since two years and a half England is using her naval power for a criminal attempt to force Germany into submission by starvation. In brutal contempt of International Law, the group of powers led by England not only curtail the legitimate trade of their opponents, but they also, by ruthless pressure, compel neutral countries either to altogether forego every trade not agreeable to the Entente Powers, or to limit it according to their arbitrary decrees. ... The English Government, however, insists upon continuing its war of starvation, which does not at all affect the military power of its opponents, but compels women and children, the sick and the aged, to suffer for their country pains and privations which endanger the vitality of the nation.[2]

Germany also correctly believed that it would take America some time to place herself on a war footing and get men into the battle line in meaningful numbers. If the Allies could be brought to their knees before then, America might be persuaded to stay her hand. So any final regard for the rules of the sea, The Treaty of London or Prize Rules went out of the window. All neutral and Allied ships at sea were at risk of sinking without warning or aid.

Lieutenant Commander Charles Poignand of HMS *Menace* was less than impressed. '[It is] reported today that the Huns propose to sink all ships on sight, hospital ships included. I wonder why they took the trouble to make the announcement as that is what they have been doing already for some time period.'[3]

Nonetheless, it did not take long for the results of this new campaign to be seen. In February 540,006grt of Allied and neutral shipping was sunk by U-boats. Food supply began to dominate the public debate on both sides of the North Sea.

The *Daily Telegraph* had reported on 5 January that a

journeyman Dutch printer, recently arrived in New York from Germany, told an American correspondent that 'Germany wants peace, and must have it at once, because the German people are starving'. This was supported on 1 March when the MP for Tower Hamlets and Mile End, Warwick Brookes, asked Lord Robert Cecil for an update on the success of isolating Germany from supply. In the House of Commons he asked if the 'Under-Secretary of State for Foreign Affairs can state whether the results of the tightening of the British blockade are proving satisfactory; and in what direction this is especially noticeable?'

Cecil was pleased to reply smugly that:

> For some months past no substantial quantity of goods imported overseas into Scandinavia or Holland has, I believe, gone through to Germany, nor have there been any material overseas exports from Germany through those countries. Recently, as a result of negotiation with the neutral countries named, the export of their produce to Germany has been considerably diminished. As to results, it is difficult to be certain. But I think it is safe to say that there is now a serious shortage of foodstuffs and certain other vitally important materials in enemy countries.[4]

It was perhaps a case of being economical with the truth.

Meanwhile, on Friday, 23 February, Prime Minister Lloyd George rose to make a major speech in the House of Commons. The problem, he averred, was that Britain was importing too much and had not the tonnage in ships to sustain such a level of import in the face of the enemy's submarine campaign. Last year, he thundered, Britain imported 6,400,000 tons of timber including 2,000,000 tons of pit props. Surely, we could use French wood in the trenches and cut more English forests.* Iron ore, he added, was an essential commodity, but there was plenty of low-grade iron ore in Britain and a saving of a million tons could be effected here too, if sufficient unskilled labour were to be forthcoming, to work under skilled miners (this was presumably the same unskilled labour that was being slaughtered on the Western Front). Timber and iron ore were,

---

* Before 1914, Britain imported most of its timber from Scandinavia, with smaller amounts from Canada and Russia. As this trade became more precarious, Britain felled 450,000 acres of domestic woodland to make up the amount necessary.

of course, the very bastions of the Scandinavian trade and economy.

The Prime Minister's other concern was food. In the face of the German unrestricted submarine onslaught, he asked the country to go back to the soil. There would be a new plan for agriculture, with guaranteed wages for workers and rent controls to aid farmers. British food imports were 'colossal' he averred. Grassland should be ploughed under for wheat; 'the plough is our hope'.[5]

Elsewhere, faith leaders were urged to allow people to skip worship on Sundays so that they could plant vegetable and other crop seeds in their gardens and communal spaces. But there was no rationing; just encouragement to be frugal.

Of course Britain had ample supplies of fish, resultant upon the fish purchasing agreement with Norway (*vide supra*, Chapter 7). But there was a problem; the fish was pickled herring, much loved by Scandinavians, less so by beef-bred Britons. This led to one of the stranger questions raised in the House of Commons that year when Henry Watt, MP for Glasgow College, rose on 30 March to ask of the Parliamentary Secretary to the Ministry of Food, Captain Charles Bathurst, 'whether there are at present at Stornoway, in the Hebrides, 100,000 barrels of pickled herrings ready for consumption; whether the delay in sending these away is traceable to his Department?'

Bathurst replied:

The quantity of herrings pickled in brine in Stornoway is about 75,000 barrels. It is clearly desirable that these fish, although not usually eaten in this country, should be retained for consumption under present circumstances, and steps are being taken which, it is hoped, may render this practicable. In the meantime, the export of these fish is prohibited. I would venture to suggest to the Hon Member and his Scottish friends that it is very desirable that they should do everything in their power to popularise this article of diet, because if there is no demand in this country for this particular kind of food, which is valuable and cheap, it will be difficult to maintain the prohibition of its export.

This point was seized upon by the MP for Pontefract, Frederick Booth, who pointed out that the problem was that 'working-class wives in this country do not know how to cook them or present them at table'.

In response, and perhaps wishing to show that MPs would make any sacrifice for their country, William Thorne, representing the gourmands of West Ham South, volunteered that the herrings should be served in the House of Commons dining room. There was little applause for the suggestion*.[6]

---

* The problematic herrings continued to plague British administrators. In May 1918 Major-General Sir Charles Maynard, commanding the supply depot and base at Murmansk, Russia, asked the Treasury for a sterling grant to fund local purchases. They offered him instead a considerable number of barrels of salted herring, stored in Vardø, Norway, to use as payment in kind. 'I had strong objection to adding the running of a glorified fish shop to my other duties' he harrumphed. Eventually, the herring turned up some weeks later at Archangel, stinking in the hot sun and completely unfit for human consumption (Maynard, *The Murmansk Venture*, ch2 ff).

CHAPTER 10

Convoy, 1917

Parliamentary debate about herrings was one thing, but the real problem to be addressed was that the German campaign was finding success. Ships were being sunk all round Britain, and at a much faster rate than they could be replaced, as the figures for losses demonstrated. March's value was 593,841grt; in April it was a staggering 881,027grt. Excluding fishing craft, the neutrals lost 131,000, 149,000 and 185,000grt of shipping in February, March and April respectively.

The system of protected sailings (*vide supra*, Chapter 8) was not working. An estimated twenty-five per cent of ships on the Lerwick to Bergen route were lost in two months from the system's inception.

In March alone twenty-seven Norwegian ships were sunk in the North Sea. It was Findlay in Kristiania who brought matters to a head. On 26 March he wrote to bring a crisis of confidence amongst the Norwegian sailors to the Admiralty's attention. 'Ship owners' association inform me that Norwegian ships report not having seen any British warship on the Bergen-Lerwick route except in neighbourhood of naval ports. Norwegians are losing confidence in protection of route and regard voyage from Leith to Lerwick as dangerous, especially off Peterhead.' He needed to be able to reassure them. 'I would beg to be informed if I can give definitive assurances that this route is in fact protected and would urge expediency of letting Norwegians see that this is the case.'[1]

Jellicoe copied the note to Beatty, and there now followed one of those unedifying finger-pointing exercises that disfigure the annals of military history from time to time. Beatty took offence at what he presumed to be the accusation that it was all his fault, and in his reply sarcastically pointed out that the area in question around Peterhead was in fact the responsibility of the CinC Rosyth and the Rear Admiral commanding the East Coast of England. With a pen dripping in irony, he wrote 'request I may be informed of Their Lordships views on this matter'.[2]

Meanwhile, Findlay had discovered another problem. The Germans were bribing Norwegian merchant crews to leave their ships. In addition, shipowners were finding it difficult to obtain crews for ore carriers as 'such ships sink immediately when torpedoed and I think that if the Norwegian ore trade is to be continued it will be necessary to find armed vessels to carry ore'.[3]

One of Findlay's advisors, writing on 2 April, saw danger ahead too. He noted that 'Over half of Norway's shipping was engaged in trades that are vital to us', commodities which included nitrates, carbide, timber, iron and steel. Unless it was protected convincingly he foresaw 'the whole fabric which is based upon our use of Norwegian shipping ... collapsing with disastrous consequences'.[4]

Vice Admiral Frederic Brock now joined in the game, also on 26 March. He reported that on his own authority he had been providing escorts for the east coast southwards run, rather than using them for patrolling, the virtues of which he doubted. 'As far as I am aware the large patrol which, for many months of the year, was retained in the Fair Isle Channel, never did any damage to a single hostile vessel.'[5] As aggressive anti-submarine patrolling was part of the canon of beliefs held by Beatty, Jellicoe and much of the Admiralty, this was to step on dangerous ground indeed, but Brock went further, pointing out that since he had introduced this freelance activity (on 3 March) seventy-five ships had passed that way with only one lost.

Three days after receiving Findlay's 26 March missive, Jellicoe wrote to reassure him 'that portion of the route Bergen-Lerwick is patrolled which vessels pass through during daylight hours if they leave the Norwegian coast at dusk'. But now came more finger pointing. It was all the merchant ships' fault. 'Experience shows that neutrals pay little attention to instructions as to leaving coast at dusk and proceeding to fixed rendezvous. Frequent sweeps of the Norwegian coast are carried out. The danger of the route south from Orkneys will be greatly minimised if ships carry out the advice given them as to route.'[6]

Rather huffily, Jellicoe tried to pacify Beatty: 'It is recognised that the responsibility for the protection of traffic along the east coast does not rest with you'. But he then made his point that mutual support was vital. 'When submarines are active in the vicinity of fleet bases it is, of course, very desirable that Grand Fleet destroyers should assist in attacking them and protecting trade, so far as this is consistent with their duties with the fleet.'[7]

In April another twenty-seven Norwegian vessels were lost (together with six Danish and two Swedish). Between 10 and 15 April *U-30* alone sank nine ships between the Norwegian coast and the rendezvous point for the 'daylight leg'. These figures took no account of Scandinavian losses in the Atlantic Ocean or the English Channel coal trade.

Also in April it was noted that 'westbound traffic was failing to meet the escort at the rendezvous, with the result that grave losses were occurring. ... The gravity of the situation was accelerated by the fact that Lerwick and Kirkwall harbours became congested with shipping as a result of enemy minelaying outside both ports.'[8]

It was clear that the protected sailings scheme had proved inadequate to the challenge, at least in the North Sea. As Jellicoe himself put it, 'difficulties, of course, arose in the event of bad weather, or when the slow speed of the ships prevented passage of about 180 miles being made in approximately 24 hours and in April 1917 it was evident that further steps were necessary to meet the difficulties which were again causing heavy losses'.[9] Something had to be done, and the problem was tossed back into Admiral Brock's lap.

Sixty-two-year-old Vice Admiral Sir Frederic Edward Errington Brock KCMG, CB, had been appointed Admiral Commanding Orkneys and Shetland on 20 January 1916. Brock had joined the Royal Navy aged thirteen in 1868, reaching flag rank forty years later. Before his current appointment Brock had previously held a number of administrative appointments, being Commodore-in-Command, Royal Naval Barracks, Devonport, between January 1907 and April 1908, Rear Admiral, Portsmouth Division, Home Fleet, 1909–10, and in September 1912 had been made 'Senior Officer and in Charge of All Naval Establishments' at Gibraltar, from which position he came to the North Sea.[10]

He was an experienced committee man. In December 1908 he had been made president of a committee on naval detention barracks, for which Their Lordships expressed appreciation for the 'able manner in which the committee performed its task'. On 20 October 1909 he was appointed to an Admiralty committee to liaise with the Department of Works regarding plans for detention barracks. Then in November 1910 he joined a commission studying pay and allowances and to superintend the introduction of the detention barracks system at the three Home Ports, a task which did not end until 1912. He also chaired a committee on disciplinary matters and the system of summary punishments. He clearly knew his way around a meeting room and was an able administrator; these skills were shortly to stand him in good stead.

In 1908/09 Brock had attended the Royal Naval War College, where he was placed first out of five flag officers in order of merit. As to his character, some found him hard to get along with. Rear Admiral Alexander Duff, when with the 4th Battle Squadron, noted in his diary for 1916 that Brock was 'a difficult man to do business with'.[11] But Jellicoe thought him 'very energetic and resourceful'.[12] The moment for him to demonstrate those characteristics had now arrived.

The Longhope Conference

Brock's headquarters was at Longhope, a coastal settlement on the island of South Walls, Orkney. There had been a Royal Navy presence there since at least 1813, when a coastal artillery battery was built to protect against American privateers during the war of 1812. The Admiralty later also built one of only three Martello towers in the whole of Scotland. The original battery comprised eight 24pdr guns, replaced in 1866 with four 68pdrs, apparently in response to a perceived threat from Feinians based in America.[*]

Now Longhope was part of the great Scapa Flow naval anchorage and base. There Brock flew his flag in the fleet repair ship HMS *Cyclops*, once the passenger liner *Indrabarah*, built by Laing for the Indra Line Ltd but bought by the Admiralty while on the stocks and launched as a floating engineers' workshop on 27 October 1905.

Beatty had first suggested on 30 March 1917 that a meeting be convened to study the possible adoption of convoy. Five days later the conference commenced at Longhope under Brock's chairmanship. There were representatives from all the East Coast and Scottish naval commands and from the Admiralty's Trade (Captain Claude Seymour) and Operations Divisions (Lieutenant Lionel

---

[*] There had been plans for an Irish Republican rising in Ireland in 1865, and there was one in 1867. During late 1866 Irish Republican Brotherhood leader James Stephens endeavoured to raise funds in the United States to fund revolutionary activity.

Cazalet). Additionally, Beatty sent his Chief of Staff, another Brock, Rear Admiral Osmond de Beauvoir Brock.*

The conference soon reached a unanimous decision that 'the convoy system be used in preference to the scheme of continuous stream of traffic'.[13] 'Experience of the methods hitherto adopted led to the recommendation that a convoy system should be instituted throughout the entire route from the Humber to the Norwegian coast and vice-versa'.[14]

It further recommended that each convoy should consist of a minimum of nine merchant vessels with an escort of no less than two destroyers plus one submarine, if available, and four to six armed trawlers. This was a substantial force, and Brock's team estimated that the programme would require between twenty-three to twenty-eight destroyers and fifty to seventy trawlers. The problem was, where would they come from? The meeting suggested that perhaps twenty-three destroyers and fifty-three trawlers could be taken from various East Coast bases, but unsurprisingly those in command of them were unable or unwilling to commit to their release.

On 5 April Sir Frederic Brock sent the conclusions of the conference to Beatty, who forwarded them to the Admiralty with a letter endorsing the recommendations. On 9 April he added a further note, stating that the Admiralty would have to order those in the commands affected to give up their ships. The process of Admiralty approval was both slow and frustrating, and the proposals further met with a tepid response from those officers on the East Coast whose ships would be stripped away.

Commodore James Edward Clifford Goodrich RNR, SNO Peterhead and a sixty-six-year-old retired admiral, objected to his trawlers being taken from him; Rear Admiral East Coast (Stuart Nicholson), writing from Immingham, stated that large ships should be individually escorted by a trawler with the remainder sailing independently, drawing a pencilled comment in the file 'Lord, what fools these [illegible] be'.[15] Rear Admiral Edmund R Pears at Invergordon took issue with losing his trawlers, and Commodore Startin at Granton was concerned that he would not now be able to conduct minesweeping activity.

At the Admiralty, Captain Webb at the Trade Division concurred

---

* They were, in fact, distantly related, being of the Guernsey Brock family lineage.

with the paper on the 12th, but with the important proviso that success depended on the supply of the necessary number of escorts without detriment to the East Coast local patrols which were escorting oilers, munition ships and the like.

The Director of the Anti-Submarine Division, Rear Admiral Alexander Ludovic Duff, also concurred, although with reservations. He was concerned to make clear that while he agreed to convoy in this particular instance, he did not accept it as a general principle. 'The convoy system is one on which very different opinions are held', he minuted.[16] And on the 20th, the Chief of the War Staff, Sir Henry Oliver, agreed to the report, though expressing doubt that it would work! Old thinking died hard in Whitehall.

Meanwhile, Beatty had ordered traffic to be resumed between Shetland and Norway on 19 April and asked for two Rosyth destroyers to relieve those from Lerwick off Rattray Head, while the CinC Rosyth, Rear Admiral Sir Frederick Tower Hamilton, was pressing for a decision, for he could not go on unless the Rear Admiral East Coast, Stuart Nicholson, was able to take over convoys at the Tyne. That same day, Beatty again pushed the Admiralty for their assent.

At the Admiralty, doubts evidently still obtained as to the likely success of a scheme which called for so many destroyers. On 20 April the Director of the Operations Division, Rear Admiral Thomas Jackson, consented to a trial for the scheme but expressed serious concerns because 'convoys invite torpedo attack and the available escorts are too few for the number of ships proposed in the convoy'.[17] On the following day the Admiralty again asked Beatty if he had in any way modified his views. This crossed with a further note from Beatty himself, asking that the recommendations made on 9 April to be put into force as soon as possible. He replied that the 'convoy system has not yet had fair trial. It is an essential part of my proposals that two destroyers should accompany each convoy, utilising for purposes destroyers of 7th DF and 8th DF. Only two ships have been sunk under convoy from Lerwick to East Coast ports, in neither of which cases were destroyers present.'[18]

Finally, on 21 April, First Sea Lord Jellicoe agreed to a trial of the system; it had taken about four weeks, at a time of great loss and emergency, for Beatty to get a formal green light.

Even now it seemed that some at the Admiralty were havering. On 23 April Prime Minister Lloyd George had raised the issue of convoy in a War Cabinet meeting. Jellicoe responded that it was under consideration, that Beatty's trial of convoy on the East Coast routes had not been wholly successful, and that two ships in two separate convoys had been sunk. Lloyd George took this to be a 'told-you-so' position. Although not a reliable source when it comes to the discussion of the introduction of convoys generally, the Prime Minister's later comment that 'the [Norwegian] convoy was not a systematic convoy, was imperfectly organised and was therefore not given a fair chance'[19] seems to gel with Beatty's position, as above.

On the 24th Brock was notified by the Admiralty that he would get some old 'River'-class destroyers from the Humber, and informed that the escorts were his responsibility. At last the system was finally put into effect. The Admiralty acted as Beatty had requested, issuing detailed orders that same day for vessels to be supplied from Grand Fleet, Coast of Scotland, Invergordon, Peterhead, Granton, East Coast, Tyne, and Stornaway.

The Longhope conference recommendation had been for a force of at least twenty-three destroyers and fifty trawlers for the east coast convoys, plus two destroyers and four trawlers for each Scandinavian convoy. The latter were granted from the Grand Fleet 'although they could be ill spared'.[20] For the east coast twenty old destroyers and forty-five trawlers were scratched up. The destroyers were a particular problem, for 'owing to the age of a large majority of the destroyers and the inevitable breakdown of machinery, the number available frequently fell below twenty'.[21]

The bulk of the force provided consisted of 'River'-class vessels and '30 knotters'. They were really only suitable for coastal work. Built in 1903–05, the 'River'-class could manage 25 knots on a good day and were lightly armed with one 12pdr and five 6pdr guns plus two torpedo tubes. The '30 knotters' were older, launched in 1895–9 and with the same armament as the 'River'-class vessels. They had been designed with a 'turtleback' forecastle which was intended to clear water from the bow, but it was found that this actually had the effect of digging the bow in to any sort of a sea, resulting in a very wet conning position. The Admiralty instructed Brock that the East Coast convoys were to be escorted by one '30-knotter' and one 'River'-class.[22] Not everyone was necessarily in agreement that the 30-knotters were up to the task. Captain (D) of the 7th Destroyer Flotilla, part of the East Coast Command, noted on 10 May that 'from consideration of sea-worthiness, coal capacity, age and the distance from land at which the convoys proceed ... these vessels cannot be suitable for this work',[23] but they were all that could be spared.

In the first month of operation the loss rate fell 120-fold, to 0.24 per cent,[24] while at the same time congestion at ports was reduced. (Before implementation there had been forty neutral vessels awaiting sailing permission at the Tyne, for example.) Starting with six ships, the convoys gradually increased to twenty and even fifty vessels over time.

The implementation was not without its problems. Jellicoe noted that '[Scandinavian convoy] was composed largely of neutral vessels and therefore presented exceptional difficulties in the matter of organisation and handling. The number of destroyers which could be spared for screening the convoys was also very small.'[25] Arrangements had to be put in place to manage the system in Scandinavia as well. To this end, Captain Arthur Halsey RN was appointed naval vice-consul at Bergen in May 1917.

As with every military operation, logistics occupied much of the time of the officers controlling the Scandinavian convoys. The operation was complex and had to be changed often. Lerwick to Bergen left daily at 1600 GMT, and Bergen to Lerwick departed at 1800 GMT, with the vessels instructed as to their sailing orders by HM Consul Bergen. The convoys generally had an escort of two destroyers and not less than four Auxiliary Patrol vessels (whalers and trawlers). For this work a force of six Grand Fleet destroyers was based on Lerwick, assisted by three local coastal defence destroyers.

In the event of their being fog at Bergen, a not-uncommon occurrence that rendered merchants unable to find their escort, masters were instructed to sail independently on a direct route for Lerwick while the escort worked back along the course at 7.5 knots (the speed of the convoys being set at 7 knots), such that if the fog lifted they might have a chance of establishing contact.

Convoys from Lerwick to Britain's west coast went around the top of Scotland twice a week with an escort of armed trawlers provided by Rear Admiral, Stornaway.

East Coast convoys ran regularly north and south three days out of four. They were escorted to Immingham by old 'River'-class and '30-knotters', previously belonging to East Coast Command at Humber.

Another issue was feeding the crews of the escorts. In his initial orders, issued on 26 April, Brock instructed that three days' worth of provisions should be loaded at Immingham before sailing north, as 'there is considerable difficulty in maintaining fresh food in the Shetlands and no supplies of this nature are to be demanded or looked for at Lerwick'.[26] It was in many respects worse for the trawlers, for they were expected to spend six days at sea, with only a day in Immingham and one in Lerwick harbours every eight days.

Admiral Brock co-ordinated everything from Longhope. This was not an ideal situation. His office was on his flagship *Cyclops*, but there was no communications centre. Instead he had to go ashore and use a room in a local hotel as his comms office, and despite his many representations to the Admiralty this remained the situation right through to early 1918. The workload soon built up and he requested additional support on his staff in the form of Commander Herbert Buchanan-Wollaston and Assistant Paymaster Cecil Dedenne; both had joined him by the end of April 1917.

Initially, the commencement point for all westbound convoys was Holmengrå, thirty-eight miles north of Bergen. Soon a range of other gathering points was adopted; Marstein (twenty-four miles to the south of Bergen), Aspo (fifty-five miles north) and Batalden (ninety miles north). By November 1917 it was estimated that 100 vessels of various nationalities were awaiting convoy in Norwegian ports.[27] Besides British and Allied ships these included Norwegian, Swedish and Danish vessels, together with some flagged French, Belgian, Russian, Dutch and even Spanish.

But resource was an ongoing problem. The minimum number of destroyers asked for at the Longhope Conference had been twenty-three, but only twenty had been allocated. Admiral Brock asked for three more but, as Jellicoe put it, 'urgent requests were being received at the Admiralty from every command and it was impossible to comply with them since the vessels were not in existence'.[28]

Beatty supplied backup vessels from the Grand Fleet for a time, but became frustrated by the lack of co-operation from other commands not within his ambit. On 13 May he sent an urgent telegram to Nicholson at the Humber, and copied in the Admiralty at the same time, asking them to direct Nicholson to comply. 'Request you will use your utmost endeavour to maintain convoy escorts. Destroyers are doing far better work by escorting convoys, where there are many chances of attacking enemy submarines, than by patrolling the coast.'[29] Eventually the Admiralty approved of the escort force of destroyers being brought up to twenty-three, and also consented to the provision of better coaling facilities at Lerwick and for an additional RNR midshipman to be appointed to each destroyer to ease the workload on the wardroom.

On 25 May 1917 Brock felt comfortable enough with proceedings to write an interim review, which Beatty forwarded to the Admiralty. Brock noted that 'the system of convoy has resulted in a marked decrease in the number of ships sunk by enemy submarines and in addition it is establishing amongst neutral shipping a feeling of confidence that they are protected by the British navy'.[30] He stated that 331 ships had been convoyed between 29 April and 12 May, of which only five had been sunk by U-boats. But the problem, as ever, was a shortage of destroyers. 'The result is that the patrol of the coast by destroyers has ceased and this disability must be accepted.'[31] As noted above, Brock did not think patrolling any use in any case.

Convoy escort duty was not an easy role. There was frequent congestion at Lerwick and in the Norwegian ports, while bad weather and the variable speed of the merchant ships made accurate timing for the passage a matter of conjecture and 'the greatest difficulty was always found in keeping a hybrid collection of neutral steamers in tolerably compact formation during the night'.[32] It was not uncommon for escort commanders to find that dawn revealed their convoys scattered over many miles of sea; and then there were the U-boats to worry about.

Taking on the U-boat

Although convoy meant that there were fewer vessels sailing singly in the North Sea, the U-boats were still there in number and looking for prey; and the Royal Navy was looking out for them, too.

On 4 May at 0830, about fifteen miles north of Scarborough, HMS *Mallard*, an old '30-knotter' commanded by Lieutenant William S Nelson, RNR, was patrolling along the coast when she sighted a periscope about 1,800 yards off and then observed a U-boat attacking SS *Devereux*. Nelson, obeying the precepts of his illustrious namesake, went to full speed and opened fire with his 12pdr and 6pdr guns, driving the submarine under the waves. He then escorted *Devereux* to port. It was a lucky escape for the merchant vessel, for the German vessel was *UB-21* under Franz Walther, who two days earlier had sunk the Norwegian *Rikard Nordraak* off Whitby with two lives lost. Two days later he was to sink the Swedish *Harold* off the Tyne, killing five of her crew.

Then, on 7 May, off Montrose, the armed trawler *Vale of Clyde*, on minesweeping duty, sighted the wake of a submarine at 1650 and followed it to drop a depth charge. Some twenty minutes later a periscope was again seen, and this time the armed trawlers *Trinity* and *Cicero* dropped depth charges. The intended victim was *UC-77*, commanded by thirty-eight-year-old *Kapitänleutnant* Reinhard von Rabenau. The previous day he had sunk the Norwegian *Kaparika*, 1,232grt, on passage from Blyth to Sarpsborg with a cargo of much-needed coal. One Norwegian crewman died in the attack.

Beatty and Brock had managed to obtain aerial resources for convoy protection and for U-boat hunting, and on 14 May one of them, seaplane No 9066, attacked *UC-42* off Blyth, on the Tyne. The aircraft was a Short 184 piloted by Flight Sub-Lieutenant John Arthur (Jack) Yonge, son of a clergyman, twenty-three years old and on spotting duties with the seaplane carrier HMS *Riviera*, a cross-Channel packet of 2,400grt, completed in 1911. In August 1914 she had been requisitioned from the South East and Chatham Railway Company, and by October, after a rapid conversion, was able to carry four seaplanes. Seaplanes were also based at Catfirth, in the parish of Nesting, Shetland. The plan was for eighteen seaplanes to be stationed there, but it soon became clear that the location was not suitable. Conditions were 'at the margins of current capability' for operations.[33]

Q-ships were also deployed in convoy protection roles. In May there were fourteen Q-ships, mostly Q-trawlers, under the command of Commodore James Startin RNR at Granton, Firth of Forth. Startin was a 'character' and in his earlier days was noted as a fearless horseman, a gymnast and an athlete. Certainly he had not excelled at the more cerebral aspects of command, being rated fifth out of six flag officers when attending the Royal Naval War College in 1907/08 'in order of attention and ability'.[34]

As a Vice Admiral he had been placed on the Retired List on 14 September 1914, aged sixty, but was reactivated into the Naval Reserve four days later. Jellicoe described him as 'the life and soul of the patrols and minesweepers working from Granton, frequently at sea with decoy ships fitted out there'.[35]

Six of his Q-trawlers were out fishing on the east coast in May, but only one came into action. This was the *Roskeen*, which had left Granton in company with the *Coot* on 14 May, after intelligence had been received that a submarine was in the area. The following day she was headed SSE off the Forth, under Lieutenant Frederick Henry Peterson RNR, when fire was opened on her. Peterson ordered his panic party away but the U-boat commander was wary and kept up fire for nearly an hour, eventually resorting to shrapnel which wounded both Peterson and his fishing skipper. The trawler then opened fire and, after the U-boat dived, dropped four depth charges, but the quarry escaped. Nonetheless Peterson, already the holder of the Distinguished Service Cross*, received a Bar to his decoration.

The U-boats were active off the Orkneys, too. Two days after *Roskeen*'s engagement, HMS *Rowena*, an 'R'-class destroyer launched in 1916 and under Commander Richard Lloyd Hamer, was minesweeping in a flat calm on 16 May when a periscope was sighted only 200 yards away on the quarter. Ordering full speed and the helm hard over, Hamer attacked with depth charges. His action probably saved HMS *G-12*, a British submarine which was in sight on the surface and the presumed target for the German attack, but *Rowena* was unsuccessful and the U-boat, *UC-31*, escaped to torpedo two Swedish vessels the following day. One was the *Aspen*, 3,103grt, on passage from Philadelphia to Stockholm with vital supplies of American wheat. She was hit twenty miles east of the Orkneys but survived to be towed in to Kirkwall with no loss of life. *Viken*, 1,825grt, was less fortunate. Carrying a cargo of sulphur from Texas to Gothenburg, she was sunk in the same place as the previous attack, with eight crewmen lost.

That same day, at 0630 just off the Tees estuary, the armed yacht *Miranda II* sighted the periscope of a submarine. Armed with two 12pdr guns, she attacked with depth charges but to no avail.

The last anti-U-boat action of May took place on the 25th, when Lieutenant Commander John Ignatius Hallett, in HMS *Talisman*, took in a wireless signal at 1812 which suggested that there was a U-boat thirty miles off the Tyne estuary. Leaving his mooring at Blyth at 1915, Hallett set sail at his top speed. At 2245 he spotted a black object low in the water and attacked with depth charges. His prey was *UB-41*, commanded by twenty-seven-year-old

---

* Gazetted 14 July 1916.

Oberleutnant zur See Günther Krause, who had sunk two vessels, one Norwegian, one British, on his current cruise, which was now cut short, for he arrived home again on the 27th without sinking any other victims, indicating that *Talisman* did inflict some damage.

For Hallett this was something of a turnaround in his personal fortunes. On 24 January 1916, newly appointed to *Talisman*, Hallett was deemed to have failed to follow up on a search for a submarine and it was recommended that he be removed from command. The Admiralty disagreed with this course of action, given his previous service record, and admonished him to try harder in future. Hallett now seized this chance with both hands, for he was commended for his zeal in pursuing submarines on 21 February, the action of 25 May and then the night of 25/26 June; for the latter attack he was awarded the DSO.[36]

Despite the bravery and elan shown by the navy in these actions, it is instructive that in the seven attacks on U-boats in the North Sea during May as detailed above, which were carried out by four different weapons platforms, not one U-boat was destroyed. They were hard to find and harder to kill. But convoy made the seas empty for them and reduced their opportunity to sink merchant ships. Better that, perhaps, than futile and dangerous search-and-(try to)-sink missions by British forces.

And, although Scandinavian ships continued to be sunk in the Atlantic, English Channel and Baltic Sea, only three Swedish and five Danish vessels were lost during May in the North Sea. The Norwegians lost thirteen, of which two succumbed in an unlikely fashion, the result of Royal Navy interference (as the Norwegians might have seen it) in their lawful progress.

On 29 May, *U-28* was loitering off the Outer Skerries, Shetland. *Kapitänleutnant* Georg Schmidt had already torpedoed and sunk the Norwegian steamship *Fridtjof Nansen*, 2,190grt, on passage from the Tyne to Christiania with a cargo of coal, when he was presented with not one, but two, easy opportunities.

Karna was a barquentine of 210 tons, owned by A/S Skiens Motor (H T Realfsen) of Skien. She had sailed from Rönneby, Norway, where she was based, headed for Akureyri in Iceland with a cargo of timber; but in trying to break out of the North Sea, she had been intercepted by a Royal Navy patrol vessel, a prize crew put on board, and her captain instructed to sail to Lerwick for control and examination.

Fifty miles off the eastern edge of the Shetland Islands, the *Karna* came across *U-28*. Captain Halvor Svennungsen and his crew, together with four Royal Navy personnel, were ordered to abandon ship, and Schmidt scuttled her with charges placed on board. Although there were no casualties, the Norwegian and British sailors suffered a cold and rough twenty-four hours at sea before they were picked up by a navy vessel the following evening and taken to Lerwick and safety.

Shortly after disposing of *Karna*, *U-28* spotted another sailing ship, following the same course. This was also an A/S Skiens Motor owned sailing ship, the three-masted schooner *Kodan*, 217grt, again under the control of a British prize crew. She too had been intercepted, also while sailing from Rönneby, this time to Sandakrog, Iceland, bearing a cargo of wood, and sent to Lerwick for inspection.

Once more Schmidt ordered the sailing ship's men into the water and destroyed it by scuttling. *Kodan*'s master, Captain Ludvig Larsen, his crew and three Royal Navy guards took energetic action to improve their situation; they rowed and sailed west until they landed at Out Skerries Light House the next day. Safety could not be found, it seemed, even with British naval forces on board one's ship.

Destroyers in a Shetland harbour.

1915 'M'-class destroyer HMS *Moon* at Lerwick.

1916 'M'-class destroyer HMS *Northesk* at Lerwick.

Above: An 'E'-class submarine HMS *E-1*, similar to Commander Talbot's *E-16*.

Left: Kite balloons at Lerwick.

HMS *G-9*, sunk on 16 September 1917 and sister vessel to Charles de Burgh's *G-8*.

Above: 1915 'M'-class
destroyer HMS *Mary Rose*,
sunk on 17 October 1917
whilst defending her convoy.

Left: 'The Last Fight of the
Strongbow' by Montague
Dawson; HMS *Strongbow*
was sunk with her consort
Mary Rose.

The 'River' class destroyer HMS *Itchen*, torpedoed by *UC-44*.

The 'River'-class destroyer HMS *Ouse*, a regular East Coast convoy escort.

SS *Peel Castle*, used as an Armed Boarding Steamer.

The German *Zerstörer G-101*, part of the force which attacked HMS *Pellew* and *Partridge*.

The light cruiser SMS *Brummer* which, with SMS *Bremse*, attacked and sank HMS *Mary Rose* and *Strongbow*.

SS *Glitra*, the first British-flagged cargo vessel to be sunk by U-boat in the war.

The Hull trawler *Swallow*, taken up by the Admiralty as a minesweeper in October 1914, typical of the many such vessels so used.

The SS *Sir Ernest Cassel*, built at Hebburn by R W Hawthorn Leslie in 1910, was a Swedish iron ore carrier equipped with twelve electric cranes. She survived the war.

The Wilson Lines ship RMS *Eskimo*, captured by the Germans in 1916, depicted on a company postcard.

Left: The three Scandinavian kings meeting at Malmö, December 1914.

Below: King Gustav V of Sweden in full regalia.

Right: Eric Scavenius, Danish Foreign Minister throughout the war.

Below right: Lord Robert Cecil, minister in charge of Blockade from 1916.

Below:
Sir Edward Grey, British Foreign Minister until the end of 1916.

Left: Sir Edward Carson, First Lord of the Admiralty December 1916–July 1917.

Below left: Admiral Sir John Jellicoe, CinC Grand Fleet and subsequently First Sea Lord from November 1916 until the end of 1917.

Below: Admiral Sir David Beatty, CinC Grand Fleet from late 1916 until the end of the war.

Right:
Vice Admiral
Reinhard Scheer.

Below: Edmond
Mansel Bowley,
captain of the
Narborough when
she and *Opal* were
wrecked in 1918.

Below right: Stoker
William Drake, sole
survivor of the
sinking of HMS *G-9*
in September 1917.

The coal hoists at Immingham Docks, photographed in 1912.

Malmö on the day of the Three Kings' meeting; the defective balcony can be seen centre right.

The Minnehallen at Stavern, Norway.

The Sjomanstornet, Gothenburg, Sweden.

The Søfartsmonumentet in Copenhagen.

One of the two 6in guns which caused Rear Admiral Greatorex so much anxiety, finally installed by Royal Marines on Bressay in 1918.

Merchant vessel dazzle-painted as seen through a submarine periscope.

The same vessel on identical course painted grey.

A portrayal of how 'dazzle' camouflage was supposed to work.

Sheds built to house the airships and balloons based at Caldale in the Orkneys and briefly used for anti-submarine patrols and Scandinavian convoy escort.

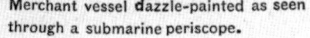

A 1918 painting by John Lavery of an aerial view from an airship looking down onto a convoy in the North Sea off Norway. Two airmen look out towards the lower left of the depiction and another walks out onto the rigging behind them.

A Short 184 seaplane similar to that used for convoy escort in 1917 and flown by Flight Sub-Lieutenant J A Yonge.

CHAPTER 11

Scandinavian Problems and Diplomacy, 1917

The Scandinavian losses in the North Sea may have been stemmed, but the tonnage losses suffered by the British mercantile marine were becoming unsustainable. Ships could not be built as fast as they were being sunk, and the available merchant fleet was shrinking with every passing month. In the last quarter of 1916 the British Empire had lost 618,000grt and built only 220,000. In the first quarter of 1917 the equivalent values were 912,000 and 316,000grt.[1]

The situation seemed so dire that on 27 April First Sea Lord Sir John Jellicoe was moved to tell the War Cabinet, via the First Lord:

> The real fact of the matter is this. We are carrying on the war at the present time as if we had the absolute command of the sea, whereas we have not such command or anything approaching it. It is quite true that we are masters of the situation so far as surface ships are concerned, but it must be realised – and realised at once – that this will be quite useless if the enemy's submarines paralyse, as they do now, our lines of communication.
>
> Without some such relief as I have indicated [*inter alia* 'the import of everything that is not essential to the life of the country is ruthlessly and immediately stopped'.] – and that given immediately – the navy will fail in its responsibilities to the country and the country itself will suffer starvation.[2]

Neutral tonnage was an inestimable boon as an addition to British merchant bottoms but the major shipping owner nations were also suffering. In the final three months of 1916 the 'rest of the world', excluding Germany and her allies, lost 1,159,000grt and built exactly none. In the first quarter of 1917 the values were 1,619,000 and 587,000grt respectively (most of the latter being American tonnage).[3]

In Britain, government had long been afraid that all freight carried in neutral bottoms could be brought to a halt from fear of German predation. Unlike British merchant ships which were increasingly carrying defensive armaments (usually a lone 4.7in gun manned by Royal Navy ratings), neutrals were afraid to arm their vessels in case it compromised their non-combatant status. As a result they were comparatively easier to sink.

During February the British government made overtures to several neutral countries regarding a possible purchase of their merchant fleets, which would put their cargo vessels safely under British control and direction.

No neutral country took up the offer, but in negotiation with Norway over the resumption of coal supplies, the value of coal as a weapon was once more demonstrated. Desperate to regain their favoured purchaser status, the Norwegians were willing to consider a transfer of their merchant fleet if it could be structured in such a manner as to avoid German retaliation. This was a realistic position, for the government of Norway considered itself to have no choice. 'If the British wishes were rejected, it was feared that Britain would simply requisition all Norwegian ships within the area under her control – without providing for supplies.'[4] Prime Minister Knudsen himself thought that a new coal crisis would lead to mass unemployment and social discontent, possibly even revolution.

Thus it was suggested that, as an alternative to buying the Norwegian merchant fleet, it would be simpler to charter it and switch the unarmed Norwegian ships with armed Allied ships on the most exposed routes where the heaviest losses were occurring. The Norwegian government proposed that in return for, and conditional upon the concessions contained in the new trade agreement with regard to the supply and transport of coal to Norway, the *Rederforbund* (the Norwegian Ship Owners' Association) could declare itself willing to transfer its ships by means of charter or requisition. This was formally known as 'The Tonnage Agreement'. The deal between Norway and Britain was signed by representatives from the *Rederforbund* and the British Ministry of Shipping and thus camouflaged the Norwegian government's active role. One hundred and thirty merchant vessels were placed at Britain's disposal, some 200,000grt. It bought some time. And in return, Britain guaranteed Norway 250,000 tons of coal per month.

Norway had become both neutral and ally. Small and vulnerable to disruption of its food and essentials supply chain, Norway had taken the pragmatic option.

A German War Against Norway?

During the early part of 1917 the German Naval Staff completed *Kriegsfall Norwegen*, a plan for war with Norway. The plan was posited on a situation in which Norway had joined Britain and her allies who thus gained access to the Norwegian coast. The plan did not involve invasion or territorial ambition, except for the use of Zeppelins to bomb industrial targets in the south of the country. But it did involve the laying of minefields and occasional sorties by the High Seas Fleet to attack ports and coastal towns.

The primary German concern was that, as the south coast of Norway was geographically closer to Germany than Britain, Royal Navy bases there could be used not only to control the North Sea, but also as a starting position for an invasion of Denmark. Danish territory could then be used as a jumping off point from which an attack on Schleswig-Holstein could be launched. Norwegian coastal harbours occupied by Royal Navy ships would also allow control of the exits from the Baltic.

The Tonnage Agreement might have led to the actioning of this plan and indeed during the negotiations there were rumours in Germany that Britain was trying to establish bases in the country; but nothing came of it in the end. The Germans were bought off by some trade concessions and assurances of strict neutrality by the Norwegians.

In fact, as noted in Chapter 8, the Royal Navy was distinctly unenthusiastic about having to operate from Norway. But the Foreign Office raised the subject again in June 1917. Parliamentary Under-Secretary Leo Amery[*] was asked to review the position and produced a paper entitled 'The Possible Entry of Norway into the War', dated the 27th. His main concern was the impact on Sweden. 'No advantage resulting from Norway's entry', he opined, 'could

---

[*] A future First Lord of the Admiralty.

counter balance the disadvantages of Sweden's throwing herself into the arms of Germany, either by actually joining the war on the German side or by stopping communications with Russia and adopting a general attitude of unfriendly neutrality.'[5] But with a typical politician's Panglossian viewpoint he went on to propose that 'the policy of the Allies should be to bring Norway into the war under such circumstances as will create sympathy for her and for the Allies in the other Scandinavian countries, and then to use her introduction in such a fashion as to provoke Germany to some violation of Danish or Swedish neutrality so flagrant as to bring both Sweden and Denmark into the field against her'.[6]

Beatty reviewed this proposition, and the policy originally adumbrated by Jellicoe of not acquiring bases in Norway, and in July asked some of his staff and the captain of HMS *Conqueror*, Captain Herbert Richmond, quondam Assistant Director of Operations at the Admiralty, to evaluate the pros and cons of Norway formally joining the Allies. Richmond concluded, in a paper written on 13 July, that an Allied base in the south of Norway 'would be of value in naval operations against the German trade and patrols'. However, this would require 'the allocation of naval and possibly military forces. We should exchange such protection as is now afforded by Norwegian territorial waters for protection of cruising or convoy. We should have to maintain a supply to the base and we should probably be called upon to assist Norway to defend her coast, towns and shipping from cruiser, destroyer, submarine and air attacks. This would divert ships and materiel ... from their objects.' He concluded that unless Norway assured Britain that it could defend itself and the base 'it is not to our advantage that she should come into the war'.[7] In his diary entry for the day he noted that he was surprised at the conclusion he had reached.

Richmond's conclusion was rather against Beatty's instincts. His gripe was particularly focused on the insistence by the Admiralty that Royal Navy ships should not enter Norway's national waters. He had already expressed himself angry that contraband runners could use the protection of Norwegian territorial waters whereas he was prevented from intercepting them. Indeed, he had written to Foreign Secretary Arthur Balfour on 15 December 1916 that 'the blind adherence to international laws ... prevents us from winning the war and is helping us to lose it'.[8] But in January 1917 the War Cabinet had taken the same view that Captain Richmond would later come to, noting that 'it would not be in our interests to take the initiative in any violation of Norwegian neutrality'.[9] That remained the policy throughout the rest of the war.

Danish Diplomacy

It has been noted above that Scandinavian neutrals were suffering badly by mid-1917. Sweden had rationed sugar in 1916, with bread flour, milk and meat following in 1917 (and potatoes a year later). In Norway, one protest meeting took as its theme 'the sailors are drowning, the people are starving, capital reaps the profits'.[10] Around 300,000 people took to the streets in protest at food prices in June 1917, 40,000 of them in Kristiania.

Comparatively speaking, Denmark was faring much better than its Scandinavian peers. Not that its military establishment had always trusted the politicians to keep the country safe from German incursions. In September 1916, the Danish Military Staff had begun to doubt the ability of their politicians to prevent a German invasion of the south of their country. Through diplomatic channels, a request for clarification of Britain's position in that eventuality was passed to both the Admiralty and the War Office. Would Britain assist Denmark if she was invaded, they asked?

The Admiralty was doubtful that it could provide the necessary ships to either escort a counter-invasion force to Danish waters, or then protect itself and its charges from German attack, unless other pressing priorities such as blockade and the defence of the Grand Fleet were ignored. Such action would, they stated, 'be the greatest risk to our naval supremacy'.[11] The War Office claimed to have neither the men nor equipment to take on the task. As General William Robertson, Chief of the Imperial General Staff, put it: 'If we undertake now to give Denmark military support we might commit ourselves to operations which, having regard to our other commitments, we could not hope successfully to carry out.'[12] The subject was quietly dropped.

But in fact a wily and clever politician was in the right place at the right time. By deftly playing-off the two warring parties, the Allies and the Central Powers, neither of whom really wanted to have to subjugate Denmark by force and both of whom needed Danish export goods, Foreign Minister Erik Scavenius manged to ensure that Denmark remained relatively prosperous and comfortable.

Maximum-price setting and government intervention kept consumer prices under control, and fixed prices for imports such as coal and maize were underwritten by government subsidy. The administration also subsidised pork and butter produced for the home market to compensate producers for the loss of the much higher prices available on the export markets, especially in Germany. Danish farmers grew wealthy as a result, not to the entire satisfaction of other sections of the population.

Germany's declaration of unrestricted submarine war in February 1917 had led to a dramatic decline in imports, as Danish shipowners refused to sail, and so the government took control of the distribution of essentials such as animal feed, sugar and bread, which were also rationed. Additionally, the price of potatoes, a staple Danish foodstuff, was subsidised. Bread, sugar and pork were rationed from the beginning of 1917.

Scavenius also took great care to protect the Danish economy and its ability to gain income through export to Britain and her allies. He carefully balanced out German and Allied interests and refused to be bound or to kow-tow to either. In May 1917 he faced possibly his biggest challenge when the German Navy, reflecting a country increasingly short of foodstuffs and becoming obsessed by the Royal Navy's blockade (which the German leadership and press called the 'starvation blockade'), increased its efforts at sea to prevent Danish goods reaching British ports.

Scavenius, whose careful diplomacy was much appreciated in Imperial Governmental circles in Germany, threatened to resign if exports were stopped in this way. The prospect of having to deal with a new and possibly less complaint minister caused the German politicians to order their navy to back down. Supplies to Britain resumed with limited interference and a backlog of deliveries was eliminated. And as a result of this careful diplomacy Denmark did not experience the social unrest of Sweden or the hunger of Norway during 1917.

Denmark Cedes an Empire (and seeks another one)

This was not Scavenius's only success in 1917. One unexpected outcome of both Danish insistence on neutrality and the German U-boat campaign against Atlantic shipping was that, on 31 March 1917, the USA acquired the Danish West Indies (the Virgin Islands), a colonial possession held by the Danes since the late 1600s.

The USA had made several previous attempts to acquire the islands, beginning in 1867, but these had all foundered on opposition within the American Senate or the Danish parliament.

But by 1915, and especially following the sinking of the *Lusitania* on 7 May, the issue of a US purchase of the territory again reared its head. Both President Wilson and Secretary of State Robert Lansing became concerned that the German government might annex or otherwise invade Denmark, in which case the Germans would also secure the Danish West Indies as a naval or submarine base from where they could launch additional attacks on shipping in the Caribbean and the Atlantic, particularly American shipping. There were many in the Danish government who would have been happy for the islands to be sold, both for the sake of the residents and for reasons of Danish security, but a concern for her neutrality meant that any such transfer would have to be realised before the United States entered the war, so that the transfer would not become a violation of neutral status and encourage German aggression. Accordingly, and recognising the long-term likelihood of the USA joining Germany's opponents, the wily Scavenius contacted the American government in May 1915 with a message that he personally believed that the islands ought to be sold to the United States, and that although he would not, indeed could not, make an official proposal, if the United States gave any encouragement to the consideration of the possibility of such a sale it might be feasible.

Thus heartened, Lansing was authorised to approach Constantin Brun, the Danish Minister to the United States, about the possible purchase of the Danish West Indies in the October. But Brun was ordered to reject the proposal. A plebiscite in Denmark would be required to authorise the sale, and Parliament felt that many Danes were concerned that the segregation polices of the USA would have disastrous consequences for the predominantly black population of their colony. So the Danish government tried to insist that the United States would make provisions for a local plebiscite, US citizenship for the islanders, and free trade. Lansing rejected these provisions, claiming that these issues fell under the jurisdiction of Congress and thus could not be bestowed by treaty.

Having tried the velvet glove, Lansing now deployed *force majeure*, implying that if Denmark was unwilling to sell, the United States might occupy the islands to prevent their seizure by

Germany. Faced with something of a *fait accompli*, and driven on by Scavenius, the Danish government decided to trade, and a treaty was signed in New York on 14 August 1916, the same day that it was simultaneously approved by the Danish Lower House. There then followed approval by a Danish referendum (though not a Virgin Islands one) and ratification by King Christian X. The US Senate ratified the treaty on 6 September and it was signed by Woodrow Wilson on 16 January 1917, formal transfer of the islands occurring on 31 March, days before the USA entered the war.* That same day, in Washington, DC, a warrant for $25 million in gold** was presented to Danish Minister Brun by Secretary of State Lansing, as payment for the territory. As part of the negotiation the United States accepted a Danish request for a declaration stating that it would not object to the Danish government extending its political and economic interests to the whole of Greenland. New empires were born on both sides of the Atlantic.

America Enters the War

The USA declared war on Germany on 6 April 1917. As well as bringing to the Allied cause the wealth, *materiel*, manpower and other resources she possessed, the entry of America into the lists had one further, important, impact. Most of the war contraband which so exercised Jellicoe, Beatty, the 10th Cruiser Squadron, Grey, Cecil and the British government, and which found its way to Germany via Sweden, Norway or Denmark, originated in the USA. America had made enormous trade gains from supplying all sides in the conflict. Her net gain in foreign trade since the start of the conflict until April 1917 had been around $4.5–5.0 billion. Cotton farmers in the South, wheat growers in the Mid-west and manufacturers in the North-east had all benefited massively from war and cared little for where their goods were eventually consigned***, but now it was in America's interests to stop the flow of goods to

---

* The US Virgin Islands were administered by the US Navy from 1917 to 1931. Full US citizenship to all residents born in the US Virgin Islands was extended in 1932 by an act of Congress.

** About $1,450,750,000 at today's values.

*** It might be noted *en passant* that the five major US meat-packing companies (Amour, Swift, Wilson, Morris and Cudahy) made profits in the three years 1915–17 of $140 million, as opposed to $19 million in the three preceding years (*New York Times*, 29 June 1918).

Germany and her allies; and to stop them getting there via the Scandinavian neutrals.

The USA was not long in bringing its power to bear. On 9 July an embargo was placed on all US exports to Scandinavia. President Wilson issued a proclamation forbidding the shipment of any goods to Europe for neutrals, except under licence. This included such staples as meat, sugar and cotton, which were the most commonly sought-after US exports. He declared that his intention was that no American products would cause 'the occasion of benefit to the enemy either directly or indirectly'.[13] America also notified the neutrals that it expected them to come up with proposals which would form the basis of war trade negotiations.

Under the sub-heading 'Retribution for Sweden', the *Daily Telegraph*'s Washington correspondent commented that 'of all the neutrals affected by this embargo, the least sympathy is felt by Americans for Sweden, which will suffer most'. He went on to editorialise: 'From the start of the war, Washington knew perfectly well that Stockholm had been a second to Berlin'. Referring to the Swedish political process, the reporter added: 'the growing spirit of Swedish democracy alone prevented the raising of the German flag by Court circles and the large group of profiteering exporters'.[14]

One undesirable result (at least to the Allied powers) of the dire situation that the neutrals were now in was to drive them towards deals with Germany. Denmark agreed credit terms with Germany for the supply of coal, salt, iron and shipbuilding materials in return for Danish pork and butter. Sweden gained access to coal in return for iron ore, cellulose and paper. The countries also tried to increase the level of trade between themselves.

But all three Scandic powers recognised that they needed American co-operation and resources. Norway sent a trade negotiating mission to Washington in July, as did Sweden and Denmark. However, no agreements were signed until 1918. The delay was not entirely the fault of the Americans. The Scandinavian countries all had reasons to fear German reaction to any trade pacts. They were also concerned that any further constraint on supply would result in further hardship for their citizens. As one historian has noted: 'Norway in particular was reluctant to introduce rationing, even though the Americans made it clear at an early stage that it was a precondition for agreement'.[15]

Norway was, in fact, regarded as something of a special case, as it had been extremely co-operative in the issues surrounding the use of its mercantile marine. German-leaning Sweden suffered most, for on 2 October 1917 Britain, frustrated at the continued supply of ores and materials to Germany, imposed further restrictions on exports (these also applied in a lesser manner to Norway and Denmark). For ordinary Swedes 1918 would be the hardest year of the war. From a peak in 1916, when Swedish exports were up sixty per cent on 1910, they plummeted in 1917, reaching levels which, in real money terms, were less than 1905 and causing major falls in national wealth and social spending. In April 1917 there were food riots throughout Sweden and demonstrations in Stockholm in support of the Russian revolution.

The USA's entry into the war had immediate effects for the Royal Navy, too. The need for the 10th Cruiser Squadron to patrol the northern entrance to the North Sea was reduced by the fact that the main source of contraband had now embargoed itself. Slowly the AMCs were stripped away from patrolling work and used instead as escorts for the transatlantic convoys. And, increasingly, US naval forces arrived in Britain to supplement and assist Royal Navy vessels.

The Luxberg Affair

After the fall of the right wing, German-leaning government of Hammarskjöld the leadership of Sweden fell to Prime Minister Carl Swartz and Foreign Minister Arvid Lindman. This was a weak ministry, but still one which followed the basic precepts of its predecessor. A general election was slated to be held in the September, and the debate was dominated by those of the government party who wished to maintain the status quo and those of the left who wanted to alleviate the food poverty now being endured and reach trade agreements with the USA and Britain.

On 8 September, in the middle of the election campaign, the United States government published the 'Luxburg telegrams'. These were despatches from the German minister in Buenos Aires, Karl Ludwig Graf von Luxburg, which had been sent via Swedish diplomatic channels to Berlin and intercepted by British intelligence. Among other things they revealed the routing of Argentine ships carrying wheat and meat to the Allies and advised that they should be 'sunk without trace'. The cables also revealed that the Swedes were openly allowing German access to their communications network, the so-called 'Swedish Roundabout'*. As historian Patrick Salmon noted: 'The British hoped the Luxburg affair discredited the existing right wing government and contributed to their electoral defeat.'[16]

This defeat brought to power, on 19 October, a Liberal-Social Democratic coalition with Professor Nils Edén as Prime Minister, the socialist leader Hjalmar Branting as Finance Minister, and Johannes Hellner as Foreign Minister. Hellner been part of the team negotiating trade with Britain in 1916–17 and was now looked on as the man in Sweden who would bring about an agreement with the western powers: as he was in Britain too.

---

* In 1915 the Swedes had begun to allow German messages to be sent to the German embassy in the USA via Swedish diplomatic systems. The British complained at this abuse of diplomatic channels, nicknamed the 'Swedish Roundabout', and the Swedes pleaded contrition but simply redirected the German messages to the German embassy in Buenos Aires, from whence they were retransmitted to Washington.

CHAPTER 12
Labour and Loss, June–October 1917

While the USA entered the war and the politicians negotiated, the system of convoy for the Scandinavian trade had proved an instant success. Between 29 and 30 April 1917 Brock sailed two eastbound (Humber-Lerwick, Lerwick-Bergen) convoys without loss; twenty-seven merchant ships in total. Twenty-six vessels were safely convoyed in the opposite direction. In May there were twenty-four Humber-Lerwick and twenty-five Lerwick-Bergen convoys accounting for 289 and 146 ships respectively, and a similar number on the westward route.

Although the introduction of convoy markedly reduced the attrition, a determined U-boat commander could still find victims. Britain needed coal; and coal mining needs pit props, a vital export from Scandinavia. These formed the cargo of the SS *Arfinn Jarl*, 1,097grt, which left Ålesund on 19 May, bound for the Tyne and under orders to proceed to Holmengrå to join a convoy to Lerwick, and hence down Britain's east coast. Two hours after arriving, Captain Oscar Hauge received instructions to put to sea and join up with the other convoyed vessels, course north 88 degrees west, at a speed of 8 knots; it was additionally signalled that the vessels being convoyed were to keep as close together as possible. The Norwegian steamer was the last on the northern line, having on her port side an armed British cargo ship, which was a little astern, and on the port bow an armed Romanian vessel. Three destroyers circled the convoy and armed trawlers provided the close escort.

This was the most vulnerable time, when convoys formed up or dispersed close to land, where U-boats could lurk in coastal waters with a fair chance of guessing where their prey might be. At 2105 on the 20th the convoy had travelled just sixteen miles to the west of

Holmengrå when the *Arnfinn Jarl* was struck on the port side of the after hold by a torpedo from *U-19*. Part of the deck cargo and one of the floats standing abaft the mainmast were thrown clear of the vessel, falling overboard, while the mainmast was bent to an angle of thirty degrees. The vessel's stern rose but then immediately fell until the well deck was in the water.

With his ship doomed, Captain Hauge ordered the boats lowered and they were rowed clear of the sinking ship, where the '30-knotter' destroyer HMS *Sylvia*, Lieutenant Peter Shaw RNR in command, picked up the crew before dashing off to look for the submarine[*]. Aided by her timber cargo, *Arnfinn Jarl* was reported still afloat around 2200, but had disappeared by midnight.

Late in the afternoon of the 21st her nineteen-strong crew was landed at Lerwick, grateful that they were alive to tell their story and with no human cost. But it was another ship and cargo lost.

One of the more resourceful and successful U-boat commanders operating in the North Sea was *Kapitänleutnant* Martin Schelle, commanding the minelayer *UC-33*. Between 23 and 25 May he sank thirteen vessels, eight of which were Danish fishing smacks, operating on the Faroe Bank; but he also took bigger fish.

The sailing vessel *Whinlatter* was a 1,378grt Norwegian-flagged, iron-hulled barque, on passage from New Orleans to Copenhagen with a cargo of wood. On 25 May she was picking her way between the Faroes and the Shetland Islands when she was sunk by *UC-33*.

That same day the small Norwegian steamer *Glyg* was working her way from Fraserburgh, from whence she had departed on the 18th, to Iceland. Her cargo was such that a U-boat captain might have had cause to regret sinking her, for she was full of fish-curing equipment, 2,200 barrels of salt and 2,254 empty barrels for storage, all intended for the making of the very same salted herring that Norway was still exporting, however surreptitiously, to Germany. Having stayed some five days in Lerwick she was directed by the harassed naval staff at the port to sail and follow a Norway-bound convoy which was leaving Lerwick in a northerly direction. The *Glyg* was to accompany the convoy only for five miles to the north of Shetland, and then leave its protection and take a direct course

---

[*] Such a procedure was counter to the doctrine used in the Western Approaches, where warships were enjoined to attack the submarine first and rescue survivors later.

for Iceland. Captain Ole M Pudersen complied with his instructions, leaving his fellow merchantmen behind during the afternoon.

At about 1900 *Glyg* was around seventeen miles NNW of Muckle Flugga, at the very tip of Shetland, when a German submarine appeared astern and fired three shots. It was *UC-33* again. All hands immediately got into the boats and pulled clear of the ship, but the submarine came nearer and ordered the captain and three others to come on board the U-boat. Schelle then sent a boarding party to place scuttling charges on the *Glyg*, but before setting them live he showed an unexpectedly compassionate side by allowing any sailor who desired to go back on board to save any clothing or effects to do so.

The charges were then detonated and *Glyg* sank by the stern. All night the men sat in their lifeboats, bitterly cold and buffeted by the waves. It was not until 1500 the following afternoon that they were rescued by a trawler, the *Loch Katrine* of Hartlepool, whose skipper at once discontinued fishing and took the men to land. The brotherhood of the sea was more important than money to this man, but it was not to profit him. Just six weeks later, on 4 July, his trawler was sunk by gunfire from *U-87* east of the Faroe Islands.

HMS *Cheerful*

The destroyers for the convoy escort were detached from the Grand Fleet 8th and 13th Flotillas in April to make up the Lerwick-based forces, while the 7th Flotilla (assigned to the Harwich Force) provided thirteen for the Humber and Tyne leg. By June twenty-three destroyers were available for the Humber-Tyne-Lerwick route and a further eighteen were based at Shetland for the cross-sea passage. Armed trawlers and whalers completed the resources, and all were divided up into six 'teams' designated A to F. On average, the escort comprised two or three destroyers and six armed trawlers; it was often a dangerous duty where a moment's inattention could spell disaster.

One of the 8th Flotilla destroyers stationed at Lerwick was HMS *Cheerful*, a '30-knotter' (later known as 'C'-class) launched in 1897 and armed with a 12pdr gun, together with five 6pdrs and two torpedo tubes. Her captain was Lieutenant in Command Harman Arthur Lewis Bond RNR, a thirty-five-year-old reservist who had been appointed to *Cheerful* in September the previous year.

On 30 June Bond and *Cheerful* were escorting a convoy into Shetland. She was the rearmost ship, and in front of her were nine merchant steamers, safely conducted to Bressay Sound and entering the swept channel from the south which would take them to Lerwick and their moorings, and with the Kirkabister light guiding them home. Only six miles of the passage remained.

Just before midnight *Cheerful* was abreast of Hilli Ness. Suddenly the night was shattered by the roar of an explosion under her boiler room. The ship immediately split in two and the forward part rolled over and floated upside down for about fifteen minutes before sliding under the waves. The after part stayed upright a little longer before it too sank.

Out of a crew of fifty-eight, only eighteen men survived. Stokers accounted for twenty-six of the dead. She had hit a mine, laid two days earlier by Schelle in *UC-33*. The subsequent court of enquiry established that it was commonplace for destroyers to stray outside the swept channel limits, a strange, self-harming departure from instructions. Following *Cheerful's* sinking, standing orders were reinforced that vessels should stay within the safe channel. The loss of men was to be regretted, but the loss of a valuable escort was also a problem. There were so few destroyers to go round. Lieutenant Bond had survived the ordeal, and six weeks later was appointed to command the torpedo boat *TB-17* in the slightly more congenial waters of the Mediterranean.

For *UC-33*, under her commander Martin Schelle, it was proving another very successful cruise. Between 28 June and 7 July she sank twelve vessels. They were mainly fishing vessels, but not so the sailing ship *Ariel*. Sailing ships could not travel in a convoy; they were too dependent on the vagaries of wind power and unable to maintain the necessary formation, or so it was thought. They sailed alone and often into danger. Without doubt the oldest ship to be sunk in the pursuit of the Scandinavian trade was the 108grt Lerwick-based schooner *Ariel*. She had first graced the seas in 1844 as a pilot boat in the Channel, but in 1860 she was sold to a new owner on Shetland and there she stayed for the rest of her life.

In 1917, and after two major refits, she was still engaged in shipping. On 29 June she had loaded with a cargo of coal and oil at Methil, on the Firth of Forth, and set sail for Lerwick. Thirty-six miles north-east of Peterhead she was intercepted by Schelle, who fired eight shells at her without achieving a hit. *Ariel's* crew took to the boats, the U-boat came alongside and put men aboard to scuttle the schooner with charges, and her sixty-three-year career at sea was over. Fortunately an armed trawler from Peterhead was sighted and the U-boat dived to escape. The patrol craft was left to take on board the schooner's crew and return them to dry land.

On the day that HMS *Cheerful* hit one of the *UC-33*'s mines, the U-boat sank the Swedish steamer *Germania,* 1,046grt, on passage from Gothenburg to Hull with general cargo, just forty miles east of Lerwick. She was in convoy and under escort, but it made no difference.

HMS *Itchen*

Six days later the escorts suffered another loss. Twenty-six-year-old Australian-born Lieutenant in Command Frederick Langton Cavaye RN had charge of HMS *Itchen*, a 'River'-class destroyer launched in 1903. On the morning of 6 July *Itchen* was part of an escorting force of two destroyers and four armed trawlers for a small Immingham-Lerwick convoy of four vessels. Two, *Luna* and *Liberty*, were Norwegian and two, *Tyskkland* and *Randelsborg*, were Danish*. Just before 0830 *Itchen* was east of the Pentland Firth and zigzagging on the starboard side of the convoy (i.e. the seaward side). Cavaye went aft to the head and left the bridge in the charge of Gunner Jones. Lieutenant E J Hicks, the first lieutenant, was having breakfast in the wardroom.

On the port side, hugging the lee shore and hidden from sight underwater, was the German U-boat *UC-44***, commanded by *Kapitänleutnant* Kurt Tebbenjohanns. He had spotted the convoy and, targeting a small steamer of around 1,000 tons, he fired a single torpedo. In the U-boat's war diary it was reported that an explosion was heard some ninety seconds after firing.

In fact, Tebbenjohann's missile had passed through the whole of the convoy without hitting anything before ramming into the port aft side of *Itchen* and triggering off a secondary explosion of one of *Itchen*'s depth charges, which had been shaken loose by the

---

* The *Luna* and the *Randelsborg* failed to survive the convoys. The former was torpedoed by *UC-63* on 14 August 1917, beached and later refloated. The latter was attacked and sunk by *UB-34* in the Skagerrak on passage to the Firth of Forth on 9 March 1918.

** Many sources attribute the sinking to *U-99* (for example Hepper, *Warship Losses*), but this has been proven not to be the case. *UC-44*'s log books were recovered after the U-boat was sunk on her next cruise, off Waterford, Ireland. The Admiralty Intelligence Department made some comments in red pencil on the right-hand side of the translation, and it is clear that they believed that *UC-44* had sunk *Itchen* (ADM 137/4244).

detonation and exploded at 80ft depth under the destroyer. Eight men were killed outright by the torpedo blast, four of them in the engine room. The accompanying escorts swung into action, the destroyer *Flying Fish* dropping a depth charge, as did the trawler *Isaac Walton*, which also fired at a suspected periscope. Neither hit anything.

The after part of the ship was completely wrecked and her back was broken. Cavaye, shaken out of his ablutions and fighting his way through smoke and wreckage, emerged on deck to find that he was trapped in the stern of the vessel, unable to get forward due to the wreckage of the decks. Together with his Chief ERA he managed to throw the confidential chests overboard.

Meanwhile, with the engine room wrecked, the ship sinking, and unable to communicate with his captain, Gunner Jones ordered 'abandon ship' and the Grimsby-registered hired trawler *Gardenia* came alongside to lift off the survivors, first forward and then again aft. As she shoved off, two badly scalded men, Stoker Albert Lyons and a shipmate, emerged from the engine-room wreckage and *Gardenia* hauled them aboard too. It proved to be just in time, for *Itchen* suddenly heeled over to port, rolled and sank by the stern. It was eighteen minutes since she had been hit.

But the convoy had to go on. Brock sent *Mary Rose* and *Nessus* out at 1030 to take over the convoy, and called on patrolling destroyers to hunt the U-boat. They did not find it.

The subsequent court of enquiry, held two days later, determined that the U-boat had fired a 'browning shot', hoping to hit something without a specific aim. The captain of the *Flying Fish* particularly drew the court's attention to the skill and bravery of Skipper E W Freshwater of the *Gardenia*, who 'most ably put his ship alongside HMS *Itchen*, then in a sinking condition and took off all survivors'.[1] Brock later commended the skipper to Their Lordships. The court attributed no blame for the sinking to Cavaye[*] or anyone else, but it was another loss of an escort which could be ill-afforded.

*　　*　　*

[*] Five months later Cavaye would face another court of enquiry for the loss of his command, the destroyer HMS *Wolverine,* when that ship was lost in collision with HMS *Rosemary* off the coast of Ireland. Cavaye was again exonerated, the blame being ascribed to the Officer of the Watch on board *Rosemary*. See Dunn, S R, *Bayly's War*, Seaforth Publishing (Barnsley, 2018).

Between the commencement of convoy on the Scandinavian routes and the end of June an average of 368 ships per month, in both directions, made the Lerwick-Bergen or Bergen-Lerwick trip. Only twenty were lost. In July ten ships were sunk out of 454.[2]

U-67 was stationed off the Norwegian coast, looking to pick off ships as they joined or left convoys. In July she sank two Danish vessels and a Swedish one. The Danish *Harrildsborg* was despatched on 19 July as she approached Bergen with a cargo of much-needed coal. Her crew was picked up by the escorting destroyer HMS *Arab*. The Swedish *Viking*, also carrying coal from Sunderland to Gothenburg, was sunk on the 24th, fifteen miles off Sognefjord, and another Danish ship, the *Rigmor*, was torpedoed four days later.

The *U-60* sank a Russian and a Norwegian vessel at the end of July, having arrived from the Western Approaches. The *U-52* sank five ships in July; two Swedish, one Norwegian, one British and the Royal Navy submarine *C-34*, sunk on 17 July off the Fair Isle, Shetland, with the loss of all but one of the crew of nineteen. Convoy had reduced the losses, but the Royal Navy had still to find a way to stop them. The desire to take an aggressive rather than passive stance still pervaded naval thinking.

Operation BB – Another Exercise in Futility

Despite the demonstrable success of convoy on the Scandinavian and East Coast routes, the idea that U-boats could be aggressively hunted to perdition, like the foxes that so many Royal Navy officers chased in peacetime, appeared to die hard.

In June 1917 Beatty planned and authorised 'Operation BB', a massive U-boat hunt around the north of Scotland. The areas chosen were based on Admiralty intelligence that a number of U-boats would be in those zones between 15 and 24 June, either working the Scandinavian convoy route or transiting to the North Atlantic.

Four flotilla leaders, forty-nine badly-needed destroyers and seventeen submarines were deployed, and the operation was given priority over all other activities, including convoy escorts. The results were disappointing, to say the least. Despite there being some twenty-four U-boats in the area, five of which were working the Lerwick-Bergen route, and after twenty-six sighting reports and eight attacks by destroyers, not a single U-boat was sunk. The submarine HMS *K-1* did fire a torpedo at *U-95* but it failed to explode.

Beatty claimed nonetheless that the operation had prevented heavy losses on the Scandinavian passages, and recommended that even more destroyers should be deployed, in smaller areas. He commented in a letter to his wife on 7 July: 'It is a prodigious job, as it is like looking for a needle in a bundle of hay and, when you have found it, trying to strike it with another needle. But we must stick to it and I am sure an answer to the conundrum will be found ...'[3]

This comment by Beatty rather ignored the fact that a solution had been found – convoy, which hid merchant vessels from submarines. It was unnecessary to kill the U-boats if they were not sinking any ships. This obvious point was seemingly not apparent at the time, for Beatty went on to sanction two more such exercises in futility, 'Operation CC' in July (which deployed kite balloons for the first time) and 'Operation HS' (which used towed nets as well) in October. No U-boats were sunk, although the Admiralty claimed three for the October action.[*] As the historian Paul Halpern noted, 'Despite the persistent efforts of the men in the small ships during appalling weather [the operation] had not been worth the considerable efforts devoted to it'.[4]

Submarine Patrol

Alongside these large-scale hunts, the Admiralty also ordered new submarine deployments. Charles de Burgh, last encountered in 1914 on HMS *Antrim*, had returned to the submarine service the following year, and in 1917 was a lieutenant commander and captain of HMS *G-8*, a modern vessel built specifically for operations in the North Sea and part of the 10th Submarine Flotilla based at Scapa.

German U-boats, deprived of isolated prey by the Scandinavian convoys, had taken to lying off the Norwegian coast waiting for the convoy to disperse, when merchant ships would sail individually to their respective destinations. As well as using light cruisers and destroyers in sweeps looking for them, the Admiralty, in its wisdom, also decided to deploy submarines to hunt U-boats. Given that both hunter and hunted would be low-lying (or submerged) in the water, and thus difficult to spot, this seemed a tall order.

---

[*] The three U-boats claimed had in fact been sunk south of the operation in minefields.

De Burgh was sent to the Scandinavian coast in May, and on the 30th was patrolling near Holmengrå Island. All he saw were two fishing vessels and a large sailing ship. The following day was more interesting. 'Sighted Hun submarine, attacked and got two tubes ready ... got within 2,000yds before raising periscope'. It was no good. 'Hun last seen 5,000yds', he recorded.[5]

The first day of June saw *G-8* back on the Norway coast at 0500. 'Rolling heavily all night, big sea, blowing gale. Surface patrol till 2000, dived for the night to fifty feet'.[6] De Burgh stayed out, cruising up and down the coast until 7 June, but saw nothing.

There was better sport on his next visit to Norway. On 19 June: 'sighted enemy ... full speed on motors, trimmed down. 0125 fired port and 0126 fired starboard torpedoes at 5,000 yards, both missed.' The next diary entry just reads 'surface patrol'.[7]

On 8 July he sighted smoke and thought it was a trimmed-down U-boat. The *G-8* went to action stations but the sighting turned out to be a trawler, hull down some six miles away. And then, the culmination of a submariner's dream. As de Burgh's diary for 23 July laconically records: 'Sighted two Huns and bagged one and chased round ahead of the other'.[8] As he sailed back into harbour he 'showed one finger to Captain [S]. Very pleased.' But the gloss was rather taken off the moment as he learned at the same time of his appointment to *K-22*.* 'Took gilt off gingerbread' he gloomily noted.[9]

De Burgh was awarded a DSO** for his exploit of sinking a German U-boat. Except that he had not; post-war records show that no German submarine was lost that day.

Sabotage

U-boats were not the only weapon that the Germans brought to bear on the Scandinavian trade. Sabotage also played a role.

Walter von Rautenfels was a German diplomatic courier attached to the German legation in Kristiania; except that he was not. Actually he was Walter Harald von Gerich, a Finnish one-time military officer, who had served in the Imperial Russian Guard, worked as a civil servant, and was now a German saboteur.

---

* The 'K'-class of steam-driven 'fleet submarines' were much unloved by their crews, being dangerous and difficult to handle and nicknamed 'Kalamity class'. Of eighteen built, none was lost through enemy action but six sank through accidents.

** Gazetted 2 November 1917.

But the Norwegian security services became interested in him. He was arrested in Grynerlockken, Kristiania, on 16 June 1917, and at the town's main railway station his diplomatic baggage was found to contain 188 kilograms of explosives in suitcases and packing cases. The haul included ninety-five large and twelve small explosive bombs, 104 fire bombs, detonators and percussion caps, all clearly intended to be placed on merchant ships. Some were shaped to resemble pieces of coal, others cigars and cigarettes[*].

The Norwegian government had been desperate to avoid a row with Germany over Rautenfels' detention. Faced with a request by its intelligence service to open the courier's diplomatic baggage, the Norwegians notified the German legation and invited them to have a representative present. The German minister raised a strong protest and sent an attaché, Prince zu Wied, to remonstrate in person.

After honour had been satisfied, and perhaps diplomatically, the Prince left the station before the bags were finally opened, revealing their treasure trove of explosives together with poisoned sugar containing anthrax.

Even now, Norway's carefully protected neutrality was its first concern. Despite Rautenfels/Gerich admitting his crime, after German governmental pressure for his release had been applied, he was set free. With a claim of diplomatic immunity due to his role as a courier to the German Kaiser, he was escorted by police to Germany on 27 June. His Norwegian and Finnish accomplices were less fortunate. William Person was sentenced to six years in prison, Wäino Pesonen to two years, Hjalmar Wirtanen to one-and-a-half years, Johannes Sandvik to four-and-a-half years and Allan Sandstrøm to the same.

But the damage has been done. As the *Daily Telegraph* noted: 'It is feared that some of the infernal machines already had been used in Scandinavian vessels which have been lost. It has been substantiated that the whole stock is of German make.' And the same newspaper reported the Kristiania *Tidens Tegn* as stating: 'The Norwegian press is now convinced that the activities which have been discovered have cost the lives of hundreds of Norwegian seamen.'[10]

---

[*] The 'cigars' were lead piping, shaped to resemble a torpedo 'cuban', hollow inside with a copper disc halfway down the pipe creating two compartments. One held picric acid, an explosive under certain conditions, the other sulphuric acid. The time delay was the time it took for the acids to eat through the copper disc and mix, causing an explosion and fire. The device was the invention of Dr Walter Theodore von Scheele, a pharmacist and German 'sleeper' agent in New York.

Problems and Solutions

Despite the relative success of the convoy system across the North Sea and down the eastern coast of Britain, Admiral Brock foresaw problems with the approaching winter. In a report of 1 July he pointed out that the old '30-knotters' would experience problems come the equinoctial gales and bad weather. Six of the slightly more modern 'River'-class, vessels with better seakeeping abilities, were ordered to Immingham in lieu, and the HMS *Garry* ('River'-class, launched 1905) and *Dee* (another 'River'-class vessel, launched 1903) were sent to Shetland from the Coast of Ireland Command at Larne.

Brock was also concerned about the performance of his trawlers. He reported eleven of them as being unsuitable for duty because of their poor steaming qualities, and once again the Admiralty obliged him in July by replacing them with vessels claimed capable of at least 9 knots.

The organisation of the convoys at sea was a constant problem, and 'it was found necessary to establish a connecting link between the westbound convoys and the escort force that awaited them'.[11] As a result, six specially trained RNR lieutenants were appointed as convoy pilots, commencing in August 1917. They sailed in selected merchant ships with each eastbound convoy, proceeded to Bergen, and after consultation with Halsey and his staff, organised the subsequent westbound convoy to the point of departure.

Problems soon became apparent. Their orders were often ignored by the merchant masters, even in the ship in which they were sailing, and there were issues regarding authority and divided and unaccountable responsibility with the escort commanders. The system was not a satisfactory solution, and eventually the pilots were embarked on armed trawlers which were meant to function as convoy 'leaders'. But this too was difficult, as the trawlers were too slow and not good for signalling from.

Eventually, armed boarding steamers were drafted into the escort and the pilots were based on these.

Another logistical problem was food supply for the merchant ships. The British Board of Trade was responsible for allocating rations to the masters and crew, but the allowance it made paid no heed to the vagaries of transit time caused by bad weather or the need to offer hospitality to Norwegian customs and port officials. As a result the crews were often on reduced rations or none at all.

Captain Halsey in Kristiania worked hard and was eventually successful in getting the allowances increased.

Sailing Alone

Despite the relative success of convoy, many ships still sailed alone. The SS *Oslo*, 2,296grt, was a Wilson Line vessel built in 1906 to work the routes from Norway to Hull. At her peak she could carry 598 passengers, sixty-two of them in first class, at a maximum of 13 knots.

There was no first class complement on board on 21 August 1917, however, for she was carrying a polyglot collection of seventy refugees from the European fighting, together with a much-needed cargo of copper ore, from Trondheim, via Bergen, to Liverpool. She was not sailing in convoy, relying on her speed for safety, a technique which had already once saved her, for she had outrun an attacking U-boat in October two years previously.

It did not work this time. Fifteen miles north of the Out Skerries she was torpedoed without warning in rough seas by *U-87*. The lifeboats were got out and the passengers ordered to jump into them via the companion ladders. Sisters Marie and Olga Rusanesco were Romanians, fleeing the war which had engulfed their land, with their father, mother and brother. Olga successfully made it into a boat, but as sixteen-year-old Marie was coming down the companion of the sinking ship the boat rose on the crest of the wave. Crewmen shouted to her to let go and jump, but she hesitated, and by the time she did let go the boat had fallen away. Marie fell between the ship and the lifeboat and was never seen again.

The boats eventually reached Lerwick pier at 1900. In the first boat was a Frenchwoman, Madame Lambertine Dupone, desperate for news of her husband Joseph and unaware if he was alive or dead. Soaking wet and shivering with cold, she stood on the pier awaiting him. The second boat arrived with no news of Joseph. Finally the third lifeboat limped in to view and her husband was found to be on board. 'Those who witnessed the reunion of the wife and husband will never forget it; but that is too sacred to discuss in the columns of a newspaper. It was at once pathetic and sublime', wrote a contemporary observer.[12]

Olga Rusanesco was saved and brought ashore but was in a terrible state. Almost naked and rolled in a blanket, she was wet and cold. She had seen her sister drown alongside the boat in which she was seated waiting for her and was hysterical with grief. Along with the rest of her family she was taken to the Grand Hotel, where a local lady sat all night with her to comfort her. Her father, although badly shaken himself, kept visiting the bedroom where his remaining daughter lay to reassure himself that she was still with him.

Oslo had been sunk by *Kapitänleutnant* Rudolf Schneider, notorious in Royal Navy circles as the man who had sunk the battleship HMS *Formidable* on New Year's Day 1915, with the loss of nearly 600 men and boys. He was to sink four more ships on this cruise, three Danish and a Norwegian in addition to *Oslo*, for a total of 7,195grt.

The Sinking of HMS *G-9*

The waters of the North Sea were dangerous in so many different ways. The weather and U-boats were the major threats, but sometimes the danger came from simple human error.

The British submarine HMS *G-9* was launched in 1916. Armed with five torpedo tubes and both 3in and 12pdr guns, she had sailed on 9 September on patrol duty in the North Sea, but on the 15th she was ordered north, to between latitudes 60.30 N and 61.30 N, to keep clear of units of the Grand Fleet which were exercising while on passage from Rosyth to Scapa Flow. A day later she was to the east of the Shetland Islands, patrolling in heavy seas and rain squalls, conditions which made observation difficult. The submarine's commander was thirty-year-old Lieutenant Commander The Honourable Byron Plantagenet Cary, second son of another Byron Plantagenet Cary, 12th Viscount Falkland. As a younger son of the nobility he had, almost by definition, to join the Royal Navy, and had been a submarine captain since 1909, commissioning his current vessel. He had been advised that a U-boat was in the vicinity of Muckle Flugga and was on the look-out for it.

Unknown to Cary, a Lerwick-bound convoy* was slowly steaming towards his position. They had set out from Aspö Fjord, around 60 miles north of Bergen, but the convoy and its destroyer escort, the 'M'-class HMS *Pasley*, had become separated in the atrocious conditions. Her captain, Commander Charles Gordon

---

* One of twenty-five such convoys, comprising 196 ships, which sailed Bergen-Lerwick in the month of September.

Ramsey, had been reduced to displaying a white light halfway up the mast in an attempt to find his missing flock.

Just after midnight Cary spotted what he took to be a surfaced U-boat and fired two torpedoes at his target. On *Pasley*, the officer of the watch, Midshipman Frank Arthur George Wallis RNR, suddenly saw the wash of torpedoes in the water; the first one hit a glancing blow on the starboard quarter but failed to detonate, and the second passed astern. Wallis ordered a hard starboard turn and went to full speed. He could now see a submarine in the sea ahead of him and, sounding the collision siren, set course to ram.

On board *G-9* the terrible realisation that they had just attacked one of their own ships now set in. Moreover, their intended victim was set on revenge. Cary ordered the connection of the cruiser arc lamp to signal the destroyer, but the process of so doing was cumbersome and time-consuming. By the time the signal was made it was already too late. On *Pasley*, Commander Ramsey saw the recognition signal. A signalman shouted 'She's one of ours!'. 'Hard to port, stop both!', yelled Ramsey. It made no difference; his ship ploughed into the submarine and nearly cut it into two pieces.

In the stricken sub, Cary ordered his crew to assemble beneath the conning tower. Stoker William Drake saw one man climb the ladder above him, and followed. Of robust build, he nearly became trapped by the stomach at the lower conning tower door, which had been ordered shut in the hope of keeping the boat afloat. Drake managed to struggle free and reach the bridge, only to be swept into the seas as the boat rolled over and sank by the stern beneath him. He later related that he thought five men had escaped before his vessel went down, but he was the only one of them who managed to survive the terrible conditions and reach *Pasley*, which had stopped to pick up survivors. Weakened by exposure, Drake was unable to pull himself up on the lifeline proffered from the destroyer, so Able Seaman Henry Old clambered over the side of the destroyer to secure a rope around him and both were hauled aboard. The remainder of *G-9*'s thirty-four-man complement died with their vessel. They included Lieutenant H T Lesley, on board only because he was conducting WT trials, and an able seaman and an ERA who were there for training.

The court of enquiry was held on board *Indomitable* four days later. It exonerated *Pasley* and Ramsey, concluding that no one would ever know what led Lieutenant Commander Cary to act as he did. Beatty noted that the incident 'was ... one of those that are inseparable from war', but deplored the delay in introducing improved signalling facilities on submarines, in particular the substitution of the slow and unreliable cruiser arc lamps with Aldis lamps.[13] Their Lordships directed Commander Ramsey to inform Midshipman Wallis that in the opinion of the Court of Enquiry the action taken by him 'was the right action to take under the circumstances, and that its result, so deeply to be regretted, is evidence that it was taken with commendable promptness and precision'.[14]

Lerwick

The growth of convoy meant that Lerwick was increasingly busy, and the size of Lerwick Harbour was becoming a problem. As early as 31 March Beatty had written to the Admiralty that 'congestion at Lerwick is becoming severe; it has been accentuated by bad weather and the number of ships awaiting orders for Prize Courting [sic]'.[15]

The introduction of separate convoys through the White Sea to Archangel meant that there were often an additional fifteen to twenty ships moored there awaiting despatch northwards on this service, as well as the Scandinavian convoys. One way to solve the problem was thought to be double convoys, one fast (over 11 knots) and one slow, but Admiral Hamilton* at Rosyth and in charge of the Coast of Scotland rejected the idea as he thought there were insufficient escorts. The issues surrounding the weather and Lerwick Harbour would come round again as winter drew near.

Until March 1917 Lerwick had merely been an examination centre for ships sent in for contraband inspection, but this was discontinued when the port became the collection point for the newly instituted Scandinavian convoys. The port's increased importance as a base was now reflected in the provision of additional defences and facilities. The old cruiser *Leander* (a second-class protected cruiser launched in 1882) arrived as an extra destroyer depot ship, together with the water vessel *Aquarius* (the former SS *Hampstead*, purchased in 1902 as a distillery vessel). Two 4.7in guns taken from HMS *Brilliant* (the pre-existing depot ship since 1915) were stationed overlooking the southern approaches.

With Lerwick's new status, shipping transiting through the port

---

* This was to be one of Hamilton's last contributions to the convoy debate, for he died in post on 4 October aged sixty-one. He was replaced by Admiral Cecil Burney, previously 2nd Sea Lord.

expanded exponentially. Between March and November 5,560 ship movements passed through. The largest number on one day was 139 vessels, including seventeen destroyers, twenty-six trawlers, twenty-two drifters, four whalers, two yachts, one salvage steamer, one tug, four motor patrol boats, three oilers and fifty-five steamers and sailing ships, all on 23 September. Often ships had to moor outside the defences, in Breiwick to the south of the harbour, and it was 'not uncommon to see sixty to seventy ships in harbour at one time'.[16] A salvage depot was established in August, not least because an average of four shipwrecked crews a week arrived in the harbour and there was always a chance of recovering the victims' vessels. The townspeople provided a regular supply of clothing and hot meals for the survivors.

There was also the ever-present danger of German minelaying. Trawlers and drifters swept the approaches to the harbour daily, but despite these precautions eleven vessels were sunk in and around the approaches to Lerwick in the three months from 10 September; four by mines and the remainder by torpedoes. These comprised three Russian-flagged ships on the White Sea run, a Royal Navy trawler, two Danish vessels and five British. All had fallen victim to the German minelayer *UC-40*, under *Kapitänleutnant* Hermann Menzel.

Not that the Germans had it all their own way in Shetland. The minelaying U-boat *UC-55*, commanded by *Oberleutnant zur See* Horst Rühle von Lilienstern, aged twenty-seven and on his second command patrol, had departed Heligoland on 25 September to lay mines in the Lerwick channel. On 29 September, just as she started dropping her mines, she suffered a loss of trim which resulted in her suddenly diving beyond her rated maximum depth. This critical loss of control caused the forward compartment to flood and the batteries to fail, which in turn triggered the emission of chlorine gas as seawater and battery acid mixed, filling the submarine with noxious fumes.

Von Lilienstern was forced to surface to ventilate the boat, but when she surfaced the rudder refused to answer the helm owing to the lack of (battery-provided) electric power. Sensing that his vessel was lost, he gave orders to destroy secret documents and codebooks and set scuttling charges in the mine and engine rooms. Meanwhile, the U-boat's sudden appearance on the surface had been observed by the minesweeping trawler *Moravia*, which engaged the submarine with its solitary gun and called up reinforcements. The destroyer *Tirade* (Lieutenant Commander Henry Dawson Crawford Stanistreet) arrived in response, hotly pursued by HMS *Sylvia* (Lieutenant Peter Shaw RNR), last noted rescuing the survivors of the *Arfinn Jarl*. Perhaps glad of a break from convoy escort duty at slow speed, they came charging in and opened fire at a range of 3,400 yards, *Tirade*'s third 4in shell struck near the conning tower of the submarine, and her fifth hit the aft casing below the waterline. *Tirade* then attempted to ram and drop depth charges while *Sylvia* charged in, firing three rounds from her forward 12pdr. One shell certainly hit the conning tower, for it killed von Lilienstern outright. The U-boat blew up and *Moravia* then closed to the wreck, fired two more shots into her and dropped a final depth charge, before rescuing the German crew. Seventeen were taken prisoner and ten men were killed. Lieutenant Commander Stanistreet claimed the prize as his.

The more experienced Hermann Menzel and *UC-40* were back at work off Lerwick again in October. The SS *Anglo Dane* was an old collier, owned and operated by the Danish company Det Forenede Dampskibs Selskab. In late October 1917 she left the Tyne, where fifty-three years previously she had been built in the Hebburn yards of Andrew Leslie and Company, sailing in convoy for Helsingør, via Lerwick. On the 21st she was approaching Lerwick Harbour, about three-quarters of a mile south-west of Bressay Lighthouse, as the leading vessel in the starboard column of the convoy. Suddenly the air was rent by a huge explosion, clearly heard and seen on shore. She had hit a mine, opposite number two hold on the starboard side. The detonation blew the ship in two, the fore part sinking immediately while the after section remained afloat for four minutes or so and then disappeared below the waves, as did the precious cargo of coal. One crewman was killed outright, but Captain Hans Lemmeke managed to get the rest of his men into the ship's boats, from where they were rescued by an armed trawler and landed at Alexandra wharf.

This latest cruise was a particularly profitable one for Menzel. Two days previously his Lerwick minefield had accounted for the Russian *Slavonic*, 3,604grt, inbound from Archangel. The same day that *Anglo-Dane* met her end, and to the east of Shetland, *UC-40* torpedoed the Danish SS *Flynderborg*, 1,400grt, in ballast from Copenhagen to Leith to pick up coal, and three days later she torpedoed the British *Novington*, 3,442grt, twenty-five miles ESE of Bard Island, Shetland, a cargo vessel bound for France from Archangel with a cargo of sawn wood. These were all substantial vessels and their loss could be ill afforded.

*   *   *

The increased workload and U-boat activity brought additional resources in its wake. On 8 October Rear Admiral Clement Greatorex raised his flag as Senior Officer Shetland, based at Lerwick and responsible to Brock for the management of the port. A Route Instruction Office was opened for briefing merchant masters. Telegraphists were kept busy sending manifests and other documentation. A female office staff, some fifteen in total, was recruited and then joined the newly-formed WRNS while the commanding officer's secretary, Lena Mouat, was promoted WRNS Assistant Principal*.[17]

However, there was no doubt that using Lerwick as the centre point of the Scandinavian trade was becoming a problem, for the port was simply too small and too weather-wracked to serve the volume of trade now passing through it; some five million tons in 1917.[18]

---

* The lowest commissioned WRNS rank, equivalent to a sub-lieutenant.

CHAPTER 13

Surface Warfare and the Disaster of the Convoy of 17 October 1917

By mid-October 1917 the Scandinavian convoy system was an established part of Brock's command and had more than proved its worth. Some 4,500 vessels had been conveyed since the end of April with minimal losses, and none at all to surface action.

U-boats found the convoys hard to encounter and attack, but were able to report to High Seas Fleet commander Admiral Scheer that there were large convoys regularly transiting between Shetland and the Norwegian coast. Scheer's paramount interest was the U-boat attacks on Britain's supply chain in the Western Approaches, but by attacking the Scandinavian convoys he could force the Royal Navy to deplete its forces in that battle zone to strengthen the defence of the Scandinavian trade. He also had the tactical advantage that his surface ships could access the eastern end of the convoy routeing from his own bases,[*] passing up along the Scandinavian coastline. The idea of surface attacks on the convoys thus commended itself to him on at least two levels.

His eventual weapon of choice for this mission was two light cruisers, specially adapted for minelaying and originally ordered for the Russian navy. The SMS *Brummer* and *Bremse* were modern, fast (28 knots), well-armed (four 5.9in guns, two 3.5in, two torpedo tubes, 400 mines) and of longer range (6,700 miles) than the typical German light cruiser. Against a light escort they would be a formidable foe.

---

[*] The route passed within 350 miles of Horns Reef.

The Grand Fleet, 15 October

At the Admiralty, Jellicoe had developed a plan for carrying mining operations right up to the German coasts and the German rivers, and had sent it to Beatty at Scapa for comment. Beatty suggested some alterations on points of detail but approved of the plan as a whole. As a preliminary operation to pave the way for implementation he had detailed a force of four light cruisers, twelve destroyers and a flotilla leader to attack the German minesweepers in the Heligoland Bight. This had been briefed in, and the relevant forces were about to sail, when Beatty received another message from London, marked 'urgent'.

This instead instructed him to raise steam in all his light cruisers and in a further twelve destroyers. He was to intercept a force now believed to be on the move. As his new orders did not tell him from where or to where this force might be travelling, he effectively had to put the whole of the North Sea under observation. What had happened?

At 1623 on the 15th Room 40, the Admiralty's cryptography department, had decoded a message from *Brummer* stating that she had postponed her orders until the following day and gave details of her course and speed. This led Admiral Oliver to cable Beatty 'minelayer *Brummer* leaves Norman Deep tomorrow 16th probably for minelaying. She should be intercepted.'[1]

This was not the only intercept that related to the Scandinavian convoys on that evening. Room 40 became convinced that *Brummer*'s objective was not minelaying. U-boats reported a heavy convoy off Shetland, and U-boats in the North Sea were specifically ordered not to attack cruisers unless they were convinced that they were British. Unaccountably, Oliver passed on none of this information to Beatty, or indeed to anyone else.

Meanwhile, Beatty was issuing new orders to his commands, setting up patrol lines in the central and eastern North Sea areas. But the admiral always seemed to have problems with signals, as his communication issues and mistakes at Dogger Bank and Jutland testify. The squadrons from Scapa occupied their stations at the times appointed, but the disposition of the Rosyth forces did not go so well. Beatty's orders cancelled others which he had issued earlier in the afternoon for the attack on the Bight; and the Rosyth squadrons were preparing for sea – some vessels were actually under way – when his new orders were received. Not all the forces concerned received the signal, and in consequence there was muddle and confusion and not all the ships were able to reach their appointed patrol lines at the necessary time or in the required numbers.

No sign of minelaying activity was observed, and the Germans maintained radio silence. Beatty began to doubt the original hypothesis. On the 16th he ordered up further reinforcements to his patrols. The 'large light cruisers' *Courageous* and *Glorious**, and four destroyers of the 13th Flotilla were sent to reinforce the 2nd Light Cruiser Squadron; *Furious* was told off to remain at sea and to concentrate on the same squadron. Then, later in the evening, the Admiralty decided to despatch increased resources to the line of approach to the Tyne and Humber. Now three cruisers, twenty-seven light cruisers and fifty-four destroyers were at sea engaged in searching for a force which, so far as could be deduced, consisted of only one minelayer and a handful of destroyers.

No reason had been seen to delay the sailing of the eastbound convoy leaving Lerwick on the 15th, or the westbound one which would make the return journey on the 16th.

Escorts

Two destroyers and two or more armed trawlers were the usual escorts for the Scandinavian convoys, the destroyers being provided from the Grand Fleet flotillas. During October eight were assigned to duty at Lerwick: *Marmion*, *Sarpedon*, *Morning Star* (all 11th Flotilla); and *Mary Rose*, *Obedient*, *Strongbow*, *Tirade* and *Marvel* (all from the 12th Flotilla). The old cruisers *Brilliant* and *Leander* (Senior Naval Officer) acted as depot ships.

On 15 October it was the turn of HMS *Mary Rose* and *Strongbow* to act as escorts, and they had left Lerwick with the eastbound convoy in company with the armed trawlers *Elise* and *P Fannon*.

Mary Rose was an 'M'-class destroyer, launched in 1915. She carried three 4in guns, three 2pdrs and two torpedo tubes at a maximum speed of 34 knots. With a complement of ninety-two men, her captain was thirty-three-year-old Lieutenant Commander Charles Leonard Fox RN.

Fox and *Mary Rose* had previously been attached to the Coast of Ireland command, and there had earned a unique distinction. On 3 May 1917 she was the first vessel to find and greet the initial

---

* Otherwise known to the Royal Navy as *Outrageous* and *Uproarious*.

detachment of American destroyers coming to join the fight against U-boats in the Western Approaches. Fox hoisted the international signal 'Welcome to the American colours', and USS *Wadsworth* answered 'Thank you, I am glad of your company'. The following day the US Navy destroyers arrived at Queenstown, together with *Mary Rose*, and America truly entered the war.

However, Fox's Royal Navy career had not been one of unblemished success. On 11 March 1916 he had been relieved of the command of the destroyer HMS *Munster* over the loss of some private signals from his ship. His appointment to *Mary Rose* came nearly a year later, in February 1917.[2]

Strongbow was another 'M'-class destroyer, launched in 1916. Two knots faster than her companion, she had the same main armament but only one 2pdr and four torpedo tubes instead of two. Her captain was thirty-one-year-old Lieutenant Commander Edward Brooke. Brooke had commanded the destroyer *Lizard* at Jutland, for which he had been Mentioned in Despatches,[*] and had taken charge of *Strongbow* in October 1916.

Both of the trawlers carried only a single 6pdr gun. *Elise* was a Peterhead-registered hired vessel, built in 1907 and taken up initially for minesweeping purposes; *P Fannon* was a 1915-built Aberdeen boat, also originally hired as a minesweeper. Neither was capable of more than around 9 knots.

Just before noon on the 16th the two destroyers parted company. *Mary Rose* went ahead to collect the westbound convoy gathered in the Bergen leads near Marstein. As senior officer, Fox ordered Brooke to take the eastbound ships, disperse them off the Norwegian coast, and then rejoin him at sea for the return journey. While Brooke undertook that duty, Fox collected his new charges and left Marstein in the afternoon. He had twelve merchant ships in company, which were grouped in no very regular formation. To add to the complication of convoy control, it was a polyglot assembly that the navy were to protect; two were British, one Belgian, one Danish, five Norwegian and three Swedish. The weather was poor, and SS *Glodale*, a vessel in the eastbound group, had become separated from her own convoy owing to her cargo of timber having shifted. Fox detached the whaler *Beluga* to stand by her, and she eventually got back to Lerwick the following day.

---

[*] *London Gazette* 29751, 15 Sept 1916.

The Death of a Convoy

The German ships had passed unseen along the Norwegian coast. They had been rigged to resemble Royal Navy 'C'-class cruisers and were also painted dark grey, a British rather than German paint scheme. In the murk of an autumnal North Sea day, and certainly at night, they might confuse an observer long enough to gain an advantage. *Fregattenkapitän* Leonhardi, commanding SMS *Brummer*, and *Fregattenkapitän* Westerkamp in the *Bremse*, certainly hoped so as they headed for where they thought a convoy might be encountered.

Mary Rose had somehow got ahead of her retinue of merchant ships, and when *Strongbow* rejoined the convoy it was dark and neither commanding officer could see or communicate with the other. Brooke tried to call up Fox by W/T but was unable to make contact. He therefore decided to take his station on the port side of the convoy, which was then to the relative north and north-west of his ship.

Dawn broke at 0530. The wind was fresh from the south-west and there was a heavy sea. The light was poor but the lookouts reported that they could see at least 400 yards. *Mary Rose* had managed to get some six to eight miles ahead of her charges and was out of visual contact. Brooke in *Strongbow* was still in company with the convoy. Neither commander knew that a general alert had been declared in the North Sea two days previously, or that a German force was out, or that a large proportion of the Grand Fleet's scouting forces were at sea looking for the enemy. It was just another quotidian day of escort duty.

Just after 0600 *Strongbow*'s lookouts reported that two unidentified vessels were approaching from the south on a converging course. Brooke was below, and the officer of the watch, Lieutenant Rupert Warden James, sent for him. When he arrived on deck he ordered the challenge of the day; there was no reply. The cruisers, as he now believed they were (possibly 'County'-class, they mused on the bridge), kept on coming. Brooke ordered a second challenge. This too brought no reply. A third challenge received the gobbledegook reply 'AW'. Brooke hesitated no longer. At 0615 he sounded action stations, called for 24 knots and the third boiler to be lit, and ordered a wireless message to be sent, but it was all too late. Before her crew could reach their guns and torpedoes, the ship was smothered by a barrage of 5.9in shells at 3,000 yards' range.

Strongbow was crippled immediately. The first salvo severed the main steam pipe, taking away her ability to manoeuvre and scalding to death many of the men below. On deck there was carnage as a murderous fire cut men down as they raced to their action stations. Brooke was hit in the leg by a shell splinter which left him bleeding profusely and in great pain. The wireless office was hit by a shell and destroyed, its one attempt at sending a signal jammed by the German cruisers. Below decks it was bedlam, but Surgeon Probationer Ian McClean Thomson RNVR, despite having his own leg shattered above the knee, continued to attend to the wounded, including the captain, until he could no longer stand. He was credited with saving many lives.

The German ships veered away. It was clear to Brooke that his ship was doomed, and despite his injury he would not allow anybody to abandon it until he was certain that every confidential book and paper had been destroyed and that the enemy would get nothing of use if they manged to board his ship; this despite two further attacks by the cruisers. He then ordered abandonment and that the ship should be sunk. Unable to move unaided, he determined to stay on board to ensure this was done.

However, his crew had other ideas. Brooke was bodily carried from the shattered bridge and placed on a Carley float. It was 0730 on 17 October. They were less than seventy nautical miles from Lerwick.

Freed from the need to deal with *Strongbow*, the German cruisers swiftly sank four merchant ships by gunfire. Meanwhile, ahead of the convoy, Lieutenant Commander Fox heard the noise of the guns, though he could see nothing of the action. Thinking the ships were being attacked by a surfaced U-boat he turned back, ordered his men to action stations and went to high speed. He did not have enough men to fight his guns and torpedoes simultaneously, and now discovered that the range and deflection transmitters for the guns were out of order and individual gunlayers would have to rely on the naked eye. Surely his worst shock came when, at about 7,000 yards' distance, he realised that the convoys' attackers were *Kaiserliche Marine* cruisers.

Fox had at least two choices. He could attack with guns and torpedoes, but would be heavily outgunned, or he could radio his position and wait for assistance. For a Royal Navy commander there was really only one choice. Following Nelson's dictum that 'no captain can do very wrong if he places his ship alongside that of an enemy', Fox opened fire at long range. He continued to drive his destroyer towards the enemy, which returned fire, until at 2,000 yards he turned broadside-on to launch a torpedo attack. As the helm went over, the enemy gunners found the range and *Mary Rose* was smothered with heavy shells. Her superstructure was shattered and the decks were suddenly full of dead and wounded men. Only the after gun was left operational, the others and their crews having been destroyed. Sub-Lieutenant Frederick William Marsh RNVR continued to fight this gun until it would no longer bear on the enemy. The torpedo tubes and crews were also badly hit, only Able Seamen French and Bailey being left alive. On their own initiative they laid and fired the one functioning torpedo tube. The next shell to hit killed French and left Bailey badly wounded in the leg.[3] Unable to fight and with his ship in sinking condition, Fox ordered Gunner Isaac Handcock to scuttle the ship and at 0700 gave the order 'every man for himself'.

The ship's boats had been smashed to matchwood. Many men took to the ice-cold sea and died of exposure. Fox himself was observed swimming away from the ship but was never seen again. Of a complement of ninety-eight sailors only ten survived; five of them first on a Carley float and then subsequently picked up by a lifeboat from a merchant vessel, which eventually landed them on the Norwegian coast. It appears that twenty-two-year-old Sub-Lieutenant John Richard Dudley Freeman takes much of the credit for the survival of this small group. As *The Times* later related:

> ... but the handful of survivors, in charge of Sub Lieutenant J R D Freeman RN, on the Carley raft, fell in some hours later with a lifeboat belonging to one of the ships of the convoy. Sailing and rowing, they made the Norwegian coast some forty-eight hours later, and were tended with the utmost kindness by the Norwegian authorities. All survivors unite in testifying to the cheerful courage of the surviving officer Sub Lieutenant Freeman, throughout the last phase of the ordeal. Able Seaman Bailey, who despite severe shrapnel wounds in the leg persisted in taking his turn at the oar, is also specially mentioned for an invincible light heartedness throughout.[4]

Others were not so lucky. Of the wardroom, Fox, his First Lieutenant Anthony Bavin, Gunner Handcock, Surgeon Probationer

Ivan Curror Christie Barclay, Engineer Lieutenant Commander William H Cleghorn and Midshipman Archibald Douglas Moir were all lost. Moir, Alloa born, was doubly unlucky, for he had only transferred to *Mary Rose* from the battleship HMS *Marlborough* for fourteen days' training. He was on day eight when he died, aged just seventeen. Only Sub-Lieutenants Freeman and Marsh survived.

Now unhampered, the *Brummer* and *Bremse* were able to sink a further five neutral ships. The rules of the sea, prize rules, were ignored. They poured broadsides into the merchant vessels without allowing them to launch their boats and get away. The Danish *Margrethe* had stopped engines immediately the attack on the merchant ships developed, and all the crew took to her boats. The German ships continued firing on the vessel while the boats were being lowered, and as they pulled to safety astern several shells fell a few yards away. The bridge and the chartroom were set on fire, the boilers blew up, and a shell landed on the after hold and exploded. Thinking her finished, the cruisers turned their attention to other vessels, but as the *Margrethe* had still not sunk they returned to her and opened fire from both sides.

The Swedish ship *H Wicander* had sixteen crew killed. On the Norwegian *Kristine* ten of the eleven aboard were dead. Men in boats or struggling in the water filled the area. Worse, the German vessels fired on the Carley float and motorboat carrying *Strongbow's* survivors. *Kristine's* mate, Simensen, was found dead in a boat with a bullet through his heart and another in his left shoulder. Next to him was a seaman with a shattered right arm and a bullet in his right side. A third had a bullet wound in his abdomen, and a fourth was wounded in the left foot and had a severely injured head.

Captain Roeneviz of the *Kristine* was picked up by a lifeboat from the *Habil*. He claimed that when the firing started he ordered the crew to the lifeboats, but a shell struck the after boat and killed seven men. In despair he and his crew tried to reboard their ship and signalled to the Germans to stop firing, but without result. 'The shells were now directed at us amidships and my men were swept down into the sea, together with the vessel's superstructure', he later told reporters.[5] The old fellowship of the sea seemed no longer to have any meaning. At 0820 the German ships had completed their work and turned away for home.

The two trawlers and the British and Belgian-flagged ships had manged to escape the slaughter, but nine merchant ships totalling nearly 9,000grt had been sunk (see also Appendix 5). Now the skipper of *Elise* brought her back to pick up survivors, including Brooke and a party from *Strongbow*. When a final count was possible the destroyer had lost forty-seven out of eighty-six crewmen. Of the merchant men '119 had been landed on the Norwegian coast and thirty-six perished'.[6]

Where was the Fleet?

Neither destroyer had been able to send a radio message (although they had tried, *vide infra*) and Beatty's forces were still south of the position of the attack, looking for a supposed minelayer. At the Admiralty it was suspected that the German vessels had not even left harbour; or if they had, some other mission was intended. They ordered the regular Lerwick convoy due to sail on the 18th to stay in port, which led Beatty to ask why. At 1420 Oliver sent Beatty an appreciation in which he suggested that the German ships were after convoys (they were in fact just north of Bergen off the Norwegian coast at this time, and steaming south at full speed for Horns Reef).

At around 1530 the *Elise,* crammed with survivors from the battle, came across the destroyers HMS *Marmion* and *Obedient*, escorting an eastbound convoy. She passed on the information of the attack and Lieutenant Commander Herbert I N Lyon in *Marmion* relayed the news to the commodore of flotillas.

This message was also received by Admiral Brock at Longhope at 1550, the first time that anyone connected with the Grand Fleet had heard of the events. Beatty finally received the information between 1600 and 1700, at which point the Germans were north of Stavanger, still heading south at speed.

At 1815 Beatty issued new instructions to his patrolling forces, ordering the majority to the east in an attempt to cut the Germans off at Horns Reef at daybreak the following morning. It was too little, too late. Before dawn the German force was off the Danish coast. They were home by 0500. Beatty thought it was all down to fortune; 'luck was against us' he wrote.[7]

The German press were not slow to gloat over the losses. 'Where is the British Fleet?', asked the *Cologne Gazette*. 'It can neither guard its own waters nor those of its Allies.' The paper continued: 'Ever since the Skagerrak, little England has been aware that she has to deal with an adversary of equal strength and therefore avoids a chivalrous battle on the sea and only wages a hunger war.'[8] The Germans gave wide publicity to the claim by the Swedish master of the SS *Visbur* that the British trawlers rescued their own men but ignored the shipwrecked Scandinavians; a claim that was vigorously denied.

Nor were sections of the British press supportive. The Northcliffe press, especially the *Daily Mail*, railed against the failure to intercept the German cruisers and criticised both the government and the naval leadership, familiar targets for the megalomaniac Lord Northcliffe, who probably felt he should be in charge of both. This made some in the navy bridle with rage. Lieutenant Herbert Wyndham Williams, serving with HMS *Nonpareil* and a regular on the Scandinavian convoy route, was enraged. 'What a beastly paper the *Daily Mail* is, up against the navy and going off half-cock every day.' He was particularly distressed by the paper's lack of understanding of the difficulties faced in Scandinavian waters. 'I should like to have the editor up on the bridge with me on some of the Skagerrak stunts', he confided to his diary.[9]

A Wife's Questions

Engineer Lieutenant Commander William Howie Cleghorn had been a popular member of the officers' mess. He was the third son of John Cleghorn of Clifton, Alyth (in northern Scotland), and the third of Mr Cleghorn's sons to make 'the supreme sacrifice'.[10] His wife Hilda, also a Scot and seemingly a very determined lady, wanted to find out how he had met his end.

She wrote to Seaman Bailey and Sub-Lieutenants Freeman and Marsh, seeking information. Bailey, incarcerated in 'Ward Six, Royal Infirmary' with a leg full of shrapnel, was unable to help her, but she sent him a carton of cigarettes anyway. Freeman told her that her husband had gone forward to report to Fox after the engines were hit but was killed by shell fire, and Marsh stated that he could tell her nothing for they had been 'sworn to secrecy'[11] and that he had clung to a raft in the sea for four hours.[*]

Freeman's letter to Hilda conveys something of the terror of the attack. 'I am leaving home on Saturday for Chatham Barracks', he wrote on 7 November. 'I do not know for how long or what for, but

---

[*] Hilda also wrote to the King, enclosing a history of all the ships named *Mary Rose* that she and her husband had compiled. The Office of the Privy Purse wrote back on 7 November 1917 to thank her for it.

I am certainly going to go sick if they try to send me to sea again just yet, as my nerves are considerably shaken and I cannot sleep but I dream of this horrible massacre, for massacre it was little else.'[12]

Court of Enquiry

The courts of enquiry into the sinkings were held at Lerwick for *Strongbow* and at Rosyth for *Mary Rose*.

With regard to the *Mary Rose*, the court found that 'the behaviour of the officers and men appears to have been admirable. Everybody ... remained cool and collected and perfect discipline maintained under the most trying circumstances of being under heavy fire from a vastly superior enemy.'[13] Sub-Lieutenant Marsh and his assistants, Petty Officer Walter Webb and Able Seaman James Skidmore, were noted for fighting the one remaining gun until it was finally put out of action, as was Able Seaman French, who managed to fire a torpedo.

But there was criticism, too.

> Whilst being full of admiration for the gallantry which actuated Lieutenant Commander Charles Fox ... we are strongly of the opinion that his decision was ill-advised. His action was obviously premeditated as he himself closed the enemy . ... the reasons for attacking are obscure, as it must have been evident that he would soon be put out of action and his convoy left unguarded, whereas if he had remained at long range he might have drawn ... enemy forces from the convoy ... [and] could have furnished valuable reports.
>
> Lieutenant Commander Fox fought his ship with coolness and marked bravery to the last and it is a cause of much regret to have to adversely criticise the judgement and action of a gallant officer.[14]

Admiral Beatty added a comment to the file on 28 October. 'While admiring the spirit which actuated the captain of *Mary Rose* it is considered that in this case, where a single destroyer was engaging an overwhelming force of light cruisers in daytime, more discretion would have been shown by keeping at long range.'[15] As regards *Strongbow*, the criticism was more muted. Greatorex thought that 'Lieutenant Commander Brooke and his men behaved magnificently in a desperate situation and they speak of Skipper Wood of HM

Trawler *Elise* in terms of highest praise'. But Brock 'regretted that *Strongbow* challenged three times before taking any action'.[16]

Greatorex was also concerned about the public relations side of the battle, perhaps with the mess that the Admiralty made of their communications after the Battle of Jutland in 1916 in his mind. 'This murderous and devilish act of the German cruisers, contrary to all the laws of humanity and the unwritten chivalry of the sea, will doubtless be made use of as necessary by Their Lordships as propaganda in the Allied and neutral cause', he wrote, adding: 'A great impression seems to exist that the convoy was destroyed by armed merchant vessels rather than light cruisers.'[17] The subsequent courts martial, on 3 December, noted that Fox should have attacked with torpedoes, but considered that the action was 'in accordance with the highest traditions of the service'.[18] Brooke, who was too ill to attend, was censured for not turning away, but it was stated that this was an error of judgement, not a disciplinary matter.

Thus the general finding was that Fox in *Mary Rose* should have stood off and radioed for help and Brooke should have turned away. These findings seem unfair on two counts. Firstly, post-war German sources indicate that *Mary Rose* did transmit a W/T message and another station picked it up and asked for a repeat, but subsequent signalling was blocked by German jamming.[19] Secondly, it rather ignores the ingrained Royal Navy culture. Most navy commanders saw the navy as an offensive weapon. They disliked standing on the defensive as the Fleet had done for most of the war. The duty of convoy escort and blockade was neither exciting nor bred into the psychology of the officer corps. Admiral William Pakenham, sitting on the court of enquiry, knew this when he described Fox's actions as 'not less glorious than that in which Sir Richard Grenville perished',[20] reflecting the *Revenge* under Grenville fighting the whole Spanish fleet at the Battle of Flores in 1591 and Tennyson's lines which Fox had perhaps unconsciously mirrored: 'Sink me the ship, Master Gunner – sink her, split her in twain! Fall into the hands of God, not into the hands of Spain!'* In reality, the blame was not to Fox or Brooke. Colonel Sir Maurice Hankey, Secretary of the Imperial War Cabinet, knew this when he confided to his diary on 26

---

* A Tennyson, '*The Revenge, a Ballad of the Fleet*' (1878).

October 1917: 'The Admiralty had been fully warned by highly secret but absolutely reliable information of the probability of an attack on the Norwegian convoy and had failed to act. Geddes[*] regards this as an example of Jellicoe's lack of energy, if not timidity, and wants to replace him with Admiral Wemyss.'[21]

Aftermath

On 20 October 1916 the Norwegian government had delivered a diplomatic note of protest to Germany in which it complained about the sinking of its ships in 'an ice-cold sea by German submarines'.[22] Now its minister in Berlin delivered a further note to the German Foreign Affairs ministry, protesting the sinking of the 17 October convoy.

This was, the note stated, 'a violation of the principle of the freedom of the high seas incurred by the proclamation of large tracts of the ocean as a war zone'.[23] Furthermore: 'It is owing to various measures of these kind that Norwegian ships, as well as other neutral countries, have been compelled in order to procure for Norway essential imports, to seek protection in the past, as they will in the future, by allowing themselves to be convoyed by warships belonging to Germany's enemies.'[24]

In conclusion, the Norwegian government enjoined Germany to instruct their submarine commanders not to expose the lives of Norwegian sailors to danger.

It made no difference at all.

Lieutenant Commander Fox received a posthumous special Mention in Despatches in August 1918. His father was livid at what he took to be a lack of recognition. Writing to the *Evening Standard,* he complained that this was 'an imaginary entry in a non-existent document', and that the Admiralty, having praised his son's bravery, were being 'inconsistent, if not an intentional insult'.[25]

Brooke, who had lost an eye and a leg as a result of the action, was awarded the DSO[**], but he was never a well man again. He died on 10 February 1919 of pneumonia, aged just thirty-three.[***] There

---

[*] Sir Eric Campbell Geddes, appointed First Lord of the Admiralty by Lloyd George in July 1917 with a brief to inject new thinking and drive into that body.

[**] *London Gazette* 30833, 6 August 1918.

[***] He was buried in Almondsbury cemetery, Huddersfield; his gravestone bears the maudlin inscription 'would God that I had died for thee my son. Mother'.

was recognition for Freeman and Marsh, too. The former received the DSC, while Marsh was Mentioned in Despatches*.

First Lord Geddes paid immediate tribute to the men involved. In the House of Commons he declared that: 'The officers and men of the Royal Navy upheld the proudest traditions of his Majesty's service. They immediately attacked against superior forces.'[26] Sir Richard Grenville would no doubt have approved. And the Official History later noted that:

> Throughout the attack the Germans displayed a severity which is hard to distinguish from downright cruelty. They gave the neutral masters and crews no chance to lower their boats and get away, but poured their broadsides into them without warning, as though they had been armed enemies ... In the case of the destroyers the enemy's conduct was even worse; to their everlasting discredit fire was opened and maintained upon the *Strongbow*'s survivors.**[27]

The outcry in the press 'was not entirely quelled by Geddes pointing out to Parliament on 1 November that since April over 4,500 ships had been safely escorted to and from Norway'.[28] Beatty himself wrote to his mistress, complaining bitterly about 'the press campaign vilifying the Admiralty in general and Jellicoe in particular ... somebody in government was at the bottom of it, probably L G'.[29] In this he was not very wide of the mark, for Lloyd George, in cahoots with Lord Northcliffe, had definitely taken against Jellicoe and the way the navy prosecuted the war.

The attack had also provoked consternation at the Admiralty. On 22 October a conference was held there, with Beatty, urgently called down to London, in attendance, to discuss the questions raised by this new menace to the Scandinavian trade. Subsequently, on 5 November, Beatty's staff made proposals to the Admiralty for revisions to the system, and on 10 December Brock was once again chairing a meeting at Longhope to consider their implementation. First on their agenda was a proposal that convoys should start from

---

* *London Gazette* 30833 6 August 1918. Lieutenant Marsh clearly had a taste for adventure, for in February 1917 he had been accepted as a Probationary Flight Officer in the RNAS 'for temporary service' (*Flight*, 8 March 1917).

** The Germans claimed that this was due to fire falling short.

Methil rather than Lerwick; the former was a much better-equipped harbour and was closer in distance for the Swedish and Danish trade. Admiral Beatty supported this suggestion, but with the caveat that 'though the new plan would increase the carrying power of vessels engaged in Scandinavian trade, it would at the same time make the convoys more vulnerable to surface attack, as the new route would be appreciably nearer the German bases'. The only remedy, in his opinion, would be 'to assimilate the Scandinavian into the Atlantic convoy system, and so put the convoys between Scotland and Norway under the protection of the cruisers engaged in oceanic escort work'.[30]

However, before any changes could be put into effect, further disasters struck, and the navy lost more valuable ships and men.

CHAPTER 14

Trouble at Sea and the Sinking of the Convoy of 12 December 1917

While the conferences and planning commenced and continued, the Lerwick convoys had resumed as soon as it was clear that *Brummer* and *Bremse* had left the North Sea. Three days after the disaster that befell *Mary Rose* and *Strongbow* it seemed like just another clockwork run as a convoy set off from its gathering point near Marstein Light to head for Lerwick. In Lerwick, another sailed to the east. The two convoys were to meet up midway at a central rendezvous, passing it on either side. They had done it scores of times by now; it was routine.

As usual, on this occasion the westward passage was escorted by two destroyers, HMS *Tirade*, an 'R'-class vessel commissioned only that June, and *Sarpedon*, of the same class but launched a year earlier than her sister. They were steering a course, as planned, which took them to the north of the designated meeting point.

The Lerwick departure was accompanied by HMS *Obedient* and *Narwhal*, both 'M'-class vessels built in 1915. However, not all went to plan, as *Obedient* fouled her propellers on a wire and was forced to remain in harbour. Orders were issued for HMS *Marmion*, another 'M'-class ship, to raise steam and join the now departed convoy with all haste.

Marmion was captained by Lieutenant Commander Herbert Inglis Nigel Lyon, who three days earlier had been the first person to report the loss of *Mary Rose* and *Strongbow*. Lyon came from a naval family; his father was Admiral Herbert Lyon CB, who had served in the Zulu Wars and the blockade of Venezuela before becoming Commodore at Hong Kong and retiring from the navy in January 1913. Like so many retirees, war brought him back to the service as a volunteer, and he was commissioned as captain RNR, serving in command of the yacht *Safa el Bahr* on patrol duty in the Mediterranean and then as Commodore RNR in charge of patrols at Malta.

Lyon junior had taken command of *Marmion* in May 1917, having previously commanded HMS *Nonsuch* at Jutland, for which he was officially commended for his services.[*][6] He was her second captain, her first having been The Right Honourable William Spencer Leveson-Gower,[**] son of a three-time Liberal Foreign Secretary.

Marmion set sail as soon as readied and worked up to 16 knots. Lyon laid a course to intercept *Narwhal* and the convoy at first light on the 21st, Trafalgar Day. It was a filthy night, pitch black and with high seas and strong winds. *Narwhal* signalled her position to guide her intended consort, but her captain, Lieutenant Commander Henry Victor Hudson, had made an error in his navigation. He was actually passing to the north of the rendezvous point, and on a collision course with the similarly positioned westbound convoy.

At 0130 *Tirade* sighted a darkened unknown vessel, fine on her starboard bow, less than half a nautical mile away. On her bridge the officer of the watch was Sub-Lieutenant Arthur Guy Dennis Bagot. His vison was suddenly full of a ship, one point off the starboard bow and four cables distant. Although Bagot did not know it, the vessel was *Marmion*, racing to find her convoy. Bagot at once switched on the navigation lights (destroyers habitually sailed without them, a darkened ship being harder for a U-boat to spot) and turned hard to starboard. At the same time, Lyon ordered his onrushing vessel to starboard as well. A collision seemed inevitable. *Tirade* went full astern. As she responded to the propellers, *Marmion* shot across her bows, going starboard to port at an angle of about twenty degrees. *Tirade* had reared up on a wave, and as she came crashing down her bows dropped on to Lyon's ship, striking it amidships and almost cutting the destroyer in two. A depth charge, shaken free in the crash, exploded under her, adding to the confusion. *Marmion* filled with water in both engine rooms and began to sink. In atrocious weather conditions, *Tirade*'s captain,

---

[*] *London Gazette* 29751, 15 Sept 1916.

[**] Who in 1916 married Lady Rose Constance Bowes-Lyon, the second surviving daughter of the 14th Earl of Strathmore and Kinghorne, and elder sister of Queen Elizabeth the Queen Mother. In 1939 he became the Fourth Earl Granville.

Lieutenant Commander Henry Dawson Crawford Stanistreet, reached the bridge to see *Marmion* signal 'Have been in collision', followed by 'Are you going to stand by me?'. 'I am coming now', Stanistreet replied, but it was already too late. 'I am sinking fast – help' was the last signal *Marmion* made.[1] On her bridge, Herbert Lyon could still be seen making distress signals; as his men left their stricken ship, Petty Officer Charles Potter counted his captain firing twelve white Very lights.

On *Tirade* there now followed some random acts of altruistic courage which are later inexplicable, but seemed natural at the time. Stanistreet turned his vessel beam-on and drifted down to some Carley floats in the water, all the time worried about his own convoy coming up on his rear. Lieutenant Reginald W Howe, her second-in-command, went over his ship's side in a bowline trying get a rope round three men he could see in the water. He managed to rescue one before he himself was hauled out of the heavy sea in an exhausted condition. Torpedo Coxswain Henry Robson also went into the water in a bowline to catch a sailor from a Carley raft. Both he and his target were only recovered with the upmost difficulty because their lifelines had become slippery with fuel oil and almost impossible to hold on to. Able Seaman Richard Boardman dived overboard with a rope and was eventually hauled back aboard entirely worn out.

Only two officers and seventeen men were picked up from the sea.[2] Lieutenant Commander Lyon went down with his ship. So did another seventy-five of the crew. Men such as Petty Officer William Spencer from Chorley, who had joined the navy aged fifteen in 1906 and served at Jutland and Heligoland; Stoker First Class Sidney John Furzeland, twenty-two years old and from Yealmpton in Devon, whose brother, also a stoker, would die the following year; and twenty-one-year-old seaman John Wallace Andrew, from Inverness. Another was Leading Telegraphist William Henry Cash from Walsall, about as far away from the sea as one could get. He had been one of only six of his parent's twenty children to make it through infancy; by the war's end the family's survivors would be reduced to three.

There was a man with three names among the missing. Winchester-born Stoker Petty Officer Frank Cole served as Frank Cator and was awarded a 1914–15 Star in the name of Clator. Surgeon Probationer G T Brown RNVR was a medical student. Sub-

Lieutenant William Stewart Batson RN, a twenty-year-old from Exeter, had been on HMS *Cornwall* at the Battle of the Falkland Islands and HMS *Warspite* at Jutland. A keen cricketer at Dartmouth College, his innings came to an end in the cold dark waters of the North Sea. So the list goes on; men lost in a pointless accident.

At the time the newspapers claimed it was the result of an enemy submarine attack, a better message for the public than poor navigation by its naval officers. The court of enquiry was, however, clear in allocating responsibility. The court found that 'We are of the opinion that the primary cause of the collision was the fact that *Marmion* was some thirty miles to the north of the position she was intended to be in'.[3] Moreover, its chairman, Admiral Charles Madden, commanding the 1st Battle Squadron, commented: 'I consider that the responsibility for the course steered by the eastbound convoy rests with Lieutenant Commander Hudson of HMS *Narwhal* and that, if the weather conditions prevented the convoy proceeding by the route ordered, he should have informed the Senior Officer of the westbound convoy.'[4]

Hudson had tried to exculpate himself by claiming that he had no responsibility for the course taken by the merchant ships. 'I understand that the duties of the escort are purely for screening purposes and the pilot is responsible for the navigation of the convoy', he had told the court.[5] This was palpably not the position, for an order had been promulgated on 25 May 1917, instructing that the ultimate responsibility lay with the senior officer of the escorting vessels; in this case Hudson himself. On the file jacket an unknown hand wrote: 'Submitted for consideration whether Lieutenant Commander Hudson should be tried by court martial or, if not, what disciplinary action should be taken'.[*][6]

Later, from Malta, a grieving Admiral Lyon sent an *In Memoriam* to all the relatives of the dead crewmen. It was a small booklet, which listed all those lost with their rank or rate, and included an extract from a sailor's letter, together with several poems and bible quotations. On the inside of the back cover it was inscribed 'With deep sympathy from Vice Admiral & Mrs Lyon, October 1918, Malta'.[7]

---

[*] Hudson was not in fact court martialled, but he was arraigned on 15 December to answer a different charge, that he 'did cowardly abandon' ships of a convoy. He was found not guilty.

The Convoy of 11/12 December 1917

As a result of the *Mary Rose* and *Strongbow* affair, Beatty and Brock had taken two immediate decisions. Firstly, a reduction in frequency and increase in size of the convoys; secondly, new orders to escort commanders. These specified that, if attacked by surface ships, 'the destroyers themselves, while using their utmost endeavours to damage the enemy, are not to engage superior forces. They are to use their speed to maintain a safe distance from the enemy; they cannot protect the convoy after it has scattered and are not to be risked uselessly.'[8] Additionally, the four or five cruisers always kept waiting for convoys at Liverpool, Glasgow and Portsmouth were told to keep at twenty-four hours' notice, to provide support if necessary (although how they were to make a timely arrival in the North Sea was left moot).

Admiral Scheer had been pleased with the attack by his two cruisers but disappointed that it had not discouraged the Scandinavian master mariners from sailing. He decided on another foray, this time using destroyers. To add to the effect, he determined to attack in two places simultaneously.

On 11 December Scheer despatched the 2nd Flotilla, comprising the 3rd and 4th Half-Flotillas. Under the overall command of Commodore Heinrich, a half-flotilla of destroyers was to attack the convoy in the channel along the east coast. Another half-flotilla was to operate at the eastern end of the Bergen-Lerwick line. They left harbour escorted by the light cruiser *Emden,* and by 1500 were off the north-eastern corner of the Dogger Bank. There they divided, the 3rd Half-Flotilla, under the command of *Korvettenkapitän* Hans Kolbe, held on to the north, while the 4th steered WSW towards the British coast near Newcastle. The *Emden* remained behind to act as a communications relay vessel.

Meanwhile, at 1400 on the 10th, the destroyers *Ouse* and *Garry* had left Lerwick with the southbound coastal convoy. On the following day the eastbound Scandinavian convoy left harbour. Although they could not know it, both were heading into danger, notwithstanding that they might have been comforted by the knowledge – had they been told of it – that during the afternoon and evening of the same day two cruiser squadrons put to sea. The 3rd Light Cruiser Squadron (*Chatham, Yarmouth* and *Birkenhead*) had left Rosyth with four destroyers at 1715. They were under orders to be thirty miles WSW of Jaederen at 0830 on the following morning

(12 December), to sweep across the mouth of the Skagerrak towards Bovbierg and to return home after dark. 'This force', Beatty's Chief of Staff later attested, 'was sent out in accordance with the general policy of making periodical sweeps to cover the approach of vessels on the Bergen-Lerwick route; and, in addition, of giving early information of enemy forces coming out of the Bight.'[9]

In addition, at 2200 on 11 December the armoured cruisers *Shannon* and *Minotaur* of the 2nd Cruiser Squadron, in company with four destroyers, left Scapa Flow to patrol the convoy route between Lerwick and Norway. They were known as the 'covering force', and Captain Vincent B Molteno of the *Shannon* was the designated SNO. His orders were to make contact with the westbound convoy on the morning after he left harbour and then to move eastwards across the convoy route and cover the eastbound convoy, which would be crossing during the day.

Thus a complex ballet of ships, men and merchantmen was set in play. The game was afoot.

*   *   *

In charge of a southbound convoy of six merchant ships were HMS *Ouse* and HMS *Garry*, both 'River'-class vessels launched in 1905. From intercepted radio information, Commodore Heinrich believed that there was the potential for plentiful prey in the area but, apart from the convoy under *Ouse* and *Garry*, there were no ship movements planned for that time. At 2130 the convoy was off the Longstone Light;* to the east of them lay the 3rd Half-Flotilla, each party unaware of the other.

It was a murky night, with heavy rain, and in the darkness two of the merchant vessels, the Danish *Peter Willemoes* and the Swedish *Nike*, became detached from their escort and brethren. On the destroyers it was believed that they had fallen out deliberately in order to make for Blyth direct, and therefore no attempt was made to try to find them. It was probably this decision that saved the rest of the convoy, for Heinrich and his ships were now close at hand.

At 0030 on the12th the German destroyers found the Danish steamer east of the channel and (as it subsequently transpired) uncertain of her position. She was sunk by torpedo. Heinrich then

---

* Off Seahouses on the Northumbrian coast.

steered for the coast. There now came one of those fortunate turns of fate that no one could have anticipated. As the Official History put it:

> The German half flotilla commander now steamed in towards the coast, expecting to make the Longstone Light; but was quite baffled to find that it was not burning. As very little shipping moved along the war channel during the dark hours, the Admiralty had long before made arrangements with the Trinity House that certain coastal lights should be lit up only at particular specified times, and extinguished when no longer required. On this particular night the commanding officer of the escort that was bringing the convoy south had asked that the Longstone Light should be shown between half past nine and half past eleven. The result was that the light was extinguished when the German half flotilla approached the land, and its commander, finding that the whole coast was in utter darkness, was compelled to round the Farne Islands at a safe distance. He fell in with nothing on his northerly course, and so, thinking that the convoy he believed to have left the Firth of Forth that evening had slipped past him, he soon turned south again.[10]

In fact, when the *Peter Willemoes* had been torpedoed the convoy was abreast of Coquet Island, only thirty miles to the south. They could easily have been overtaken and dealt with by the German ships, but in the night and rain they slipped away. Nonetheless, Commodore Heinrich had more success that day when the unfortunate *Nike* stumbled into his path and was torpedoed at 0400 off Blyth. Sixteen Swedish crewmen died in the attack.

As the German destroyers steamed away they sighted four steam trawlers. These were mistaken for the convoy, and the destroyers opened a heavy fire at 0430. The *Ranter* was damaged and the *J J Smart* sunk. A quickly conducted search found no more targets, and at 0500 Heinrich turned for home.

The convoy arrived at Immingham around 1600 on the 12th. Neither of the destroyer captains was at all aware that the stragglers from the convoy had been attacked by surface craft during the night. But what of the 3rd Half-Flotilla?

*   *   *

The eastbound convoy from Lerwick comprised six merchant ships: *Bollsta*, *Kong Magnus*, *Bothnia*, *Maracaibo*, *Torlief* and *Cordova*, all Scandinavian bar the last, which was British-registered. They were escorted by four armed trawlers, each armed with one 3pdr gun: *Livingstone*, *Commander Fullerton*, *Lord Alverstone* and *Tokio*, together with two 'M'-class destroyers, HMS *Pellew* and *Partridge*, each carrying three 4in and two 2pdr guns and two twin torpedo tubes. They were due to arrive in the Marstein leads early in the afternoon of the following day.

At around 1145 *Pellew*'s convoy was to the south-west of the Bjorne Fiord. The *Partridge* was astern of her, and behind the two ships followed the convoy of six vessels, an armed trawler to the front and trawlers on each flank. It was windy, from the north-west, with a heavy swell which defeated the efforts of the destroyers to increase their speed without creating a washout of water over the bows.

Lookouts on both destroyers sighted a strange ship to the port of the convoy. *Partridge* attempted to send a challenge by light, but the searchlight would not work. By the time it had been fixed ten minutes had elapsed; when the challenge was finally sent it was wrongly answered. And now the strange ships were much closer, and could be seen to be German destroyers.

Kolbe's forces were considerably stronger than the combined convoy escort. The *torpedobootzerstörers* SMS *G-101*, *G-103* and *G-104* had in fact been ordered for the Argentine navy and were seized on the outbreak of war. They were armed with four 10.5cm (4.1in) guns plus torpedoes, and were capable of 33.5 knots. The fourth vessel, SMS *V-100*, was equipped with four 8.8cm (3.5in) guns and six torpedo tubes, and had a top speed of 36 knots; but on this occasion she was having mechanical trouble which restricted her to 25. Kolbe sent her off to deal with the merchantmen while he formed a line of battle with his three G-ships and signalled the attack.

On the Royal Navy destroyers, action stations rang out at 1150. The men raced for their guns and five minutes later were in action. On *Pellew*, Lieutenant Commander James Robert Carnegie Cavendish RN, whose only sign of emotion in a crisis was apparently 'to take off his hat and stamp on it'[11], ordered the convoy to scatter (hoist 'commercial G') and sent off a signal to the

Commander-in-Chief, informing him that the convoy escort was in contact with an enemy. Neither of the destroyer captains had been told that there was a covering force of cruisers at sea, so they could only send their warning to Scapa. Had they known, would it have changed what they now did? Ignoring their orders not to engage a superior force, Cavendish steamed across the convoy's bows to get on to their exposed flank, and *Partridge* followed her sister. The Germans took up a line of battle, with the British ships on the weather side, spray and wind blowing into the gunners' faces. Both sides opened fire at close range.

There could be only one outcome to the unequal contest. At 1215 *Partridge* was hit by a shell which severed her main steam pipe. The escaping scalding steam killed everyone working the engines. She was now effectively a static practice target for the German gunners, who wreaked devastation upon her. A few minutes later another shell struck the after gun, putting it out of action. Almost simultaneously a torpedo struck the ship forward and she began to settle down.

Despite the chaos and carnage, *Partridge* continued to fight back. First Lieutenant Lancelot J B Walters, the twenty-two-year-old son of a vicar, and Lieutenant Aubrey A D Grey manned the torpedo tubes and scored a hit on *V-100* which failed to explode, but it was to no avail. At 1220 *Partridge*'s captain, Lieutenant Commander Reginald Hugh Ransome, ordered 'abandon ship', after which she was struck by two more torpedoes.

There followed two acts of personal sacrifice and bravery which defy explanation. In the bowels of the ship, Engineer Commander P L Butt and his Chief Engine Room Artificer, George Wood, attempted repeatedly to enter the engine room to give assistance and rescue any survivors, but were driven out by the red-hot steam each time. On Butt's final trip he manged to open the starboard condenser to let in water to ensure the ship sank and could not be salvaged by the enemy. While he was so doing, a torpedo exploded against the ship, putting the matter beyond doubt. Butt then came on deck and remained on board with Ransome until the stern alone was above water, when they both jumped into the sea.

Lieutenants Walters and Grey also went over the side. They found a raft and got in it, but it was overturned by the waves. The sea was rough, and Walters, a poor swimmer, quickly became exhausted and was close to drowning. Grey had been wounded in the thigh, and was losing blood, but was an accomplished swimmer. He supported his colleague in the water and got them to a life raft, which quite clearly had room for only one man more. Grey insisted that Walters take the spot, helped him on to the float and then drifted off, leaving a trail of blood behind him. Thirty minutes later he was spotted by *V-100*, whose crew got him aboard at the third attempt and made him a prisoner.

Another sailor saved by the Germans was ERA John Bradley[*]. With some of the crew he had managed to get the midships raft into the water. Fishing a hat out of the sea, he discovered it was his own and put it back on. As the German ships moved closer, another sailor suddenly jumped of the raft crying 'they're not getting me' and swam off. He was never seen again.[12]

Meanwhile, *Pellew* too had taken punishment. She was hit several times in the engine room and had only one torpedo tube working. But she manged to loose off seventy rounds of Lyddite shell in 'controlled salvoes' before retiring in the face of overwhelming odds, escaping under the cover of a rain squall and eventually reaching Selbjorn Fjord.

She was the only ship to survive the engagement. All six merchants were sunk by Kolbe's force (see also Appendix 6). As for the armed trawlers, all four were sunk by the German destroyers. They were there to protect the convoy from submarines or mines, not surface ships, and their 3pdr guns were as pop-guns compared with the enemy's weapons. *Commander Fullerton*, Hull-registered, was hit near the gun platform, in the mess deck and then on the winch while it was being used to lower the lifeboat, causing the men in it to fall into the water. Her survivors were eventually picked up by the destroyer HMS *Sable* in the evening. Her skipper, forty-year-old John William Whelan RNR, was not amongst them. *Livingston,* another Hull vessel, was struck in the engine room, cabin and mess deck before foundering. Some of her crew were made prisoner by the Germans, and three were fished from the water by another destroyer, *Sorceress*, at 1420. *Lord Alverstone*, from Grimsby, was speedily sunk and all twelve members of her crew managed to escape in a boat, reaching Stolmen Island, where they were collected by a Norwegian naval vessel. And *Tokio*, of Hull, was also sunk, slipping beneath the waves with little fuss or bother.

---

[*] According to his son, after the war Bradly read in a book that he had died in the action.

The whole action, which had taken place forty miles from the Norwegian shore, lasted only forty-five minutes. The Germans claimed four officers and forty-eight ratings taken prisoner from *Partridge*. At the final tally she had five officers and ninety-two men[*] dead, including her captain, Reginald Ransome, Chief ERA George Wood and the luckless Lancelot Walters.

Pellew lost only four men. Five sailors whose bodies were recovered were buried at Fredrikstad Military Cemetery in Norway. Lieutenant Aubrey Grey was awarded the Silver Medal and Certificate of the Royal Humane Society, on the recommendation of Commander Butt, who himself received the DSO.

Perhaps the best analysis of the attack was entered in his diary by Lieutenant Herbert Williams of HMS *Relentless*. 'The Norway convoy has been attacked and sunk again ... what good are two destroyers with the convoy, alone? Too few to screen for submarines and too weak to defend them from anything else.'[13]

Where were the Shadowing Forces?
The 2nd Cruiser Squadron and the 3rd Light Cruiser Squadron were at sea specifically to defend against such an eventuality as had just taken place. What had gone wrong?

Firstly, and unlike the attack in October, the Admiralty had no forewarning of the raid. The *Kaiserliche Marine* had managed to conceal their intentions and radio traffic was minimised. Secondly, the attack on the southbound convoy went unreported. As noted above, the escorting destroyers were unaware of the fate of their two lost merchant ships. Various shore stations reported hearing firing, but it was assumed to be a U-boat. When the noise of gunfire was pointed out to him, the SNO at the Tyne had asked the escort commander whether he had heard any firing. He received the reply that the destroyers had, but it seemed a long way off. That reassured the SNO, as it meant the convoy was not in danger.

Thus nobody suspected that the Germans were out, or that a second attack would now take place. *Partridge*'s attempt to send a radio signal had been jammed by the 3rd Half-Flotilla, but it eventually reached Captain Molteno in the *Shannon* at 1215, unfortunately in garbled form, but with a location. Molteno signalled his

---

[*] Most sources give these figures, for example Hepper, but Naval-History.net only lists seventy-three names. Using either figure, the German claim cannot have been true.

course and speed to *Partridge*, went to 20 knots and ordered his destroyers on ahead of him, led by *Rosalind*. He was, of course, already too late. When his destroyers did arrive at the scene they could only pick up survivors.

When the information reached Beatty he directed several squadrons of the Grand Fleet to raise steam, and at 1303 he despatched the 3rd Light Cruiser Squadron to sweep towards the position where the enemy had been reported. And the SNO Shetland was instructed 'Priority. Eastbound convoy is not to sail. If already sailed, recall it.'[14] The same instructions were sent to the pending westbound ships.

Now came news from *Pellew*. Having finally gained a safe anchorage, Lieutenant Commander Cavendish signalled Molteno at 1505 that he had reached Slotteroe but could not steam. Meanwhile, *Shannon's* destroyers had arrived at the position of the action and *Sable* began to pick up survivors.

Thus 3rd Half-Flotilla had about two-and-a-half hours' start on the Royal Navy forces. It was clear that 2nd Cruiser Squadron would not meet them, but there was still a chance, for the 3rd LCS was patrolling between the south-western coast of Norway and Bovbierg, and was thus right across the line of the German retirement. It was not to be. The light cruisers did indeed intercept the line of retreat, but the enemy ships had passed the spot three hours earlier. In the dark, gales and squally rain, the German ships slipped away.

Badly holed but assisted by misty weather and squalls, *Pellew* had managed to creep into Norwegian waters around 1500. Unable to assess his vessel's condition, Cavendish had headed for the safety of territorial waters to examine the damage. He was now about one mile from Slotteroe Island, having at last succeeded in shutting off the escaping steam in the engine room and anchor up.

There now began a strange gavotte in which the essential decency of Norwegian navy men was compromised by the political need to show that Norway was resolutely neutral to all belligerents, come what may.

Pellew was found by the Norwegian 1st class torpedo boat *Hvas* (two 1pdr guns, two torpedo tubes), whose captain offered a tow to a safer anchorage. In attempting the task he got the tow wire foul of his own propeller and *Pellew* had to raise steam, against all the odds, and tow *Hvas* instead.

Lieutenant Commander Cavendish then took his vessel a further seven miles into Bekkevig Sound, where the next day she was found by HMS *Sabrina*, sent to search for her and take off the crew, leaving the ship to be interned if it was not capable of sailing, for under international law any combatant vessel might only stay in a neutral harbour for twenty-four hours.

Next to arrive was the Norwegian torpedo boat *Brand*, under Lieutenant Evensen, with a message from the Norwegian powers-that-be that *Pellew* must leave by 1500 that day. Cavendish argued that under the Hague Convention, article 14, he could stay longer, as his ship was damaged, and Evensen escorted him to a local farmhouse where he might send a message to the British Vice-Consul in Bergen, asking for his intervention. Evensen had to carry out the conversation on behalf of Cavendish, as it was stated that no English could be spoken on the Norwegian telephone system. At 1300 the Norwegian commander received a message stating that *Pellew* was to be detained in any event.

Cavendish's engineers were working flat-out to fix the ship, with assistance from *Sabrina*'s Chief ERA, and there was now insufficient time to transfer men and arms to *Sabrina* ahead of the deadline, so Cavendish asked if another phone call could be made to the Vice-Consul, only to be told that, rather mysteriously, the system was now out of order.

However, the diplomats in Bergen had taken action, sending the *Princess Dagmar* and a convoy pilot by sea with orders to tow *Pellew* to sea; but she was not yet seaworthy.

At 1730 Cavendish declared the ship able to be towed, and by 2130 she had steam up. But she had definitely overstayed the twenty-four-hour limit and the *Brand* still had orders to detain her. The Norwegian commanders were now entertained to dinner on *Sabrina*, and were bluntly asked would they use force of arms to prevent the two Royal Navy vessels leaving. The Norwegians considered that they would not.

However, a new message was received from Bergen at 0030 on the 14th which averred that the Norwegian Admiralty would probably make a decision that day to release the *Pellew*, and therefore it would be better not to attempt a 'break-out'. But *Sabrina* had to leave at 0630 to avoid overstaying the time limit herself. Finally the diplomats came good; some heavy lifting overnight with Norway's government resulted in the commanding officer of *Brand* receiving a message at 0620 that *Pellew* could sail freely and, after some heartfelt best wishes to the Norwegian navy captains, she did. Honour had been satisfied on all sides.[*]

In London the War Cabinet[**] was briefed on the disaster at its 14 December meeting. It was stated that reports suggested two German destroyers had been sunk, and First Sea Lord Jellicoe (who attended *ex-officio*) was requested to produce a full communique by the 15th.[15] It was not until Monday 17th that they were told the true story (by Admiral Wemyss as Deputy First Sea Lord), and only on 9 January that a report from the Red Cross informed the War Cabinet that sixty-one men were held as prisoners of war in Germany, comprising sailors from *Partridge*, *Tokio*, *Livingstone* and the British-registered merchant ship SS *Cordova*.[16] One of those captured was the convoy pilot, Lieutenant Lane RNR, who had sailed on *Tokio*.

*   *   *

First Lord of the Admiralty Eric Geddes, thoroughly frustrated by what he saw as the quite unsatisfactory handling of the events around the action, had usurped both Jellicoe's and Beatty's preroga-tives and authority by personally ordering a court of enquiry into the affair and nominating the members himself. Jellicoe was ill in bed at the time, and tried to prevent Geddes behaving as he did but, inexcusably, Geddes 'altered the text of a telegram from Jellicoe to Beatty and despatched it with an additional offensive message from himself'.[17] Beatty was incandescent with rage at this presumption, and when Jellicoe next visited him he had to spend a long time pacifying the Grand Fleet's CinC.

Nonetheless, the court of enquiry into the events of 11/12 December was convened. Its chairman was Admiral F C Doveton Sturdee, the (perhaps rather fortunate) victor of the Battle of the Falkland Islands and now commanding the 4th Battle Squadron. He was joined by Vice-Admiral John de Robeck (2nd Battle Squadron) and Rear Admiral William Goodenough (Robeck's second-in-

---

[*] *Pellew* finally returned to Scapa on 15 December, escorted by *Shannon*, *Minotaur* and four destroyers.

[**] At this time comprising Lloyd George, Lord Milner, Andrew Bonar Law, Lord Curzon, Jan Smuts and Sir Edward Carson.

command). Despite Geddes' intervention it was a high-powered and well-respected court. Beatty briefed Sturdee and specifically directed him to examine the loss of the convoy and of HMS *Partridge*, and to express an opinion as to whether her confidential books could have fallen into the enemy's hands.

After taking evidence from the survivors and making its own assessments of the position, the court came to some cogent, not to say trenchant, conclusions. It acquitted any of the officers afloat during the action of any culpability; but some pointed barbs were thrown in the direction of the Admiralty.

Amongst other points, the court noted that:

There was a lack of co-ordination in the rather complex problem of arranging protection of convoys ...

The possibility of attack from surface craft has been recognised by both the Admiralty and all naval authorities since 17 October but, due to delay caused by various conferences being held, no definite action was taken ...

The evidence shows that responsibilities are divided and that no definite orders for guidance have been given.

The responsibilities have not been defined and this, together with a lack of community of thought and action between the Admiralty and those who have forces under their immediate command, would appear to have been a cause of the loss of the convoy and its small protecting escort.

[Captains] were certainly not furnished with the information that it might reasonably be expected that they should possess ...

We are strongly of the opinion that the control and immediate responsibility for these convoys should be undertaken by a flag officer afloat (under the CinC Grand Fleet) as we consider that it is impossible for an officer placed as the Admiral Orkneys and Shetlands is to have satisfactory supervision of the work required.

In conclusion they summarised that: 'It is therefore our opinion that the cause of this regrettable incident was the continuation of a system of control of convoys which had previously proved ineffective ...'[18]

Writing on 21 December, Beatty endorsed all of these findings except for the need for command by a flag officer afloat. He noted that the cause was found to be the continuation in force of a system whereby only one covering force could be arranged for, 'having regard to other requirements and the serious shortage in number of destroyers'.[19] He concluded by saying that the whole North Sea strategy should be reconsidered. 'We are endeavouring to pass trade of vital importance to us over the North Sea with a powerful enemy within striking distance. To render these communications secure is a problem of extreme complexity and necessitates a reconsideration of our naval forces ...'[20]

Such conclusions probably pleased Geddes, for the verdicts reached clearly took aim at the process for decision-making, at Jellicoe, Oliver and the Admiralty in general, together with Brock. Beatty's rather frustrated hand can be seen in these findings too, for they were the very recommendations which he had been agitating for since October and arrogated to Beatty the overall command and freedom from Admiralty interference that he wished he had.[*]

Jellicoe Falls

On Christmas Eve 1917 Admiral Sir John Jellicoe received a letter from Geddes asking for his resignation. Jellicoe himself believed that it was due to his determination not to 'acquiesce in his [Geddes'] high-handed treatment of senior flag officers', coupled with the issues around convoys. Writing on Christmas Day to his friend Admiral Reginald Bacon, he noted: 'I have had many disputes of late with the First Lord on this subject. The latest was the convoy enquiry.'[21] The argument about the 11/12 December action and the subsequent court of enquiry had claimed another victim.

---

[*] Nonetheless, Their Lordships wrote to Beatty on 5 February 1918, telling him that they rejected the criticism of the Admiralty contained in the court of enquiry findings.

CHAPTER 15

A Change of Plan

Three days after the attack on the convoy of 12 December 1917, a group of officers gathered at the Admiralty to consider the outputs from the second Longhope conference. Lerwick was now deemed unsuitable for continued use for several reasons. Firstly, its facilities for loading and unloading were thought to be inadequate. For example, iron ore shipments from Narvik had declined from 866,000 tons in 1916 to 268,000 in 1917[1] as a result of congestion and offloading difficulties. Additionally, Lerwick made for a longer journey to Scandinavia than the alternatives, and it was proving difficult to route ships safely around the top of Scotland for Britain's west coast to ports such as Liverpool, where paper pulp deliveries from Scandinavia were necessary for the board-making industries.

Methil[*], on the Firth of Forth, was considered a better alternative. An existing railway link would facilitate deliveries across to the west of England, Methil was an established coal port with three docks, ten coal hoists and eight cranes, and the journey times to the east were shorter. Movement from the pitheads to the docks was by rail. There were over twenty-five miles of sidings, and this network could hold up to 50,000 tonnes of coal, some 3,000 wagons, at any one time.

Before the war, a Tyne-Kristiania trip would take three days. With Lerwick as the assembly point, convoys were taking ten to twelve days. From Methil they would average five to six.

Admiralty approval for a new process was forthcoming in January, and the revised convoy system commenced on the 20th.

---

[*] A stone harbour had been built at Methil by David, Second Earl of Wemyss, in 1664 for the export of coal and salt. He was an ancestor of Admiral Rosslyn Wemyss, First Sea Lord at the time the decision to move to Methil was approved.

Eastbound convoys were given the designation OZ from Methil to Marstein and HZ for the return trip. Tyne convoys to Methil were TM and MT for the southern run. From Immingham to Methil the designator was UM. Finally, Immingham to the Tyne was coded UT and the return TU.

By 15 February standing orders had been developed for all ships sailing in the convoys; 'Standing Orders for Scandinavian Convoy and Humber-Tyne-Methil convoy', secret memorandum no. 057/19, portentously endorsed 'not to be allowed to fall into the hands of the enemy', and signed by Cecil Burney as admiral for the coast of Scotland. These noted that:

a) Coastal convoy. A convoy will sail from the Humber to the Tyne and from the Tyne to the Humber every day.
b) Coastal convoy. A convoy will sail from the Tyne to Methil and from Methil to the Tyne every day.
c) Scandinavian convoy. A convoy of ships bound for Scandinavia will sail every day from the Humber to Methil; and a convoy from Methil to Norway will sail approximately every three days, composed of three or more days' collection of such vessels at Methil. To ensure irregularities, the sailings will be periodically retarded one day.[2]

In all, 10,000 copies of the orders were printed in English, 4,000 in Norwegian and 1,000 each in French and Spanish.

Beatty was still concerned that using Methil took the convoys closer to the German bases, so they were routed north up the coast of Britain until they were in the latitudes of Aberdeen, before turning east for Norway. This was, of course, still nearer to Germany than before, but reflected a compromise. The main destination was now Marstein, but Slottero (thirty-seven miles south of Begen) and Skudesnales, aka Selbjornes fjord, (sixty miles south) were also used[*]. Eventually, German mining meant that only the northern ports could be used.

It was always a problem to pull together sufficient escorts for the Scandinavian convoys. Apart from the obvious fact that there were many calls on a finite number of vessels, there was also the issue of mechanical wear and tear and concomitant breakdowns. And pilots

---

[*] In October 1918 the nineteenth-century herring port of Florø became the collecting port.

had to be carried on suitable ships (*vide supra*), which increasingly meant the deployment of armed civilian steamships, originally taken up for use as armed boarding steamers (ABS). Between January and March a small force of four such ships was allocated to the Scandinavian convoys, the *Duke of Cornwall* and *Amsterdam*, taken from the 2nd Cruiser Squadron at Scapa, the *Duke of Clarence*, previously on Atlantic convoy duty, and *Tithonus*, which had been operating in the White Sea.

One of these vessels had almost immediately come to grief when, on 29 January, the *Amsterdam*, 1,777grt, 17 knots, built in 1894 for the Great Eastern Railway's ferry service to the Hook of Holland, struck a submerged rock off the Norwegian coast near Slottero. She was holed in the side and quickly took six inches of water into her engine room.

Commander John McInnes Borland RD RNR DSO*, her captain, managed to get her to shallow waters and a salvage vessel was despatched from Bergen. All through the night a Norwegian torpedo boat stood by her and reported on her condition to Captain Halsey, who was worried that she could be interned if she overstayed the permitted twenty-four hours. Fortunately *Amsterdam*'s wounds were repaired, she got under way again by 1800 on the following day, and the Norwegian interpretation of twenty-four hours proved to be fairly flexible.

The convoys themselves started on 20 January with OZ 1 (actually destined for Gothenburg), comprising vessels mainly carrying coal. The ABS *Duke of Clarence* was the convoy leader under the overall command of the SNO in the destroyer escort. The destroyer *Lucifer* was designated as escort, but the Vice Admiral Commanding Battle Cruiser Fleet, Vice Admiral William Pakenham, had to be leant on to loan two more from the 13th Destroyer Flotilla.

Convoy OZ 2 sailed a day late, predictably delayed by fog, and OZ 3, on 27 January, was the largest convoy yet, comprising forty vessels mainly loaded with coal and salt. The ABS HMS *Amsterdam* was designated convoy leader with destroyers *Lark*, *Lucifer* and nine trawlers.

The convoys were always a multinational affair. For example, OZ 6 comprised five British merchant vessels, three Norwegian, eight

---

* Borland had spent the war in boarding steamers and had received his DSO in 1917 (Gazetted 22 May) for 'services in the Armed Boarding Steamers, &c., during the period which ended on the 30th September 1916'.

Danish and nine from Sweden. It made land at Slottero, from whence vessels travelled along the coast line to twelve different destinations.

But the problem was to find enough close escorts. Admiral Sir Cecil Burney, CinC Coast of Scotland, wrote to the Admiralty on 22 February that he had had to designate the yacht *Shemara* as convoy leader 'as no more suitable vessel was available for the purpose'. He added: 'It is important that the vessels allocated permanently for the duty should be ready at the earliest possible date; at present only two ABS are available.'[3] Obviously promised ships were being withheld. *Shemara* was clearly of limited use in the role; she was the one-time *Victoria*, 477 tons, built in 1899 and armed with a 12pdr and a 6pdr gun.

German U-boats were not the only enemy; the weather was a constant worry. Convoy OZ 8, which sailed on 14 February, lost two merchant ships, one British, one Danish, in a storm. As the convoy commander noted, 'A strong easterly gale arose with heavy seas and the ships were scattered and quite unable to hold their courses. A Danish ship ... was broken up by heavy seas as it was heavily laden and could make little heading. Some of the ships that followed tried to cast out lines and life belts but as far as it is known it was impossible to save anybody.' As for the British ship, 'an English steamer had the cargo shifted by the storm and went under. It was bound for Bergen with coal. Eighteen men lost and six saved.'[4]

The opposite convoy, HZ 8, also suffered loss, but a U-boat, *UC-71*, was the cause, torpedoing SS *Atlas*.

At 0730 on 4 March OZ 14, twenty-eight vessels, left Methil. Once again there was an issue with providing close escorts, and the convoy leader was the yacht *Zoraide*, ex-*Sylvabelle,* 532 tons, armed with a 12pdr gun and a 6pdr anti-aircraft weapon. She had been built in Hull in 1894 as a pleasure yacht for one T J Waller.

It proved a trying job. The SS *Mortlake* stopped with steering problems and a trawler had to be detached to watch over her. Then the vessels *Cito* and *Fidda* were unable to maintain the speed of the convoy, a common problem for the escort commanders, and another trawler had to be dropped astern to guard them. The unique feature of this convoy was that it was escorted from Methil until 1500 by two seaplanes, a first for the OZ route.

The convoys from Methil to Immingham ran daily, but those from Methil across the North Sea were despatched every three days (soon increased to four and then to five at the end of April), in order that the Grand Fleet could provide distant cover and to prevent two convoys being at sea at the same time. Beatty was made responsible for all escort provision, and regularly attached a division or battle squadron to the distant escort; but he lost his fight with the Admiralty over full control, for the management of the convoys remained in Whitehall.

Beatty had upped the resources he was prepared to commit to convoy escort. Between 9 and 11 January the dreadnoughts *Royal Oak* and *Royal Sovereign* covered the Norway convoy. OZ 8 was escorted by a battleship and seven destroyers as close escort, and OZ 18 of 16 March was supported by the 3rd Battleship Division under HMS *Orion*, plus three ships from the 4th Light Cruiser Squadron. This convoy was attacked by a U-boat but it was driven off, having been first spotted by Skipper A J MacDonald of the trawler *Choysea*, one of Commodore Startin's brood at Granton. MacDonald was later to receive Their Lordships' Appreciation for his actions.

The fact that Beatty felt able to detach a division (four ships) or a squadron (eight vessels) of battleships from the Grand Fleet was in stark contradiction to the earlier doctrine of maximum concentration of heavy ships, ready to meet the High Seas Fleet in fleet-to-fleet combat. It reflected the way in which thinking about the war had changed. Britain no longer expected to win the fight by wiping the German fleet from the seas. Rather it was the blockade of German supplies and the protection of trade and commerce which now engaged people's concerns.

Lost in a Storm

The 'M'-class destroyers HMS *Opal* and HMS *Narborough*, launched in 1915 and 1916 respectively, could both achieve speeds of 34 knots, and carried three 4in guns and two (*Narborough*) or three (*Opal*) 2pdrs, with two twin torpedo tubes. They were regulars on the Scandinavian convoy escort run, being detached from the 12th Destroyer Flotilla at Scapa to Lerwick for that purpose.

On 12 January both vessels were detailed for a Dark Night Patrol, in company with the scout cruiser *Boadicea* (launched 1908 and converted into a minelayer in 1917), searching for German minelaying ships believed to be operating off the Scottish coast. The destroyers met the cruiser at 1530 off the Pentland Skerries and sailed east in the teeth of poor and deteriorating weather. By 1700 the seas were washing over them, and at 1830, in snow, heavy seas and wind, Captain Edwin Harold Edwards, commanding the cruiser, decided that the conditions were too dangerous for the destroyers to continue and ordered them back to Scapa Flow.

Between 1840 and 2115, Lieutenant Commander Charles Caesar de Merindol Malan, commanding *Opal*, transmitted several RT messages indicating that he was proceeding directly to the anchorage at Scapa and requesting that lights be shown for guidance. But at 2127 there was a garbled transmission, picked up at Longhope, that she was in trouble; 'urgent, have run aground'.[5] This was followed by fragmentary signals, probably from *Narborough*, which were not comprehensible. Then, nothing.

Weather conditions were terrible, and it was impossible to send out search vessels until 0900 the following day. It was not until the 14th that the destroyer *Peyton* discovered both vessels wrecked on the shore of the Clett of Crura, near Hesta Rock. Only one survivor was found, Able Seaman William Sissons, gunlayer second class on *Opal*. After managing to put on a lifebelt he had jumped into the sea and clambered on to a rock before losing consciousness. When he came to, his hands and feet were frozen, but he somehow climbed up to a cave above the wreck, where he sheltered for thirty-six hours until rescued.

He related that the ships had been sailing a regular slow course, taking frequent soundings and making radio reports, but had suddenly crashed headlong into the rocks. *Opal* struck two or three times and was pooped by the following sea, which filled her after part with water and carried away her funnels and mast. She then slid into deeper water and the ship's fore part broke off at the forecastle. According to Sissons's testimony, Sub Lieutenant Henry Shaw had been on the bridge of *Opal* at the time the vessel stranded. On striking, *Opal* had sounded three blasts on her siren which *Narborough* had acknowledged, before she too ran aground, striking the rocks on *Opal*'s port quarter and immediately heeling over. 'Abandon ship' was ordered on both vessels, but men were carried away by the sea and dashed against the rocks. Those that survived that experience tried to climb the cliff face to safety, but it was so cold that their hands could not grip and one by one they plunged back into the sea, except for Sissons.

Pounded by heavy seas, both ships rapidly broke up. When the tugs and rescue vessels sent out finally arrived on the 14th both destroyers were total wrecks, and awash at high tide, although salvage experts thought that the guns and torpedo tubes might be salvaged, weather permitting.

Lieutenant Herbert Wyndham Williams was an eyewitness to Sissons's rescue and the wreckage, having been despatched south on HMS *Nonpareil* to search for the lost vessels. 'The funnels of *Opal* were visible above water and there was one survivor. This man was at his last gasp and had been walking up and down a narrow ledge of rock ... living on snow and oysters.' In his diary Williams noted: 'Apparently a few others got ashore and there were marks on the cliff where they had tried to scale them and failed and finally dropped back into the sea, frozen ... the temperature never rose above freezing point and there was snow.'[6] Sissons spent three months in a hospital ship before he was fit enough to be discharged.

Lieutenant Commander Malan, Lieutenant in Command Edmond Mansel Bowly of the *Narborough* and 186 of their men died in the wreck. Among *Opal*'s dead was Surgeon Probationer Louis Percival St John Story RNVR, known to his friends as Percy, a twenty-one-year-old third-year medical student from Antrim, serving as ship's surgeon. Just twelve days before he died he had written to his father, a Church of Ireland vicar, that he had 'sent in his application for domobilisation ... I expect I shall mange to get it alright'.[7] He wanted to go back to medical school to finish his course and fully qualify.

Another who died was Engine Room Artificer Stanley Cubiss, who had married his wife Florence just six months earlier. His gold engagement ring, inscribed 'To Stanley from Flo, 6 March 1916' was found on the seabed by divers eighty-nine years later.

The subsequent court of enquiry ruled that a navigational error was at fault and that Malan had not allowed for a northerly set of the tide, steering 272 degrees instead of 268 degrees. Beatty's judgement was more damming. 'The accident was, in my opinion, due to a want of seamanlike caution in making the land and this should not have been attempted in the weather conditions prevailing at the time.'[8] Perhaps Admiral Beatty might also have considered if the mission should not have been attempted at all, given the climatic circumstances. Nevertheless, in such small errors of navigation and inexperience a tragedy was born. Two more hard-to-replace convoy escorts were no more, together with their equally valuable crews.

Diplomatic Cargo

While the disaster of *Opal* and *Narborough* unfolded, and apart from trade and commerce, governmental concerns were also engaged by events in Russia. On 15 January 1918 the light cruiser HMS *Yarmouth*, commanded by Captain H Edgar Grace, son of the famous cricketer Dr W G Grace, was despatched on a special mission to Norway, and carried a human 'cargo'. On board was the British diplomat R H Bruce Lockhart, returning to Russia via Scandinavia, who had been given the responsibility for 'establishing relations'[9] with the new Bolshevik regime. Lockhart was to replace the long-term ambassador to Russia, Sir George Buchanan, who had been close to the Tsar and the Provisional Government of Alexander Kerensky. Buchanan, disappointed that the fledgling democracy offered by the Provisional Government had been strangled by the Bolshevik coups of November 1917, and *persona non grata* to the new rulers whose government was not recognised by the Allies, was to be brought home by the same route, having had what was 'tantamount to a nervous breakdown'.[10]

Lockhart and his suite boarded *Yarmouth* at 1800 on the14th, but it was not until 0800 the following day that they left the Forth, in company with two escorting destroyers. They sailed into terrible weather; heavy seas, raging wind and occasional snow squalls. Lockhart slept in the captain's cabin for most of the journey and his staff was distributed around the ship, some sleeping in the sick bay, and all bar Lockhart himself were violently seasick.

The weather soon accounted for one of the escorting vessels, which had to return to port having been badly damaged by heavy seas. After ten hours at sea they reached the Norwegian coast, but it was too dark and rough for a safe entrance to a harbour and *Yarmouth* was forced to cruise around all night until daybreak, when she anchored up in Bergen Fjord.

There, with three inches of ice on the rigging, the cruiser met with Buchanan and his party, who had come out in a yacht. A transfer of diplomatic personnel followed, and at 1230 *Yarmouth* proceeded to sea at full speed with Buchanan, his wife, Lady Georgina, daughter Meriel and his staff (including Rear Admiral Victor Albert Stanley, quondam head of the naval mission to Russia). The weather was terrible and Captain Grace was forced to reduce speed; even so, his passengers still had 'an uncomfortable night'.[11]

They finally arrived at Leith on the 17th. Buchanan, scion of a Scottish family, was greeted by a kilted bagpipe band. Given the voyage he had just endured, he might rather not have been.

This was not, in fact, the last ambassador to Russia that the navy would convey home. On 22 May the destroyers *Nonpareil* and *Menace* escorted the SS *Vulture* to Korsfjord, arriving at midnight. In the morning *Vulture* went in to pick up the French ambassador to St Petersburg, Maurice Paléologue, coming out at 1730; the destroyers collected her at 1800 and covered her return to Aberdeen.

Lerwick

With the move from Lerwick to Methil, and the concomitant reduction of forces in the Shetland Islands, Rear Admiral Greatorex became concerned as to his abilities to defend the islands. On 13 January 1918 he wrote to Brock, asking him to bring to Their Lordships' attention that he had only one old destroyer, the '30-knotter' HMS *Otter*, then under repair, with which to defend the whole of Lerwick and Shetland. In addition he had five whalers, eight minesweeping trawlers, five hydrophone trawlers and seven drifters with a few 3pdr and 6pdr guns and two static 4.7in guns on the Nabb, which had a very limited arc of fire. He stated that with this tin-pot force he had to defend the seaplane and kite-balloon stations now under construction, the hydrophone station, W/T, coal depot, salvage plant, Lerwick itself and the fishing fleet.

With the nearest support at Scapa, he felt vulnerable. '[There is] ample time for an enemy force of no more than two destroyers, by a suitable choice of time during the dark period of the year, to effect a raid with impunity';[12] and destroy the lot.

'I request', he added portentously, 'that I be informed when other defences will be sent'.[13]

Brock was unsympathetic:

The question of providing further protection at Lerwick depends on the extent the base will be used in the future, both from a strategic point of view and as a port of call. The arguments put forward by the Senior Naval Officer, Shetlands, can be advanced to some extent as regards the majority of towns on the east coast of Great Britain and, under present conditions, I do not consider Lerwick is sufficiently important to be granted preferential treatment.[14]

197

Beatty concurred. On 23 January he wrote: 'Lerwick … is defended by the Grand Fleet. … You should take every step to hasten the placing a two 6in guns on Bressay*, which should not be beyond the capabilities of local resources.'[15] There simply were not enough ships to go round.

This was, incidentally, virtually Brock's last contribution to the fight. On the 28th he was relieved by Vice Admiral Herbert Goodenough King-Hall. Brock was placed on the retired list at his own request that August.

Convoys and Losses

The SS *Destro* was a regular on the Scandinavian run, before and after the introduction of the convoys. An 859grt coaster built in 1914 for the T Wilson Line of Hull, she had her moment of fame when, on 3 August 1916, she was attacked by *UB-39* while on a solo run from Stavanger to Hull. The submarine had already sunk three trawlers that day when she found *Destro* ten miles NEE of Coquet Island and opened fire with her deck gun. Skilful manoeuvring by the coaster's master, Captain Edward Borrowdale Johnson, saw off the U-boat and, although damaged, *Destro* lived to sail another day. Captain Johnson was awarded the DSC for his efforts, 'in recognition of zeal and devotion to duty shown in carrying on the trade of the country during the war'.**

By 1918 her ownership had transferred to Ellerman's Wilson Line Limited of Hull, following Wilson's sale in late 1916 (*vide supra*, Chapter 7), and she had gained a defensive armament and a gun crew of Royal Navy gunners to man it. One of them was twenty-year-old John Walker, born in Granton, home to Commodore Startin's private navy, and before the war an apprentice turner with Messrs Bruce Peebles & Company in that same town. John had joined the RNVR, been made an Able Seaman, and was now responsible for the protection of the small merchant ship on which he served.

On 25 March *Destro* was headed for Manchester with a cargo of ferro-chrome and timber which she had loaded at Namsos in Norway. She had reached Lerwick as part of a convoy, but was now

---

* Eventually, two 6in guns were positioned, with some difficulty, at high points in the north and south of Bressay.

** *London Gazette*, 29877, 22 December 1916.

making the perilous solo voyage round the top of Scotland and down its western coast to reach her destination. Some five miles southwest of the Mull of Galloway she was torpedoed without warning by *U-96*. This time Captain Johnson's skill was not enough to save her, and she sank with the loss of six men. One of the dead was John Walker.

The background of the other lost crewmen tells of the scope of the British Empire, and also of the lengths to which it was necessary to go to find crew at this late stage of the war. Apart from Walker, the dead included a seaman and a fireman from Bombay, two seamen from Singapore and a fireman born in Jamaica and living in Manchester.

The same day that *Destro* went down, two other ships were sunk in the North Sea. The hired net drifter HMT *Border Lads* fell victim to *UB-78* in the mouth of the Tyne with the loss of four sailors, an RNVR telegraphist and three RNR, her 6pdr weapon proving of no use, and the old collier SS *Hercules*, 1,095grt, was torpedoed by *UB-21* NNW of Flamborough Head. She was a defensively armed vessel, like *Destro*, but it did her no good. One gunner, Able Seaman Christopher Oman RNVR, was killed outright by the explosion of the torpedo, which hit the magazine and brought down the mainmast, and the ship sank in three minutes. Fortunately the crew got the boats away, and the survivors were picked up by two minesweeping trawlers after only five minutes in the water, and landed at Scarborough.

Many trawlers and drifters served in the defence of the Scandinavian trade. Primarily they were used for minesweeping or for close convoy escort. Typical of the type was HMT *Swallow*, built on the Tyne for Kelsall Brothers & Beeching Ltd of Hull in 1897 as *H-97*, and taken up by the Admiralty in October 1914. Fitted with a 3pdr gun, and with her original skipper (William Dawson) and crew, she served fighting the U-boat and mine menace off the Yorkshire coast, one of over 880 vessels and 9,000 men from the fishing trade that the Humberside area contributed to the overall war effort.

On 29 March 1918 *Swallow* was on night anti-submarine patrol just off the east coast village of Skinningrove. At 2130 she was run down in the darkness by the British-flagged *Audax*. The little trawler sank in seven minutes. All the crew were saved.

Audax was a Belgian-built, 975grt defensively armed, three-masted merchant schooner, constructed in 1903. She escaped the collision unharmed but it did not profit her for long, for on 6 September she was torpedoed by *UB-80* in the very same waters that *Swallow* had been defending, while on passage to the Tyne to collect a cargo of coal. Despite attempts to tow her to safety, she sank off Whitby. Three crewmen lost their lives.

* * *

The Methil-to-Norway convoy OZ 20 sailed on 28 March; twenty-one ships escorted by two destroyers, *Llewellyn* and *Linnet*, and with the ABS *Tithonus* as convoy leader and pilot. Originally SS *Titania*, but now named for the lover of Eos, Titaness of the dawn,[*] *Tithonus* had been built in Dundee in1908 as a passenger ship of 3,463 tons, accommodating eighty-six first-, sixty-eight second- and 585 third-class passengers. She was owned by the Finska Ångfartygs Aktiebolaget, Helsinki, and used on the Copenhagen-Hull service.

In 1916 she was requisitioned by the Admiralty for use as an armed boarding steamer and armed with two 6in guns. Such vessels were intended to stop and board merchant ships in the search for contraband, being chosen because they were generally manoeu-vrable and relatively fast. (*Tithonus* could make 14.5 knots.) They were certainly not intended as combat vessels, although one such ABS, *Dundee*, distinguished herself on 16 March 1917 when she assisted in the sinking of the German raider SMS *Leopard*.[**]

Tithonus was now on convoy duty, and at the front of the third of three columns of merchant ships heading east across the North Sea some fifty nautical miles from Aberdeen. Her captain was Commander Frederick Henry Fitzroy RD RNR, a long-term reservist, who in 1916 had been advanced to the rank of commander.

Unbeknown to the surface ships, below the waves a U-boat was stalking the convoy. The *UB-72* was a modern vessel, less than twelve months old and armed with ten torpedoes (fired from four forward and one rear tubes) and an 8.8cm deck gun. Her commander, twenty-four-year-old *Oberleutnant zur See* Friedrich Traeger, was on his first command cruise and was seeking his first kill.

At 2030 he got it. A single torpedo fired from the submerged

---

[*] To the Greeks; she was Aurora to the Romans.

[**] For this story, see Dunn S R, *Blockade, Cruiser Warfare and the Starvation of Germany in World War One*, Seaforth Publishing (Barnsley, 2016).

UB-72 hit *Tithonus* on the starboard side, forward of the bridge, and exploded in number two hold. All the hatch covers were blown off and debris from the ship was scattered over a large area. The steamer started to sink immediately, going down by the head. The experienced Fitzroy knew she could not be saved, and ordered her abandoned, shortly after which her stern reared vertically into the air and *Tithonus* slipped beneath the waves.

Linnet immediately went to rescue her crew and picked up many from the water. For his actions her commander, Lieutenant in Command John Needham Knox, received Their Lordships' Appreciation.

Four seamen were killed in the attack. One was Stoker First Class Austin Clement Morley RFR from Stoke Newington. A decorator by trade, he had first enlisted in the Royal Navy in 1900 as a Stoker Second Class and had served in HMS *Terpsichore* during the Boer War. Morley was promoted Stoker First Class in July 1906, but bought himself out of the navy in 1908 and joined the Royal Fleet Reserve. Recalled for war service in August 1914, he was sent to Antwerp in Churchill's quixotic attempt to save that city with his naval reservist battalions, surviving the debacle to resume his former post in the stokehold. He was another reservist who answered his nation's call and now was lost to his country, wife Catherine and his family.

The Norwegian-flagged SS *Vafos* left Methil with the same convoy, which she had joined after sailing from Hull with general cargo for Skien, Norway. Two days into the trip she too fell victim to Traeger and *UB-72* when she was sunk south-west of the Marsteinen Light. Four crewmen lost their lives.

Falcon

The old C-class destroyer HMS *Falcon* had endured a hard war. Launched in 1899, she had started the war as part of the 6th Destroyer Flotilla in the Dover Patrol. On 28 October 1914 she had been on anti-submarine watch off Westende, supporting ships conducting a shore bombardment, when she came under heavy, accurate fire from a German shore battery. *Falcon* returned fire and stayed on station but, at 1400 between Nieuwpoort and Ostend, was hit by an 8in shell on the port forward 6pdr gun muzzle. Her captain was killed outright and the ship seriously damaged. *Falcon* was brought home in a sinking condition by acting Sub-Lieutenant

Charles John Houssemayne Du Boulay with a third of her crew dead or wounded. Although she was repaired at Dunkirk and resumed her duties,* as newer and better-armed craft took their place in the line she had been 'relegated' to work on the east coast convoys, where her limited armament of one 12pdr and five 6pdrs plus two torpedo tubes might still be effective against U-boats.

Her captain was forty-four-year-old Lieutenant Charles Herbert Lightoller RNR. Lightoller was already famous, but the reason for his fame was one he would have preferred to avoid, for he had been the Second Officer on the *Titanic* when she hit the iceberg in 1912. He enforced Captain Smith's 'woman and children first' instruction to the letter, backing up his words with a Webley pistol. After he had discharged his duty and escaped the ship, he found himself the senior ship's officer to survive the sinking.

At the outbreak of war Lightoller became first lieutenant on the ill-fated AMC *Oceanic*** and then on the seaplane carrier *Campania* before gaining command of torpedo boat HMTB *117* in 1915. In her he won the DSC for engaging a Zeppelin airship before taking over *Falcon* in July 1916.

 On 31 March 1918 *Falcon* and Lightoller were escorting convoy UT-74, departing from Immingham at 1600 to the Tyne; just another everyday journey. In company was the destroyer *Peterel*, of similar vintage to *Falcon*, and the armed trawler *John Fitzgerald*, an Admiralty trawler not yet four months old and armed with one 12pdr gun, together with six other similar vessels and the convoy of thirteen merchant ships.

It was dark, and *Falcon* was on the starboard side of the convoy, covering it from seaward attack and zig-zagging up and down the flank. At 2020 Lightoller ordered a sixteen-point turn in order to take up a position astern of the convoy. As she came around, the men on the bridge suddenly saw the trawler emerge from the darkness dead ahead. Officer of the Watch Gunner Samuel James Shonk ordered the turn stopped and altered instead to port, at the same time shouting for full ahead on the starboard engine. Despite (or because of) these last-minute efforts, at 2030 *John Fitzgerald* plunged her bow into *Falcon*'s starboard side amidships, ramming into the forward boiler room and almost cutting the little destroyer in two.

---

* And received the battle honour 'Belgian Coast 1914–17'.

** Which ran aground on Foula in 1914 and broke up.

Somehow *Falcon* remained afloat. Lightoller ordered 'abandon ship' but remained on board himself, together with his first lieutenant and Gunner Shonk. They tried to pass a tow to another trawler, HMT *St Louis*, but it was either fouled by the trawler's screws or otherwise carried away. At 2130 *Falcon* broke in two, the forward part sinking immediately. The stern still floated, and Lightoller and Shonk stayed aboard to attempt salvage at daybreak, but at 0145 on 1 April she sank. On this occasion only one sailor died, a stoker scalded to death in the initial collision.

Any loss of a Royal Navy ship brings about a court martial, and one was convened at Immingham. Perhaps sensing that Shonk would be blamed for the loss, Lightoller praised his conduct in the aftermath of the collision, testifying: 'He frequently went down the after stokehold reporting conditions to me and at other times made tea and played the gramophone.'[16] The court allocated no blame, but a senior officer review stated that Shonk should have completed the turn and, if he had, no collision would have taken place.

*   *   *

Nevertheless, despite accidents and the continued U-boat threat the system was working. In that same month of April, as *Falcon* met her end, only one Scandinavian-flagged ship was sunk in the North Sea, the SS *Superb* from Norway. The east coast and Scandinavian convoys had lost only eleven ships between January and the end of March. However, a new challenge was about rear its head; perversely one that Admiral Beatty had devoutly wished for.

CHAPTER 16

The Last Throw of the Dice and More Convoys

On 12 April 1918 Admiral Beatty moved the Grand Fleet to Rosyth, leaving only the unloved 2nd Cruiser Squadron and some destroyers behind. Ostensibly his reasoning was that it placed the fleet closer to the German bases, and this was undoubtedly true. It also fitted with his desire to take a more offensive stance if he could.

But there were other, more subtle reasons. Beatty had been based at Rosyth with the battlecruisers until his elevation to CinC. With his American wife Ethel and their children he had lived nearby in Aberdour. Life was not unpleasant. Unlike Scapa, men of the Battlecruiser Fleet could go ashore and enjoy the attractions of Rosyth or Edinburgh, although the latter was strictly for officers only. Hospitality from local landowners was generous and frequent, and the social round was constant. There were good rail connections to London, too.

Most of the Grand Fleet hated Scapa. It was always cold, wet, windy and dismal, and there was almost nothing at all to do when off duty. It had suited Fisher's, and later Jellicoe's, strategy of closing the North Sea. With the Grand Fleet so positioned, the German fleet could not hope to exit into the Atlantic. Rosyth was a more crowded and less suitable anchorage, not least because of concern that the Forth Bridge could be attacked and dropped into the water, trapping ships inside the Firth. Beatty nonetheless felt the risk worth taking, as it brought him closer to the likely scene of any action and to the Scandinavian convoy routes. As he wrote to his mistress: 'I could not bear the isolation up North any longer ... with the tragedy going on,

---

* Beatty is referring here to the 1918 German Spring Offensive or *Kaiserschlacht* (Kaiser's Battle), which commenced on 21 March and led to Haig's famous 'backs to the wall' order.

on the Western Front* … [we] are in a better strategical situation than away in those northern mists.'[1] It proved to be a prescient comment.

The High Seas Fleet Goes Hunting

The High Seas Fleet strategy had always been to try to destroy elements of the Grand Fleet in detail, avoiding a full fleet-on-fleet encounter until the numerical advantage in battleships held by the Royal Navy had been eroded. Jutland had come about as a result of such attempts, as had other fleet encounters. Flushed with the success of his two surface attacks on the Scandinavian convoys, German High Seas Fleet commander Reinhard Scheer began to formulate a plan which would encompass both the war on trade and the long-held 'erosion and reduction' strategy that had been pursued since the start of the war.

In this he was encouraged by intelligence supplied by his U-boat commanders that the 3rd Battle Squadron had been disbanded to provide crews for anti-submarine ships in the North Sea, thus lessening Grand Fleet resources, and that detachments of capital ships now routinely shadowed the crossings to and from Norway. The first of these beliefs was only partly true. The 3rd Battle Squadron, comprising the old pre-dreadnought ships of the *King Edward VII* class, had indeed been paid off on 20 April 1918, but they did not form part of the Grand Fleet, being deemed too old and slow and lacking in firepower. Instead they had been moved from Rosyth to Sheerness in April 1916, and came under the Nore Command in the Thames Estuary. (The move had been intended to make more large ships available for coastal defence duties.) The Grand Fleet was in no way depleted.

As Scheer's plans were fermenting, Beatty continued to fret about having battle squadrons detached from the Grand Fleet for escort duty in the North Sea. In so doing he correctly interpreted Scheer's intentions. Beatty could not believe that the German Staff would remain in ignorance of his dispositions, nor could he believe that they would make no move when they learned that forces detached from the battle fleet were moving across the North Sea unsupported. Unless the Admiralty could be sure of obtaining early information of an impending move by the High Seas Fleet, this could place individual squadrons in great danger. Both fleet commanders were converging on the same thoughts.

Admiral Scheer assembled his ships in the Heligoland Bight on the 22nd, keeping radio silence as far as humanly possible. Room 40 picked up nothing untoward and Beatty was informed that same day that the Bight was quiet.

At 1345 a homebound convoy of thirty-four ships left Selbjorns Fjord under the escort of the *Duke of Cornwall*, an armed boarding steamer, and the destroyers, HMS *Lark* and *Llewellyn*. They were covered by the 2nd Battlecruiser Squadron and the 7th Light Cruiser Squadron, which met them outside and steamed across the North Sea to the south of them. At daylight on the 23rd the convoy was about 140 miles to the east of the Orkneys; Admiral Scheer, his movements still unknown to the British, was beginning to take his squadrons northwards through the swept channels out of the Bight.

Almost immediately a fog descended, but Scheer continued to the edge of the British minefields, where he anchored to let his minesweepers get to work. At 2030 Beatty was again told by the Admiralty that the Bight was quiet. Once more the Germans resumed their progress, entering an area being watched by four RN submarines. One, HMS *J-6*, spotted ships and identified them provisionally as a group of destroyers and light cruisers. Lieutenant Commander J Geoffrey Warburton, captain of the submarine, had been ordered to be aware that British ships might be operating in his area. He therefore took the vessels now observed to be friendly, and no report was passed back to Rosyth. Scheer slipped into the North Sea, free and unknown.

Now the German intelligence failings began to show. Their agents and consuls in Norway could easily have supplied the intelligence that convoy sailings operated all week and to a regular schedule, but Scheer relied on information provided by his U-boat commanders and had been misinformed that movements took place in the middle of the week. Thus he planned to intercept the convoy on Wednesday the 24th. If he had sailed twenty-four hours later or earlier he would have fallen in with a large convoy. As it was, by darkness on the 23rd the westbound convoy and its covering force had reached the latitude of Buchan Ness. They had struggled through the fog all day, and towards nightfall it became thicker than ever. Nevertheless the escort reached the western rendezvous at about the scheduled time, and would be in Methil on the following morning. No other convoy was due to leave until the 24th. Admiral Scheer and his battle squadrons were steaming into an empty sea, devoid of warships and merchantmen alike.

His progress was further hindered when the battlecruiser *Moltke* suffered a mechanical failure. She had been steaming ahead in a scouting role, but now she was ordered to retire on the main fleet. For this order to be transmitted, radio silence, so assiduously kept thus far, was broken.

Confusion now reigned. Scheer reluctantly turned for Horn's Reef and home. Beatty ordered his ships out to sea, Brock was warned that the Germans might be planning an attack on the Orkney Islands, and an eastbound convoy was just passing the Firth of Tay. Beatty ordered the 2nd Battlecruiser Squadron to escort it and the 2nd Cruiser Squadron to join them, while putting the rest of the Grand Fleet to sea. Beatty was able to send out thirty-one battleships, four battlecruisers, two cruisers, twenty-four light cruisers and eighty-five destroyers. He wrote to Eugenie that: 'Thanks to the capabilities and fine qualities of my flag officers and captains we got out 193 ships in the shortest time on record without an accident.'[2] He was spoiling for a fight.

It was too late. The *J-6* saw more ships, and at 0745 surfaced to report them; *E-42* fired four torpedoes at some ships and actually hit the *Moltke* without causing much damage. At 1340 the Admiralty told Beatty that he could retire to base if he wished. Beatty was not amused. Of Warburton's failure to report his initial sightings he wrote to First Sea Lord Rosslyn Wemyss: 'It was incredibly stupid and indeed heartbreaking.'[3]

It had been proved that a viable surface threat to the convoys, and their battleship escorts, remained. The Admiralty had been unable to give any warning of Scheer's promenade across the North Sea and was unwilling to say that it could.

A Great What If?
The USA had declared war on Germany on 6 April 1917. In naval terms the immediate help provided was to send destroyers to Queenstown to work in the Western Approaches as sub-hunters and (later) convoy escorts. In July the British entreated the US Navy to send battleships to the Grand Fleet too. Somewhat grudgingly at first, they did. In December 1917 Battleship Division Nine of the Atlantic Fleet, under the command of Rear Admiral Hugh Rodman, arrived in Scapa Flow to become the Sixth Battle Squadron of the Grand Fleet. It comprised the USS *New York* (flag, ten 14in guns), *Delaware* (ten 12in), *Wyoming* (twelve 12in), *Florida* (ten 12in) and

(from the following February) *Texas* (ten 14in). They were all coal burning as there were ample supplies of coal in Britain but oil had to be imported, at considerable risk.

Apart from the Americans having to learn Royal Navy systems of deployment and signals, it was found that their gunnery was well below the British standard. Beatty and Rodman worked well together nonetheless, and made a conscious effort to do so. However, on 12 June 1918, six months after the American arrival, the Deputy Chief of Naval Staff at the Admiralty, Rear Admiral Sydney Fremantle, quoted Beatty in a memorandum as saying that the American battleships were '... rather as an incubus to the Grand Fleet than otherwise. They have not even yet been assimilated to a sufficient degree to be considered equivalent to British dread-noughts, yet for political purposes he does not care that the Grand Fleet should go to sea without them.'[4]

Had Scheer run his operation a week earlier, the convoy close-cover heavy ships would have been Rodman's squadron, deployed on 16–18 April. The Americans thus missed stumbling on to the entire High Seas Fleet by a week.

At this time the American Expeditionary Force on the Western Front had yet to be involved in any heavy fighting or take any major casualties. What would have been the effect on US public opinion on the loss of one or more heavy units and the associated deaths? Equally, on St George's Day, 23 April, the day of Scheer's adventure, Rodman's ships found themselves in the vanguard of the Grand Fleet as it deployed. It might (or might not) have been a glorious engagement and gone down in US naval history, one way or another.

CHAPTER 17

Convoys and Convoy Protection, 1918

Two East Coast Convoys

The threat of U-boat attack on the convoys was always real, as demonstrated during two days at the end of May 1918. *Dirk* was escorting Convoy TU-26 from the Tyne assembly area to Immingham. A Scottish-built vessel, she was commanded by Lieutenant James William Green RNR and armed with one 12pdr and a 6pdr fitted as a high-angle anti-aircraft weapon.

Admiralty records incorrectly state that she was a trawler. She was actually a ferry owned by David MacBrayne Limited. In peacetime *Dirk* and her sister ship, *Lochiel*, had carried passengers and mail around the Scottish isles. *Dirk* had been launched in 1909, and although of only 181 tons, the same size as a typical trawler, she had sleeping cabins as well as cargo space. She worked the Oban–Coll–Tiree–Bunessan mail services throughout her pre-war career.* The Admiralty hired both ships in September 1917 and used them for general patrol and escort work, but apparently did not know what sort of ships they were.

Dirk was at the head of the convoy and just off Flamborough Head in the early hours of 29 May when, at 0127, there was a sudden and loud explosion. She sank quickly, and in the darkness and confusion twenty men out of a complement of twenty-two lost their lives. Was it mines or a U-boat?

The destroyer for the escort was HMS *Ouse*, under Lieutenant in Command Walter Thomas Arthur Bird. He was convinced it was a U-boat and, estimating from where the submarine might have fired,

---

* The Admiralty was to lose both of these vessels during the war and had to replace them. The *Lochiel* was lost off Whitby.

he raced to the point and dropped depth charges. He saw no evidence of a hit, and for some time the authorities were unclear as to the reason for the loss.

In fact, as later German accounts showed, *Dirk* had been torpedoed by *UC-75,* commanded by *Oberleutnant sur Zee* Walter Schmitz. The U-boat had not entirely escaped *Ouse*'s attack. She was damaged and leaking oil, which would readily give her position away at daylight. Schmitz had to haul away, and spent two days effecting running repairs.

Amongst *Dirk*'s dead were her captain, Lieutenant Green, her engineering officer, Sub-Lieutenant James Stevenson RNR, and RNVR, RNR and MMR sailors, including one Alec Peddle RNR, who had come all the way from Newfoundland to meet his end in the cold, cruel waters of the North Sea.

By the 31st Schmitz had repaired his vessel and was back in the east-coast corridor, looking for new victims. In the early morning he fell in with another convoy. It had a sizeable escort; the destroyer *Fairy*, six trawlers and a whaler, shepherding thirty-plus ships. *Fairy* was the rearmost ship on the seaward side. At 0200 Schmitz was trying to identify a target when his periscope was spotted by the steamer SS *Blaydonian*, a 315grt coaster built 1915 by J P Rennoldson and Sons of South Shields for the Blaydon and London Steamship Company, Newcastle. Her Master, Captain George Francis William Sim, did not hesitate. Altering course and calling for the best speed his engine room could manage, he steamed over the U-boat's position and hit the hull, damaging the conning tower. The U-boat began to flood through the conning tower hatch. In this class of boat (UCII) there was no hatch between the conning tower and the control room below it; the flooding was thus straight into the hull, and *UC-75* was forced to surface.

Aboard *Fairy*, Officer of the Watch Gunner Arthur Bennet heard the noise of the collision at 0205 and immediately ordered his vessel to steer in the direction of the sound, increasing speed to 20 knots. The destroyer's captain, thirty-year-old Wigan-born Lieutenant Geoffrey Howard Barnish RNR, who had been taking a walk round the deck of his small (355 long tons) command, ran up to the bridge. Seeing the submarine lying low in the water, he ordered a visual challenge to be made. Receiving no reply, Barnish made several more attempts before ordering the ship to prepare to ram. She struck aft, passing over the hull and then slewed round for another attempt. The U-boat's crew were racing for her 8.8cm gun, and *Fairy* opened fire with her one 12pdr and five 6pdr weapons before slamming into the submarine amidships, which caused fatal damage to the German vessel. Schmitz ordered her to be scuttled. Fourteen members of the U-boat crew were rescued, including two who had actually climbed onto the destroyer's forecastle on the second impact, and her commander himself.

This was not an unalloyed success for Barnish. His own ship, much smaller than his victim (which displaced 545 tons), was also badly damaged. Although he steered towards the shore, the ship's mangled bows would not hold, and at 0305 she foundered and sank.

Barnish and his men now spent a very uncomfortable two hours floating in the North Sea. It is often not the initial shock of immersion or drowning which kills sailors thrown upon the sea, but exposure, and Barnish's account of his feelings at the time bears that out. 'It was bitterly cold in that Carley Float', he commented later, 'and we were very grateful when a drifter came along at 0500'.[1]

Captain Sim was honoured for his role in delivering *UC-75* to the Royal Navy. He was awarded the DSC, Gazetted on 6 August 1918, along with sixteen other merchant marine captains, 'in recognition of zeal and devotion to duty shown by him in carrying on the trade of the country during the war'.[*] Lieutenant Barnish's achievement was also acknowledged, by the award of the DSO that September,[**] and he and his crew got a rather more material award, too. A prize court, sitting at the end of 1919, awarded £155 to *Fairy* 'in recognition of *UC-75* and thirty-one crew' at £5 a German head.[2] That would be around £8,000 today, to share among sixty men.[***]

At Granton

In April 1917 seventeen-and-a-half-year-old Harry Chadwick-Smith, born and resident in the Lancashire cotton town of Leigh, had cycled the eleven miles to Warrington to enlist in the RNVR. Eight months later he was in Granton as part of Commodore James Startin's merry band, a signalman on a 110-ton Grimsby trawler

[*] Merchant masters awards were usually written in a way which avoided mention of any warlike activity, to protect the Merchant Marine from being accused of being a fighting body and thus subject to greater risk of attack or retribution.

[**] *London Gazette* 30900, 13 September 1918.

[***] After the war Barnish became Marine Superintendent and Harbour Master at Heysham.

acting as escort to the Scandinavian convoys. In this he was typical of the make-up of the trawler crews. Generally they maintained their original crew members, enlisted as RNR, and usually the skipper remained in command, with technical support provided by RNVR radio operators and signalmen. From their harbour on the Firth of Forth the Granton-based trawlers would sail up to the Norwegian coast and then pick up the return convoy and shepherd it back to Britain. Methil, Newcastle and Immingham became very familiar to the trawlermen.

One Saturday morning Chadwick-Smith and his mates were escorting a convoy off Scarborough. Their ship was carrying depth charges, but was also detailed as a smoke-laying vessel and carried a number of smoke boxes for that purpose. Two miles off the Yorkshire coast a submarine was sighted. The convoy was instructed to scatter, but two merchantmen were torpedoed before they could react. Smoke was ordered, but the rough seas of the crossing from Norway had saturated the fuses and they would not ignite. A destroyer came haring over, flying the peremptory signal 'make more smoke', but none could be made. As the destroyer skipper became increasingly irate, the trawler's second engineer solved the problem. He poured paraffin over the smoke boxes and set a match to them.

Instantly, it seemed to Smith that the whole ship was on fire. There was smoke aplenty, but the paintwork and fittings were burning too, and the flames were in danger of reaching the depth charges. All hands took to the hosepipes, and it was a blackened and sorry escort vessel that eventually limped into Immingham Harbour. They had certainly made 'more smoke'.

By June, the vessels under Commodore James Startin at Granton had expanded to include motor launches, maids of all work, designed and built in America and Canada, originally by the Elco Company of Bayonne, New Jersey. They were about 86ft long, had a crew of eight, could achieve 19 knots, and were originally armed with 12pdr guns and later with a 3pdr and depth charges.

On 10 June 1918 one of their number, *ML-64* commanded (as they usually were) by an RNVR officer, Lieutenant John Dougal Campbell, was lying in Granton Harbour when she exploded and caught fire. This was not a completely unexpected event, for they were not entirely without defects, the most dangerous of which were their Hall-Scott engines. These originally used petrol, a significant fire hazard, and problems with the engines overheating resulted in a decision in mid-1916 to convert them gradually to use a mixture of one part petrol to two parts kerosene.

The *ML-64* was immediately enveloped in flames, and Startin himself set out in *ML-324* to direct the fire-fighting operation. Arriving at the stricken vessel, Startin saw that the engine room was burning fiercely, and was informed that the engineer was trapped below. Without hesitation, the sixty-four-year-old warrior jumped down the launch's hatch and succeeded in recovering the trapped man unaided, despite the fact that the bulkhead between the engine room and the forward tanks had been blown down by the force of the explosion, and the fire was blazing at the sides and on top of the forward tanks, which were thus liable to burst at any moment.

Despite Startin's bravery, the man, another RNVR sailor, Chief Motor Mechanic Herbert Mann, died of his injuries. On 20 August the King awarded Startin the Albert Medal for Gallantry in Saving Life at Sea[*] in recognition of his efforts.

As well as trawlers and motor launches, Startin's Granton command also included the occasional yacht; HMY *Zoraide* being one such. She had previously belonged to Kenneth Mackenzie Clark[**], whose great-great-grandfather had invented the cotton spool and whose company, the Clark Thread Company of Paisley, had grown into a substantial business which allowed the founder's great-great-grandson to live a life of luxury. Of 532 tons, she had been built in 1894, and a year later the well-known marine artist Tomasso De Simone painted a study of her in the Bay of Naples. In September 1914 she was hired by the admiralty, fitted with a 12pdr and a 6pdr AA gun and sent off on patrol.

By 1918 *Zoraide* was based at Granton, one of two steam patrol yachts there, and commanded by the famous yacht-racing skipper Archibald Hogarth, who had sailed Sir Thomas Lipton's *Shamrock* in the America's Cup of 1899 without, however, securing the trophy. Her second signalman was now Harry Chadwick-Smith.

Zoraide's tasking was to patrol the edge of the minefields around the Scottish east coast, looking for drifting German or British mines. These were then to be disposed of as necessary, which usually

---

[*] *London Gazette* 20 August 1918.

[**] His son was the art historian Kenneth Clark of the television programme 'Civilisation' fame.

entailed sending a boat's crew over to the mine to make an investigation. As Chadwick-Smith recalled: 'It was no joke prodding a mine ... with boat hooks in an attempt to remove the seaweed or scrape away the barnacles, for the least touch ... would have meant curtains for the boat crew.'[3]

On one occasion it was decided to despatch a mine by gunfire from the vessel's main armament, and to ensure a good hit the Gunnery Petty Officer decided on a close-range engagement. But his shell only hit the horn of a German mine, and it went off spectacularly, showering the crew with shrapnel, dead fish, seaweed and other marine detritus. Chadwick-Smith felt that the GPO was not a popular figure after that.

Charles Lightoller Sinks a U-Boat

Since the German destroyer raid on the North Sea convoys, the 'River'-class destroyer HMS *Garry* had continued to act as escort to the East Coast convoys. Her commander was now Lieutenant Charles Lightoller RNR, appointed to *Garry* subsequent to the loss of the *Falcon*.

On 19 July 1918 *Garry* was leading a convoy of merchant ships past the Yorkshire coast when Lightoller sighted a submarine and, as it submerged, attacked with depth charges. His intended victim was *UB-110*, a brand new U-boat (commissioned on 23 March that year) under the command of the experienced 'ace' *Kapitänleutnant* Werner Fürbringer, popularly known as 'Fips'. Fips had sunk 100 vessels in six previous commands, and had added one more plus one damaged since taking charge of *UB-110*. His latest victim was the SS *Southborough*, sunk off Scarborough on passage from Tunis for the Tees with a cargo of iron ore. Thirty merchant sailors had died in the attack.

Now Fürbringer was in trouble. The depth charges had damaged his boat badly and an emergency blow brought it to the surface. He would have to fight it out with his gun. Lightoller took no chances; he ordered a high-speed ramming course, sounded three blasts on the siren, and hit the U-boat amidships, sinking it. There were twenty-one German survivors and thirteen dead.

In his memoirs, written in 1933, Fips alleged that Lightoller had ordered his crew to open fire on the unarmed survivors of the U-boat with revolvers and machine guns. He described how, during the ensuing 'massacre', the skull of an eighteen-year-old member of his crew was split open by a lump of coal hurled by a Royal Navy sailor. When Fürbringer attempted to help a wounded officer to swim, he was told: 'Let me die in peace. The swine are going to murder us anyhow.' Fürbringer further averred that the shooting stopped only when the convoy arrived in the area in which the action had taken place, when boats were lowered to pick up survivors.[4]

If these accusations were true, it would have been most unusual. German U-boat commanders were frequently accused of such atrocities, often with good cause, but the Royal Navy prided itself on retaining the moral high ground. There were few such incidents reported, the most well-known being the *Baralong* affair.[*]

Feelings were undoubtedly running high, and the war still hung in the balance, but it would have been out of character for Lightoller to act in such a fashion. He was a committed Christian, a member of the Christian Science movement, and a family man with five children. Was Fips merely trying to deflect blame away from the U-boat atrocities which had done so much to mar the German navy's reputation?

Certainly, he remained in the German navy after the war. From January 1927 to September 1933 he was a civilian employee at Naval Command. Rejoining the service, he was promoted *Korvettenkapitän* in October 1933, became an instructor and consultant to the Submarine School until 1938, and was then promoted to *Kapitän zur See.* Fürbringer served the navy all through the Second World War, rising to the rank of *Konteradmiral* in 1942, and thus clearly had no issue with Hitler or his war. Given the timing of the publication of his memoirs, 1933, and the fact that Hitler became Chancellor in January of that year, there is more than a suspicion that the accusations against Lightoller and the Royal Navy were propaganda.

In any event, the Admiralty were pleased with Lightoller. He received a bar to his DSC for the action.

Convoy Protection

As well as the provision of close and distant surface escort, the Admiralty – and the admirals concerned – constantly experimented with other forms of convoy protection on the Scandinavian convoys. Among the options tested were camouflage and air cover. The Royal Navy had tried a number of different camouflage schemes

---

[*] For details, see Dunn S R, *Bayly's War*, Seaforth Publishing (Barnsley, 2018).

in the North Sea. At the start of the war the crews of HMS *Natal* and her sisters in the 2nd Cruiser Squadron had been ordered to paint the ships and their turrets off-white. According to Midshipman Geoffrey Hawkins, 'the idea of this colour is that the ship will not show up half so much in a fog, of which there are a great many, and secondly when we are in an enemy's horizon, range finding will be much more difficult'.[5] By July 1916 different counsels prevailed, and orders were issued that 'all destroyers are now to be painted grey'.[6] Merchant ships tended to be a drab black, black and white or in house colours.

Now, amid the carnage being inflicted on merchant ships by German submarines after the declaration of unrestricted submarine warfare in February 1917, any camouflage idea which might bring a degree of protection to the victims was welcomed. One such was 'dazzle painting', a scheme for which the credit most properly belongs to the painter Norman Wilkinson, who served as an RNVR Lieutenant Commander during the conflict.

In April 1917 Wilkinson sent a letter to the Admiralty in which he detailed his proposal, noting in his sixth paragraph that 'the average merchant ship, with her all black or grey hull, offers an ideal target and shows her shape and length exactly, whereas by the scheme proposed she must, at least, present more of a problem to the attacker and confuse his judgement as to her proportions and so enormously diminish the chance of the vessels being struck'.[7]

The scheme was not intended as camouflage, for at sea the background colours change with every alteration in the light, the sky and the water. A submarine periscope sees every vessel with a background of sky, causing the vessel to appear as a dark silhouette. Additionally, smoke rising from the funnel, especially in the presence of a following wind, and the bow wave and stern wash of a ship all easily reveal a ship's position to a U-boat commander.

The idea of dazzle-painting ships was developed to cause confusion and to make it difficult for a submarine to estimate the course of a target vessel with any accuracy. It did so by breaking up the surface of a ship by the use of violently contrasting pigments, painting the bow so that its sharp edge appeared to be moved several feet to the sides and providing wide strips of different colours, carried up from the hull over the superstructure, funnels, bridge, and boats, creating such an admixture that a submarine commander at the periscope should be at a loss to know what particular part of a ship he was sighting and in which direction it might be sailing.

After some havering at the Admiralty the idea was adopted in June 1917, and Wilkinson assembled a team of artists who devised designs for the different types of vessels to be treated. The Ministry of Shipping was delighted with the feedback it received from merchant masters as to the efficacy of the scheme, and in October decreed that all ships in excess of 150ft in length should be painted in a dazzle design. By June 1918 2,300 British merchant vessels had been painted to Wilkinson's designs, including those operating on the Scandinavian trade routes.

Statistics produced at the end of the war do not show a significant advantage, or at best show only a small positive, for dazzle-painted ships in escaping sinking by U-boats. But the ships' masters were enthusiastic and the support for morale that even illusory protection gave must have had a beneficial effect.

But perhaps this was not the case in the Scandinavian convoys. The eastbound sailings would be silhouetted against a sea or coastline often white with snow or light grey with mist. The striated dazzle lines came to be thought of as less effective against such a background. In a report produced on 31 July 1918 it was recommended that dazzle painting be discontinued for ships operating on the Scandinavian trade routes. Instead they were to be painted a uniform 'dirty white', including the escorting destroyers.

Captain Arthur Halsey, the naval consul at Bergen, agreed with this decision and may even have been one of its authors. Certainly he advocated the change and was concerned that it was not being made quickly enough. In October 1918 he wrote to the Admiralty: 'I believe that an Admiralty order has been issued that British ships in Scandinavian convoy should not be camouflaged which has not been carried fully into effect and I am of the opinion that all remaining ships should be painted grey on their next return to the UK.' He was also concerned about the presence of foreign vessels in the convoys standing out: '... for purposes of obtaining homogeneity of convoy, colours on the sides of all neutral ships should be painted out and all ships in convoy should be of one colour, *viz* grey'.[8]

In the Air

From September 1916 airships had patrolled over the swept East Coast channel. They were not acting as ships' escorts and there were, of course, no convoys at this time, but airships of the 'Coastal' type were based at Howden, Yorkshire, and cruised from the Humber to the Tees estuaries, hunting U-boats.

They were not particularly successful at identifying submarines. After all, a large object in the sky would be clearly visible to a U-boat commander from twenty miles away on a clear day. An airship might only spot a semi-submerged submarine from perhaps 400 yards' distance. If a U-boat was seen, the airship would attempt to attack with small bombs, or signal sea vessels to come to assist.

In June 1917 Beatty asked for the provision of air support from Orkney and Shetland. Work commenced at Catfirth Voe, Shetland, on a seaplane station, and at Grimista a kite-balloon station was erected. Additionally, an airship station was built at Caldale, near Kirkwall, Orkney. With regard to the latter, Brock was directed to carry out patrols daily in support of Lerwick-Bergen convoys. He was also ordered to give the station details of sailings and movements such that 'airship patrols may be arranged with a view to scouting ahead of convoys and affording them as much protection as possible'.[9] When a submarine was spotted the airship crew was instructed to notify the convoys by visual signal and wireless message.

Brock was also keen on the use of seaplanes to counter the U-boat menace, and wrote to the Admiralty to request that he be given enhanced resources. On 22 September 1917 they wrote back to him favourably:

> I am to acquaint you that approval has been given for the establishment of Seaplanes of the Large America type[*] in the Orkneys to be increased to eighteen and that a further increase to a total of thirty-six machines is contemplated.
>
> These seaplanes are to be used to carry out intensive anti-submarine patrols in the summer months of next year. ... the greatest importance is attached to effective patrols being developed by the spring of 1918 ... it is probable that a large increase in the kite balloon establishment will also be required.[10]

These developments made a big impact on the local population. At Lerwick 'the arrival of the first kite balloon, towed by a destroyer, caused a great sensation ... many of the inhabitants being under the

---

[*] An improved RNAS version of the Curtiss H-12 and H-16 flying boats.

impression that it was a German airship coming to bomb the town'.[11] And when the first seaplanes arrived they 'also made a great stir, no aircraft having been previously seen so far north'.[12]

However, by the autumn of 1917, as the airships proved unable to handle the weather, the Admiralty instructed Beatty to experiment with kite balloons attached to convoys to look out for submarines, but this never happened. Vice Admiral John de Robeck, to whom Beatty entrusted the job, advised against it because 'fitting out a separate kite balloon convoy service appears to be a somewhat complicated matter involving the use of less effective vessels, new organisation and additional equipment'.[13]

The airships from Orkney had been relatively active during the summer, but, with the evidence clear that the local climate was too much for them, in January 1918 the facilities were closed down and escort abandoned.* Summer 1918 saw a resumption of airship escort from a base at East Fortune, Edinburgh. On 17 July, for example, the 'Coastal' airship *C-7* escorted a Scandinavia-bound convoy of fourteen ships, an AMC, six torpedo boats and eight armed trawlers. The *C-7* was able to sustain the patrol for seven hours before returning to base.[14]

The seaplanes and aeroplanes based in Orkney and Shetland did not carry out escort duties until mid-1918, but were used instead as fleet reconnaissance and escort and for U-boat hunts. For the last year of the war the coastal Methil/Lerwick-Humber convoys had escorts of airships based in Yorkshire and Scotland. Aircraft were added after June 1918.

The old workhorse HMS *Ouse* became the beneficiary of the provision of fixed-wing air support on 28 August. The U-boat *U-70* was lying on the seabed off the North Yorkshire coast, near Runswick Bay, when she was spotted by a Blackburn R.T.1 Kangaroo, a twin-engine reconnaissance torpedo biplane operated by 246 Squadron RAF and based at Seaton Carew in County Durham. The submarine's commander, *Oberleutnant zur See* Karl Dobberstein, might have considered himself unlucky, for the Kangaroo was new into service and was not considered to be a winning design, primarily because the rear fuselage was prone to twisting and the aircraft suffered from control problems. Only twenty ever went into service.

---

* The base was converted into a kite-balloon base for the Northern Barrier in summer 1918.

However, on this occasion Flight Lieutenant E F Waring was able to drop a 520lb bomb near enough to the U-boat to cause substantial damage. Fortuitously, Lieutenant Walter Bird in *Ouse* was nearby and was able to finish off the submarine with depth charges; *U-70* sank with all hands and thirty-one men died.

By 1918 convoy air cover on the East Coast was also provided by kite balloons, which were towed by specially equipped ships and manned by an observer trying to spot U-boats on the surface. (See also Appendix 7.)

One such ship was the SS *Peel Castle*, an Isle of Man packet launched in 1894 and owned in peacetime by the Isle of Man Steam Packet Company. In more normal times she had plied her trade between Douglas and Liverpool, but in November 1914 she had been hired into the navy. For the next three years, commanded by ex-P&O officer Lieutenant Commander P E Haynes RNR, she fulfilled the various duties of a patrol ship. Initially employed as part of the Downs Boarding Flotilla in the Dover Patrol,[*] she distinguished herself when her boarding party captured two German prisoners found hiding on a transatlantic Holland-America line vessel. One of them proved to be the notorious Franz von Rinckler, one of Admiral Tirpitz's senior spies, who had organised a campaign in the USA against Great Britain, setting fire to factories and placing bombs in ships.

Following a fire and a refit, by 1917 she was patrolling around the Shetland Islands and Orkney before being transferred to the Humber-Tyne convoy route. This was considered to be the most dangerous part of the Methil-to-Immingham run, for the deep water between Flamborough Head and the Tyne gave submarines sufficient depth to operate effectively when submerged. Indeed, the number of wrecks in the original channel became so great that a fresh channel had to be swept through the minefield.

The convoys usually consisted of between thirty to sixty ships going 7 to 9 knots, restricted by the speed of the slowest ship, and preceded by a destroyer as convoy leader. *Peel Castle*, flying its kite balloon, sailed on the seaward side of the channel, going about 14 knots up and down the convoy. If the weather was favourable, airships and aeroplanes escorted the convoy from one air base to

---

[*] See Dunn, S R, *Securing the Narrow Sea*, Seaforth Publishing (Barnsley, 2017) for details of the Dover Patrol's activities.

another. But the margins for successful flight were small in bad weather and, when flying was not possible, the escorts were once more on their own and the observation balloon assumed even more defensive importance.

A crewman later described the routine:

> We arrived at the Tyne, and proceeded next day with a convoy to the Humber, and docked at Immingham to change the balloon. On 17 August 1918, whilst going north, we received a signal that a ship of the southbound convoy had been torpedoed off Scarborough on the 16th. Left the Tyne at 0800 and at 0830 the balloon fell into the sea, so had to rip it open and pack it up. On 4 Sept 1918 we received a signal that a submarine had been sunk off Whitby, and next day, on the southbound convoy, we saw the place where the submarine had sunk. A trawler was standing by, and the place marked by four buoys. A stream of oil was rising to the surface and floating away with the current. With the balloon up 1,200 feet we could see about twenty miles radius, and get a real bird's-eye view of the coast from the Tyne to Flamborough.[15]

Peel Castle continued providing air observation in this fashion for the rest of the war. It was not without incident. One day the balloon fell into the sea but the observer on board was safely rescued. On another day the balloon winch jammed with the balloon half aloft, and neither the balloon nor the observer could go up or down, which must have worried the airman somewhat. The ship's engineers had to sort things out.

CHAPTER 18

American Power, Mining and the Armistice, 1918

The First World War made the USA an economic powerhouse. The country sold and exported to all combatants, and when the British blockade made direct trading with Germany and her allies difficult, she traded through the Scandinavian neutrals. US exports to Europe rose from $1.479 billion dollars in 1913 to $4.062 billion in 1917. Industrial production by 1918 was thirty-nine per cent ahead of the levels of 1916. GDP rose from $46 billion to $69.7 billion over the same period.[1]

America, with a population in 1914 of 99 million, had over twice the number of inhabitants of France and Britain combined.[*] Among the combatants, only Russia, with a population of 166 million, topped the USA.

As the economic historian Hugh Rockoff commented:

> The United States had long been a debtor country. The United States emerged from the war, however, as a net creditor. The turnaround was dramatic. In 1914 US investments abroad amounted to $5.0 billion, while total foreign investments in the United States amounted to $7.2 billion. Americans were net debtors to the tune of $2.2 billion. By 1919 US investments abroad had risen to $9.7 billion, while total foreign investments in the United States had fallen to $3.3 billion: Americans were net creditors to the tune of $6.4 billion. Before the war the centre of the world capital market was London, and the Bank of England was the world's most important financial institution; after the war

[*] 46 million and 40 million respectively.

leadership shifted to New York, and the role of the Federal Reserve was enhanced.[2]

Britain's economy was crippled by the cost of the war, and nearly all her gold reserves had found their way to the USA as payment for goods. Government spending rose from £190 million in the year ending March 1914 to £2,700 million in the equivalent period ending 1918. As a percentage of GDP, UK government expenditure rose from ten per cent in 1914 to fifty per cent in 1918.

France suffered similarly, and only stayed in the war through British financial assistance. Germany likewise was economically ruined, and the communist takeover of Russia in 1917 condemned a country of significant economic potential to the long winter of a socialist nightmare.

So when the USA finally entered the war, in April 1917, it was not its military might that was most valuable (the America army in 1917 stood at only 200,000 men), but its economic might. This would quickly be felt by Sweden, Norway and Denmark. On 9 July the USA proclaimed a total ban on exports to Scandinavia, and served notice that it expected the neutrals to produce proposals which might serve as the basis for war trade negotiations. Allied control over the Scandinavian neutrals' import and export trades was now almost total.

Treaties

Of the three neutrals, Sweden now found itself in the worst position. The collapse of Russia following the revolution of February 1917, and its subsequent withdrawal from the war, meant that the key bargaining chip of transit across Swedish territory for Russian war goods no longer had any value. Furthermore, her domestic politics were in turmoil and, as has been noted earlier, a stable government was not formed until 19 October 1917.

Following the USA's proclamation of a total ban on exports to Scandinavia in July, Sweden sent a diplomatic trade mission to America. But the Luxberg affair (*vide supra*, Chapter 11) could not have come at a worse time for the Swedes. Their trade delegation in the USA was actively in negotiation with the US government. Now the cable crisis looked set to derail any progress. The *Chicago Tribune* of 9 September 1917 noted: 'The revelation of Swedish duplicity comes at a time when a Swedish commission is in

Washington seeking to influence President Wilson to lift the embargo upon the export of American supplies to the Scandinavian country. The commission had already encountered great difficulties in convincing American officials that such supplies are not being sent to Germany.'[3] It appeared that the delegation members had not made a good impression on the newspaper, for it added: 'The members of the Swedish commission have been unable to conceal entirely their German sympathies', and continued: 'It is likely that in view of Mr Lansing's disclosure they will receive little consideration from the American government. Indications are clearly forthcoming that a stiffer policy towards Sweden is to be adopted by the administration.'[4]

To bolster their negotiating strength, in August 1917 the Swedes had despatched a prominent businessman, Hjalmar Lundbohm, to take over the mission. Explaining this step, their spokesman in Stockholm noted: 'Sweden needs food and other supplies from the United States and needs them badly', adding: 'We Swedes are always willing to talk business. The only trouble is that America is so far away and so big. We fear America may lose sight of us, or see us through big American spectacles, therefore not recognising our very real need.'[5]

Having tried for the sympathy vote, the unnamed spokesperson next suggested a veiled threat. 'If America does not give us sufficient grain and fodder to feed the Swedish people and the Swedish cattle, we shall be forced to direct much of our available corn and other fodder to feeding our people, making it impossible for us to maintain our present stocks of cattle, which is about 3,000,000 head. ... We shall be forced to slaughter and export cattle on a large scale'.[6] It did not need to be said that, in this event, the major purchaser of the meat would be Germany.

Sweden was not completely without bargaining strength, however. She still had a substantial merchant fleet. Regarding this, a press spokesman played a straight bat. 'As to the ship question, the statesman said that Sweden had no wish to keep her ships in port ... [but] must take care that she has tonnage enough to carry her own necessary imports.'[7] The German predation of Allied shipping meant there was a severe shipping tonnage shortage, and access to Swedish-owned and -registered ships was a key desideratum for the British negotiators, who met their Swedish opposite numbers in London on 13 December.

Moreover, Sweden's potential vulnerability certainly did not stop her being tempted by offers of territorial expansion, as had first been mooted by the German government in 1915 (see Chapter 3).

When Russia collapsed and the Bolsheviks took control, the new Soviet state wanted to conclude a separate peace with Germany. In December 1917 Germany agreed to a Russian armistice and peace talks. Lenin sent Trotsky to Brest-Litovsk in Belarus to negotiate a treaty.[*]

Finland had been part of Russia since the Treaty of Fredrikshamn of 17 September 1809, which ended the war between Sweden and Russia, and had become the Grand Duchy of Finland with the Tsar as Grand Duke. But a policy of Russification, which started in 1899 and was designed to limit the special status of the Grand Duchy to more fully integrate it into the Russian empire, was opposed by most Finns, and nationalist movements gained ground.

The October Revolution of 1917 gave the Finns the opportunity to seek independence and self-determination. On 15 November 1917 the Bolsheviks declared a general right of self-determination 'for the Peoples of Russia', including the right of complete secession. On the same day the Finnish parliament issued a declaration by which it took power in Finland. The non-socialists in the Finnish parliament proposed that parliament itself declare Finland's independence, which was voted through on 6 December 1917 and approved by the Soviets a little later. Both Germany and Sweden (on 4 January 1918) also recognised Finland's now independent status.

In parallel with these events, and as the German army advanced on Petrograd in late 1917, Germany's new Secretary of State for Foreign Affairs, Richard von Kühlmann[**], made a new offer of empire to Sweden. Knowing that King Gustav and his monarchist supporters were in favour of annexation of the Åland Islands, von Kühlmann twice secretly approached the King, on 11 November and 17 December, with an offer to support and push for Swedish sovereignty over them. In return, he asked for increased support for the German war effort from Sweden, a free hand in the Baltic Sea

---

[*] The talks broke down, and in February 1918 fighting resumed on the Eastern Front. With German troops advancing on Petrograd, a panicked Lenin authorised the signing of the Treaty of Brest-Litovsk on 3 March 1918 and Russia finally left the war.

[**] He had replaced the disgraced Arthur Zimmerman in August 1917.

and the supply of greater volumes of iron ore, which also benefited Germany by denying the ore to Britain. Von Kühlmann proposed that Germany would either occupy the islands and then hand them over to Sweden, or would negotiate for their transfer to Sweden in the peace talks with Russia.

But Finland's declaration of independence made things more difficult. The Åland Islands were linguistically Swedish and generally saw themselves as Swedish. However, the Finns claimed them as a long-standing part of the Grand Duchy of Finland.

Worried about the response of Britain and the USA, and the possible imposition of further sanctions, together with the implications of German supremacy in the Baltic, both Gustav and his government played down the German offer, writing on 23 December to Germany and her allies, Austria and Turkey, to request that Sweden's interest in the Islands be safeguarded, and proposing neutralisation of the islands as an interim solution.

In fact, Finland plunged into a civil war between pro- and anti-Bolshevik factions in January 1918. On 13 February, in response to allegations that Russian soldiers (acting in support of the 'red' Finnish faction) had committed atrocities on the Åland Islands, the Swedish government launched a military invasion of them, an incursion which was probably intended to become a permanent occupation.

A week later, Germany, acting in response to a request for support from the Finnish 'white' faction (the anti-Bolsheviks), who claimed the islands for Finland, told the Swedes that Germany intended to occupy the islands and that Swedish forces should leave immediately.[*]

While this turmoil raged around them, and having rejected the German offer of a new, if small empire, Sweden urgently wished to consolidate its position with the USA and Britain. As a result, by 29 January 1918 a draft agreement had been signed; but then the Americans further tightened their blockade policy without any regard for the needs of Sweden or Britain, and right-wing and monarchist elements in Sweden agitated for the German offer of the islands to be taken up.

Keen to help the Swedish negotiating team and government by allowing them a success which would play well domestically, on 16

---

[*] This demand was eventually translated into a joint German-Swedish occupation of the islands that lasted until 25 April 1918, when Swedish forces withdrew in the face of Finnish protests.

February the British were instrumental in bringing about an agreement which gave Sweden a generous allocation of grain and fodder imports in return for a reduction in iron ore imports to Germany of two million tons and the passing to the Allies of 500,000 tons of shipping.

Even now the Swedes felt they should clear the agreement with Germany, and in April sent a delegation to do so. Surprisingly it was a success, for the Germans made it clear that they could not meet Sweden's food import needs and had in fact secretly stockpiled sufficient iron ore to meet their short-term needs. An American/British/Swedish agreement was finally signed on 29 May.

Even now, Sweden's pro-German leanings remained in sight, for her Liberal-Social Democrat government 'silently blessed Germany's intervention in the Finnish Civil War and signed a secret treaty with Berlin after the Red defeat, according to which Germany would demolish the Russian fortifications in the Åland Islands provided Sweden would accept Germany's position as the dominant power in the Baltic region in future'.[8]

Norway gained some special treatment for its co-operation with Britain over the shipping agreement, and as early as 17 July US President Wilson had made it clear that 'he drew a distinction between shipments to Norway and the other neutral countries of Europe'.[9] Norway sent a trade delegation to Washington in July 1917, eager to gain access to American grain, as the supply previously obtained from Russia had ceased with the advent of the revolution. The Norwegian government was reluctant to introduce any further rationing, though the US negotiators made it clear that this was a precondition to any agreement. It took until 30 April the following year to sign a trade treaty.

As for Denmark, she was hit hard by the US export ban and by Britain stopping all exports after October 1917, except for coal. All imports came to a standstill and she was forced to conclude agreements with Germany, as noted in Chapter 10. A US/Danish agreement was not signed until September 1918, just two months before the war's end.

The Northern Barrage and Norway

When the USA entered the war, one of its government's immediate concerns was that the transport of troops and *materiel* from America to Britain and Europe should be as safe as possible. The introduction of transatlantic convoy and the conversion of the quondam 10th Cruiser Squadron AMCs into Atlantic convoy escorts were but two manifestations of that desire.

Another was a plan to deny U-boats access to the Atlantic by building a 250-mile mine barrier between the Scottish and Norwegian coasts. In May 1917 the US Navy Office of Operations proposed the project to the British, who found the idea faintly risible, due to their experiences with the Dover Barrage.* As Norman Friedman noted: 'Given the problems [of] maintaining the short Dover Barrage, the idea must have seemed ludicrous'.[10] But the plan was supported by Assistant Secretary of the US Navy Franklin D Roosevelt, and the Americans persisted. The Mayo Mission pressed the concept on First Sea Lord Jellicoe, who in turn brought it before the London Allied Naval Conference of 4–5 September. Roosevelt ensured that some 100,000 mines were manufactured in America, and the US Navy eventually got its way. The first mines were laid in March 1918.

The plan was to leave two corridors at either end of the Barrage to allow transit of friendly craft, one (Area B, sixty miles wide) flanking the Orkney coast, and one (Area C, seventy miles wide) the Norwegian. Area B was to be deep mined so that vessels supporting the Scandinavian convoys could pass over them and the U-boats would be driven down on to them by patrol craft which, as it transpired, could not be provided in any meaningful way. Area C was mined with deep and shallow mines, as it was considered too far away for patrolling. The main section (Area A) was an American naval responsibility, while B and C fell to the Royal Navy.

Admiral Beatty was not a supporter of the mine barrier concept. Indeed, in August 1918 Arthur Balfour wrote to Lord Robert Cecil that Beatty held a 'dislike of the whole thing'.[11] But as a good officer he followed his orders, and Rear Admiral Lewis Clinton-Baker was appointed to command the Royal Navy part of the minelaying force. The Americans sent Rear Admiral Joseph Strauss aboard the Atlantic Fleet Mine Force flagship USS *Black Hawk*, a destroyer tender launched in 1913 as SS *Santa Catalina* and purchased by the US Navy on 3 December 1917. Strauss's command included twelve minelaying vessels. They were stationed at Invergordon and Inverness.

---

* For the story of the Dover Patrol, see Dunn, S R, *Securing the Narrow Sea*, Seaforth Publishing (Barnsley, 2017).

Gaillardia

HMS *Gaillardia*, launched in 1917, was one of twelve *Aubrietia*-class convoy sloops completed for the Royal Navy. These were a sub-set of the 'Flower'-class minesweeping sloops, but were designed to look like small merchantmen in the hope of deceiving U-boat commanders when they were sailing as convoy escorts; in effect escort Q-ships. They were built by commercial shipbuilders to Lloyd's Register standards, making use of vacant capacity, and the individual builders were asked to use their existing designs for merchantmen, based on a standard 'Flower'-class hull.

On 22 March 1918 *Gaillardia* departed Kirkwall at 0500 under the command of Lieutenant John Alexander MacDonald RNR. He was not, however, the senior officer on board, for thirty-six-year-old Commander John Sharpey Schafer was also part of the wardroom. Before the war Schafer had worked in the navy's Hydrographic Department until his retirement in 1912 to take up a career in rubber planting. On the outbreak of hostilities he rejoined the service, and in January 1915 was appointed to HMS *King George V*, flagship of the 2nd Battle Squadron. He was present in her at the Battle of Jutland, and was advanced to Acting Commander and Navigator on the Staff soon after that. Schafer, a specialist navigator and naval surveyor, was reputedly instrumental in introducing improvements in tactics which were generally adopted. Then, as the Northern Barrier project gained traction, the need for specialist surveying resources to assist the minelaying project was identified, and Schafer was temporarily assigned to *Gaillardia* for special surveying service in November 1917. He was in sole charge of navigation and plotting the buoys and minelaying.

Gaillardia, in company with the destroyer *Musketeer*, was acting as escort for the minelayers *Princess Margaret* (Captain Harry Hesketh Smyth, senior officer for the little group) and *Angora*, which were deployed laying deep mines, at forty-five feet or more to allow the shallower-draft Scandinavian convoy escorts to pass over them, in 'Area B' of the mine barrier. The mines themselves were far from satisfactory and there was a constant problem with floaters[*], mines that refused to sink when laid. Around 1100 Smyth signalled *Gaillardia*:'I am afraid that there are two or three floaters.

---

[*] Or more technically 'shallow failures'.

Go along the line and help *Musketeer* to find and sink them. The last mine I laid was a floater.'[12]

Both ships proceeded along the line of buoys, searching for, and sinking, failures. But at 1140 their work was disrupted by a very heavy explosion some six cables distant, which transpired to be six mines exploding without any apparent cause. *Musketeer* signalled *Gaillardia* 'What did you think of that explosion?', to which she replied, 'Will report when in harbour'.[13]

Five minutes later they sank the last floater and increased to 15 knots. At 1155 *Gaillardia* was suddenly wracked by a huge explosion, closely followed by a second detonation. She had hit a shallow mine, which had triggered off another.

Lieutenant MacDonald was standing at the compass when the first explosion occurred. He was thrown to the back of the bridge and then hurled into the air by the second. MacDonald landed on his back on the upper deck to find a wound to his leg and the ship sinking under him. He slipped into the water alive but shaken.

Surgeon Probationer Francis Heasey Anderson RNVR was in the wardroom when the mine detonated. 'The first explosion knocked me off my feet', he recorded. 'I was sitting down and something came down from the deck overhead and hit me on the head and I tried to get out. I came up the hatchway on to the messdeck, port side, then I came out aft, through the after battery door to the well deck.'[14] Anderson thought there were three explosions (the third might have been the vessel's boilers), and at the third the ship seemed almost under water, so he jumped into the sea and scrambled into a lifeboat.

Others were not so lucky. Commander Schafer was last observed on the upper bridge, wounded in the face and adjusting his life-saving waistcoat. He was never seen again. Assistant Paymaster Thomas S Phelps RNR was noticed endeavouring to open the door to the ship's office, apparently in an effort to save the ledger and confidential books. He did not succeed or survive. The ship had been broken into four pieces by the explosions and reportedly sank in twenty seconds. In all, two officers and sixty-nine ratings were lost. Another five officers and thirty men were rescued from the waters, despite the problems causing by unmoored mines, by Lieutenant Edward Eastwick-Field, commanding *Musketeer*.

The subsequent court martial cleared all the survivors of any blame. The officers received ten days' leave, the ratings were sent to a depot prior to leave and MacDonald was despatched to Granton Hospital.

Of equal concern to the loss of the ship was the fact that the mines, new British-made H-type mines with special Mk II deep sinkers, appeared not to be reliable. There were far too many floaters and unexplained detonations such as those witnessed by *Gaillardia* and *Musketeer*. This should not have been news to anyone. Throughout the war the navy had struggled to produce an effective mine. British mines proved to be woefully inadequate, with problems concerning mooring wires, sinkers and firing pistols. Improvements were made by the simple expedient of copying German mines, which were seen to work all too well. Information about the German mines had, in fact, been obtained by the Intelligence Service pre-1914, but had not been acted upon by the time war came.

Beatty, no supporter of the Northern Mine Barrage project anyway, got straight on to the front foot. On 28 March he telegraphed the Admiralty: 'I do not consider that any further mines should be laid on Barrage until technical experts can overcome existing defects.' Three days later he followed this up with a further message: 'The chief point to settle is are these mines safe if within forty-five feet of the surface. Unless that can be guaranteed, the policy of laying mines in the vicinity of principal fleet base is wrong.'[15]

Their Lordships gave in to the demand for a technical enquiry, which quickly reported that there was a problem with the sinkers. 'Evidence shows the deep sinkers are very unreliable', the committee wrote, adding: 'We do not consider the deep switch can be relied upon to ensure the safety of a mine that breaks adrift after prolonged submersion at a depth greater than forty-eight feet.'[16]

Now the Admiralty asked Beatty to sweep the minefield up again, along a forty-mile stretch. His response was that he refused to risk his valuable fleet sweepers in such a task. It was all to no avail. The mines continued to be laid.

Pellew Again

The minelayers laying the Northern Barrier were protected by Royal Navy destroyers. There were six US Navy vessels deployed to mine the open sea, with Royal Navy ships working the line from Norwegian waters. In June HMS *Nonpareil* was on escort duty. Lieutenant Herbert Williams noticed that the US minelaying was far from competent. 'Some 200-odd exploded as they were laid,' he wrote in his diary, 'but there are a good many left to drag about the North Sea. I don't think the Yanks can teach us much about minelaying.'[17]

On 19 July the protection duty fell to HMS *Pellew*, now repaired after her adventures of the previous December and still commanded by Commander Cavendish, who had been advanced from Lieutenant Commander after the action of 12 December. Sub-Lieutenant Brian de Courcy-Ireland had been confirmed in his rank and had left *Relentless* to be part of the *Pellew*'s wardroom.

De Courcy-Ireland was in his cabin at 1030 when there was a tremendous crash. *Pellew* had been torpedoed, the missile striking the starboard propeller and blowing away part of her stern. He found himself on the deck with his bunk on top of him, while across the flat the Chief Engineer was lying upside down and looking rather dazed. 'We could hear water rushing in below and against the after side of our bulkhead; the ship was obviously settling. Worst of all the hatch had jammed and I couldn't open it. We were trapped.'[18] To compound his worries he could smell fire, which he thought was the after magazine.

Above them they heard working on the hatch. 'Are you all right?' a voice called. 'There is a fire in the after magazine', sang out de Courcy-Ireland. There was a brief wry chuckle in response: 'There is no after magazine.'[19] It was at the bottom of the sea.

Freed at last, de Courcy-Ireland ran to the bridge, tripping over a case of Plymouth Gin which the explosion had deposited at the foot of the bridge ladder. Somehow Cavendish and his crew manged to shore up the bulkheads, and six tugs were sent from Aberdeen to tow them the 100 miles back to that port. On arrival they were put straight into a dry dock, and the wardroom was informed that rooms had been booked for them at the Palace Hotel, to which they immediately repaired. On seeing the rather bedraggled state of the newly arrived 'guests', the receptionist denied all knowledge of any bookings, a situation which was not resolved until a telephone call to the Senior Naval Officer at the base brought forth a van containing packing cases full of soap. Honour satisfied, 'Without batting an eyelid, the female conducted us to our rooms'.[20]

Beatty Takes a Stand

Despite these best efforts, and perhaps not unnaturally, it was soon discovered that U-boats simply passed over the deep mines of Area

B and, in the absence of any patrols, continued steadily on their way to the Atlantic. Consequently it was decided, at the pressing of Admiral William Sims USN, the senior US Navy officer in Britain, that it would be shallow-mined as well. This would prevent support for the Scandinavian convoys getting readily through the gap, and Beatty, by now increasingly at loggerheads with the Admiralty, blew his stack. He insisted that a ten-mile gap be left to the east of the Orkneys to allow a clear passage for supporting forces to the Norway-bound convoys.

First Sea Lord Rosslyn Wemyss, who had replaced Jellicoe at the turn of the year, wrote menacingly to Beatty, claiming that the Americans were insistent and that if the barrier was not to be completed end to end, then Sims would recommend that work cease, the USA would have wasted much money and resources, and Sims would perforce be recalled, to be replaced by a possibly less supportive officer.

Beatty was unmoved. 'I have to command the sea, not Admiral Sims', he annotated on Weymss's letter, and replied to him that: 'In the original scheme it was provided that a sixty-mile area would be available for passage of surface craft, whereas now I agree to a passage of only ten miles.'[21] Eventually a compromise was reached and a corridor of three miles was provided.

There now came a further threat of falling out, owing to issues at the eastern end of the Barrage. The potential for such problems had been recognised in February 1918, when Captain Cyril Thomas Moulden Fuller RN, Director of Plans at the Admiralty, wrote in a memorandum[*] that a partial occupation of Norway, particularly the creation of an operation at Stavangar, would be critical to the success of the project, as a Barrage without a Norwegian base would be like 'some great girder supported only at one end'.[22]

So it proved. U-boat commanders avoided the mined Area C by

---

[*] This note followed one presented to the War Cabinet on 6 December 1917, 'The Position of the Northern Neutrals', which noted that 'The Committee were impressed with the great importance of using as few destroyers as possible in connection with the patrol of the barrier, in view of the urgent need of their services elsewhere, and recommended that :–
1) We should try to secure a base, such as Stavanger, on the Norwegian coast, with the assent of Norway. 2) Provided Sweden remained neutral, it would be to our advantage for Norway to enter the war on our side. 3) Norway should be informed that we will render the necessary assistance to prevent a) The landing of any considerable German force in Norway; and b) Air raids on any large scale'. (CAB/24/4, NA) Old ideas died hard.

sailing around it into unmined Norwegian territorial waters. As a consequence it was decided to ask the Norwegian government to mine their own waters to prevent such usage, and on 7 August 1918 the British minister in Kristiania handed a memorandum to the Norwegian Foreign Minister, Nils Claus Ihlen, asking for such action. On13 August the Norwegians declined, to which the Allies replied that the response was 'unsatisfactory'.

Beatty was then ordered to mine Norwegian waters; orders which implied that the Norwegian government would not be told and that resistance might be expected. He refused, writing to Foreign Secretary Arthur Balfour that: 'The insult to Norway's independence is flagrant and continuous.'[23] Paraphrasing Beatty's arguments, Balfour reported that Beatty believed that '... if we violate Norwegian neutrality, Germany will certainly do the same. In that event all the coastwise traffic which now goes round the South of Norway and gets made up into convoys at Bergen [i.e. the HZ convoys] would be interrupted'.[24]

Beatty came under considerable pressure to change his mind, but remained resolute, stating at a late August conference that such activities would be 'repugnant to the officers and men of the Grand Fleet'.[25]

Additionally, Beatty continued to maintain that the Northern Barrier was, in any case, worthless. In a conference between him and the Director of Mercantile Movements, Captain Frederic Aubrey Whitehead RN, it was recorded that the admiral could not concur that the Northern Barrage was effective. 'In his opinion it was probable that the greater number of British mines were by this time useless owing to the depth failures and non-water-tightness; and of the mines in the American minefields the larger proportion has probably disappeared owing to premature explosion.'[26]

In the face of Beatty's intransigence, and his robust defence of the Scandinavian convoys and Norway's neutrality, the government backed down, and on 23 August decided to confine its effort to an attempt to persuade the Norwegians to do the job themselves. Soft diplomacy won out, for on 29 September the Norwegians declared that they would close their territorial waters through an extension of the Northern Barrage near Utsire from the 7th of the following month, just five weeks before the armistice came into force. Admiral Beatty had protected the Scandinavian convoys, and Norway's independent survival, with more than just escort vessels.

Routine

Still the Scandinavian convoys continued, although changes were made throughout 1918. In March the direct Humber-Methil (UM) convoy had been dropped as unnecessary, given that the majority of Scandinavian traffic was now coming or departing via the Tyne. In May 1918 the Norwegian destination was changed to Holmengrå, although the Methil convoys were still given the designation OZ eastbound and HZ westbound. The UT and TU traffic was given an increased escort in July 1918, a result of losses suffered to U-boats operating off Flamborough Head and coming up the North Sea from their Flanders bases. Eventually, nearly all shipping travelling on the Humber and the north route was convoyed, UT-18 in August gaining the distinction of being the largest oceanic or coastal convoy of the war, numbering seventy-three merchant ships and eighteen escorts.[27]

The quotidian boredom of convoy at this stage in the war is well conveyed by the diary entries of ERA Charles Budden on HMS *Yarmouth*. Beatty was now deploying the light cruisers as close escort for protection against surface attack, and *Yarmouth*, a 1911 'Town'-class light cruiser mounting eight 6in guns, was on convoy duty in September 1918. On the 9th she set sail at 0400 in company with HMAS *Melbourne* and destroyers to pick up a twenty-ship convoy, which they met at 1700. Sailing through the night, they reached the Norwegian coast at 0930, delivered the convoy to harbour and then cruised around waiting for another convoy of thirty ships which was collected at 1700. On the 11th Budden noted: 'Weather choppy, noon Scotland in sight, 1800 convoy in Lerwick.' Next day: 'Anchor at Scapa 0830, 1130 proceed to sea. 1230 pick up convoy, 1700 leave convoy, return to harbour, anchored at Scapa 2200.' Then, on the 13th, they start coaling at the untimely hour of 0130.

The 20th sees *Yarmouth* back on convoy duty, 'Cold sea and choppy'. The following day: '0930 convoy and harbour Norway, 1100 pick up another convoy, about forty ships'. For the 22nd Budden merely notes 'Rotten sea'.[28] Indeed, Budden thought that 'Nothing exceptional occurred till the day the Armistice was signed 11 November, just the usual routine, plenty of convoying, etc and go out to sea scouting'.[29]

Trawler *Viola*

If the destroyers were the workhorses of the convoy escort, then the armed trawlers and whalers were the mules. Slow, poorly equipped and barely militarised, they nonetheless played a crucial role in providing protection against U-boats and mines.

The Admiralty built trawlers of its own, but the majority were hired, taken up at the outbreak of war, usually with their original crews supplemented by an RNR officer and often a RNVR telegraphist. There were 1,456 of them used through the war, of which 266 (eighteen per cent) were lost. By far the largest contributions were made by the east coast ports of Aberdeen (228, of which 33 were lost), Grimsby (514, 99 lost) and Hull (315, 62 lost).

One such vessel was the trawler *Viola*, built in 1906 for the Hellyer Steam Fishing Company fleet at Hull and taken up one month after the war began. She was renamed *Viola III* by the navy and skippered by Charles Allum RNR, a trawlerman who lived in Hessle Road, Hull, but was born in London. Her original Hull crew came with her too, the youngest of whom, Charles Turner of St Andrew's Street, was just fifteen years old.

Viola was sent to Lerwick to patrol for U-boats and sweep for mines. Many of the wives followed them, including Mary Allum, who died in Shetland in 1916, some said poisoned by chemicals used to produce field dressings for the Western Front from the sphagnum moss which the local women gathered.

In September of that same year *Viola* was transferred to the Tyne and equipped with two relatively new weapons; hydrophones to help locate submarines and depth charges with which to attack them. Allum gained 'Their Lordships' Appreciation' for his actions on 21 April 1917 in driving off a U-boat which was attacking shipping off the Farne Islands. Earlier that year he had also gained praise for the rescue of the crew of the French coal-carrying barque *Cognac*, driven ashore in a gale at Scarborough on 5 March, and he was 'Mentioned in Despatches' in 1918.[*]

In his commendation, Allum's base commander, the Senior Naval Officer Tyne, noted that Allum '... at once opened fire on the hostile submarine which ceased attacking the steamer and opened fire on Chief Skipper Allum's ship ... . With shots falling close to him, the submarine submerged. The latter was armed with a large gun whilst *Viola* had only a 6pdr. The steamer was undoubtedly saved by *Viola* seeking an engagement as soon as possible. A good leader of men, the best Skipper at the Base.'

[*] *London Gazette* No 30909, 20 September 1918.

Allum left the ship in January 1918 for another command. *Viola*'s real moment of glory came on 13 August 1918 when, patrolling with others of her kind off Whitby and on the look-out for U-boats trying to intercept the east coast convoys, a periscope was suddenly sighted. It was *UB-30*, seeking to gain a leeward position from which to attack passing merchantmen.

Together with the trawlers *John Gilman* and *John Brooker*, *Viola* attacked with her new armament. Two hours later the U-boat tried to surface and was again fired upon and depth-charged. This time the damage was fatal. *Oberleutnant zur See* Rudolf Stier and his twenty-five crew went to the bottom for good, three miles NNE of Whitby pier.[*]

A month later, on 29 September, and seventy miles up the coast, *Viola* was on convoy duty when another U-boat was sighted, this time by an airship, *R-29*, which spotted a U-boat in the water and dropped a bomb on it. The old 'River'-class destroyer HMS *Ouse* and the '30-knotter' *Star,* both from the Humber-based 7th Destroyer Flotilla, were part of a Tyne-Methil convoy escort, with *Viola* and another trawler. At 1350 they saw the airship's attack and one minute later went to full speed and attacked with depth charges. *Star* dropped five depth charges in quick succession, and at 1432 the airship reported that an oil slick could be seen. *Star* and *Ouse* went to full speed, and the former dropped a sixth charge. At 1451 she dropped a seventh, and the trawlers caught up to add to the rain of high explosive. The U-boat was *UB-115*, commissioned in the May and on only her second patrol. She went to her end some four-and-a-half miles off Beacon Point, as did her commander, twenty-seven-year-old *Oberleutnant zur See* Reinhold Thomsen, and his crew of thirty-eight. The war had just forty-three days to run.

Captain (D) 7th Destroyer Flotilla, Gordon Campbell VC, stated that *Star* '... was handled in a most creditable and satisfactory manner ... and co-operated with the Air Force in a most excellent and zealous manner'. 'Their Lordships' Appreciation' was expressed, and the officer of the watch on *Star*, Sub-Lieutenant William Edmund Liley RNR, was awarded the DSC for 'alertness to duty in the prompt alteration of helm and increasing of speed to clear the position over which Airship *R-29* had released a bomb,

---

[*] *Viola* survived the war to become a whaler, seal catcher and scientific support vessel and, eventually, the oldest surviving steam trawler of her times.

and so enabling a successful depth charge attack to be made.'[*] Lieutenant Walter Thomas Arthur Bird RN, commanding *Ouse*, who had also sunk *U-70* in August, received a DSC[**] and was described by Captain (D) as 'indefatigable in his efforts and one of the most successful officers in anti-submarine warfare that I have ever had the honour to command'. (Despite this encomium, after the war Captain (D) Portsmouth Flotilla, Richard Greville Arthur Wellington Stapleton-Cotton, recorded on 11 November 1919: 'From what I have seen of this officer he will have to show a great deal more interest in his men and destroyers if he wishes to get on in the navy'.[30])

Armistice

By October it was clear that Germany no longer had the stomach for the fight. It was not so much that she had been beaten on the battle-grounds of the Western Front; it was more that her soldiers could no longer cope with the suffering they knew their kindred at home were enduring, with no end in sight. The collapse of German morale on the Western Front in the autumn of 1918 was in some large measure due to the reports that combatants were getting of conditions for their families and friends in Germany, together with their shock at seeing the plentiful Allied rations that they captured in their last great offensive of the war, the 1918 *Kaiserschlacht* (Kaiser's Battle).

For misery prevailed in Germany. Approximately 2,500 calories per day are needed to sustain working life. By 1917 the German rationing schemes offered only a daily diet of 1,100 calories, which was insufficient even for infants. Diseases of malnutrition, such as scurvy, tuberculosis and dysentery, became commonplace throughout the country by 1917. In Austria the official ration gave only 850 calories by 1918; 'too little to live on, too much to die', the beleaguered citizenry moaned. By the last year of the war the mortality rate among civilians in Germany was thirty-eight per cent higher than in 1913; tuberculosis was rampant, and, among children, so were rickets and edema.

Morale was an issue for the *Kaiserliche Marine*, too. On 5 October the German Flanders Flotilla U-boats *UB-10*, *UB-40*, *UB-59* and

---

[*] *London Gazette* No 31248, 24 March 1919.

[**] *London Gazette* No 31039, 26 November 1918.

UC-4 all scuttled themselves off the Flemish coast. That same day Germany started to seek an Armistice under its new government of Prince Max of Baden, and asked President Woodrow Wilson of the USA to mediate between all parties. One of Wilson's preconditions for so doing was that Germany should end its submarine war. Riding over the objections of Admiral Scheer, now Chief of the Imperial Navy Staff, the German Government made this concession on 20 October. Orders were sent that all U-boats should return to Kiel.

An infuriated Scheer planned one last Valkyrean death ride, a major fleet sortie to attack the Thames and the Flanders coasts which he scheduled for dawn on 31 October. He intended that these raids would draw out the Grand Fleet from Rosyth and that the High Seas Fleet could intercept and fight them that same afternoon and evening. It never happened. Years of inactivity and poor officer-men relationships had allowed the disease of Bolshevism to infect the crews of the High Seas Fleet. The evening of 29 October was marked by serious unrest and acts of indiscipline within the German ships, with the sailors convinced their commanders were intent on sacrificing them in a provocative attempt to sabotage the peace process. Open revolt broke out in many of the larger vessels, and the men refused to follow orders. Scheer had no option but to call off his putative raid. It was perhaps just as well, for the Grand Fleet was stricken with the influenza outbreak which became the dreadful 'Spanish 'Flu'. Beatty was unafflicted himself, but the whole of his staff were struck down and he reported to his mistress, Eugenie, that 'a lot of deaths, especially amongst the officers ... and two of my best captains' had occurred.[31]

Meanwhile, Erich Ludendorff, *Erster Generalquartiermeister* of the German army and by now effectively joint dictator of the German state, had been forced to resign on 26 October and, disguised in blue spectacles and a false beard, ignominiously fled to an admirer's house in Sweden (where else?) to write his memoirs.[*]

The German Armistice delegation eventually left for France on 6 November, and negotiations finally began on the 8th. The following day Germany declared a republic and announced the abdication of the Kaiser.

On 10 November HMS *Ascot*, a 'Racecourse'-class paddlewheel minesweeper commanded by twenty-five-year-old Lieutenant

---

[*] The Swedish government did not ask him to leave until February the following year.

Donald MacDonald RNR, was headed up the east coast of England to Granton, base to James Startin and his Q-trawlers and now home to some nearly 200 auxiliary vessels as well. Off the Farne Islands she was torpedoed by *UB-67*. Despite the recall orders that had been sent twenty days earlier, *Oberleutnant zur See* Hellmuth von Doemming had pressed home his attack. It was the day after his twenty-seventh birthday. The war was effectively over, but von Doemming either did not receive his orders or chose to ignore them.

Doemming was a successful U-boat commander. He held the Iron Cross First and Second Class and had sunk fourteen ships of 18,948 tons and damaged three more. Why he acted as he did is unknown; but all fifty-three men on board *Ascot* died that day, less than twenty-four hours from peace, in the East Coast convoy sea lanes. She was the last Royal Navy ship to be sunk by enemy action in the war.

In distant Stornaway, Isle of Lewis, Lieutenant MacDonald's mother shortly received a letter from his commanding officer, Lieutenant Arthur W Taylor, senior officer of the 9th Fleet Sweeping Flotilla. 'The Commanding Officer, officers and men of the 9th Sweeping Flotilla, wish to express their sincere and heartfelt sympathy on the loss of your boy', Taylor wrote. 'Lieutenant Macdonald was held in the highest esteem by everybody and we felt his loss very deeply. Now that this terrible war has come to an end and your boy has made the supreme sacrifice, we sincerely hope that comfort will come to you during your declining years, and that you will have some comfort in knowing that your boy took a prominent part in it. We honour the mother of a hero and a lost shipmate.'[32]

*   *   *

In the morning of 11 November a small crowd gathered outside 10 Downing Street. Prime Minister Lloyd George emerged to greet them. 'At eleven o'clock this morning the war will be over', he declaimed. 'We have won a great victory and we are entitled to a bit of shouting.'[33] Earlier that day, in Lerwick, Rear Admiral Greatorex was telegraphed news of the impending Armistice at 0900. He immediately informed the *Shetland Times* and *Shetland News*, which printed handbills with the glad tidings that were distributed all round the port and town.

'A profound heart-throb ... went up from the whole community, with a fervent "Thank God, Peace has come", but no indication of hilarity', reported the *Shetland Times*, adding that there was 'no pretence at what is commonly described as "popular" rejoicings'.[34] Despite this rather downbeat view, it appears that bells were rung, ships' sirens sounded, rockets fired and flags and bunting displayed. The town brass band played and people sang patriotic songs. The next day, Tuesday, was declared a general holiday, with a parade and three united church services of thanksgiving. At last it was over.

At Kirkwall the Armistice was greeted by the ringing of the sixteenth-century bells of the Romanesque Cathedral of St Magnus, once ecclesiastically in the charge of the Norwegian Archbishop of Nidaros (Trondheim)*. All the vessels in the crowded harbour, and those standing out to sea, sounded an accompanying cacophony of sirens and whistles.

Beatty was less than pleased, however. In his pre-Armistice discussions with Wemyss he had insisted that the German fleet be made to surrender. Instead, to quote Captain Roskill, 'To be deprived of his decisive battle, taken with the decision to substitute internment of the German warships for surrender and rejection of his proposal that Heligoland should be handed over, was more than he could bear'.[35] Worse, he had not been consulted over the change to the peace terms, and a final appeal to Geddes was futile as they had already been presented to the German peace delegates.

The reaction of his fleet was rather more positive. Certainly many felt like 'a bit of shouting'. At Rosyth, Midshipman Basil Jones recalled that 'two tots of rum were issued to ship's company and as darkness spread over the Fleet the scene was transformed, as all the searchlight were switched on and waved up and down the sky ... while every ships' siren sounded. ... all ships also fired rockets'.[36] Whereas on HMS *Yarmouth* Charles Budden recorded only 'Armistice signed, 1300 splice the Main Brace'.[37]

Brian de Courcy-Ireland was by now on the brand-new destroyer HMS *Westcott*, moored at Port Edgar on the Firth. He went to Edinburgh and witnessed the 'astonishing scenes and celebrations in Princess Street'.[38] At Immingham, all the ships in the dock blew their whistles, but the *Peel Castle*'s siren made more noise than any one of them.

In the outer Firth of Forth HMY *Zoraide* was on patrol off May

---

* Between 1154 and 1472.

Island. At first light Signalman Chadwick-Smith RNVR observed the mechanical semaphore arms on the island in action, trying to contact his ship, and a flag flying. To his surprise, as he took in the signal from the semaphore machine, he realised that it read 'Armistice to be signed at eleven o'clock this morning'. His mind whirled; 'Would miracles never cease? It was astounding news. It was unbelievable', he thought.[39]

He rushed to give the glad news to his captain, Archibald Hogarth, who he found sitting on the edge of his bunk in his pyjamas. On being given the message, Hogarth simply said 'Good', and dismissed him. But the news spread like wildfire among the crew and, perhaps unsurprisingly, they felt that they could now return to base and enjoy the festivities which were bound to be resultant on such a declaration. But when they reached Granton, Startin was furious at such dereliction of duty and sent them out again to complete their mission. 'So back we went', Chadwick-Smith* remembered, 'feeling very sorry for ourselves knowing that we should miss all the fun and jollification of Armistice Day ashore.'[40]

The terms of the Armistice required Germany to 'notify the neutral Governments of the world, and particularly the Governments of Norway, Sweden, Denmark ... that all restrictions placed on the trading of their vessels with the allied and associated countries, whether by the German Government or by private German interests, and whether in return for specific concessions, such as the export of shipbuilding materials, or not, are immediately cancelled'.[41] Additionally, a ban was placed on the transfer to a neutral flag of German vessels.

In Denmark, post-notification, the first acts of the Armistice were to begin the recovery of the minefields and reopen the closed parts of the waterways. The lighthouses too were brought back into operation. It would take many months for the sea lanes around Denmark to be safe; on 14 December, more than a month after the peace, three Danish marines were killed and eight wounded when the torpedo boat *Svaerdfisken* ran into a German mine off Albuen in the Great Belt. Nonetheless, by the end of 1918 Denmark had reduced the number of her navy's ships in commission to the bare bones. Only the coastal defence ship *Herluf Trolle* (two 9.4in guns, four 5.9in), the cruiser *Hejmdal* (of 1894 vintage, two 4.7in, four

---

*After the war, Harry Chadwick-Smith became a Methodist Minister.

20pdrs) and some torpedo boats had been fitted out as the winter squadron.

The ending of hostilities did not mean that demobilisation started immediately (it took until mid-January 1919 for the Admiralty to issue the 'commence demobilisation' signal), or that the merchant sea trade immediately reverted to pre-war conditions. On the 12th *Peel Castle* was part of the escort for a convoy to the Tyne, and was able to observe the Armistice celebrations at Newcastle. The following day she took the last convoy south. They docked at Immingham, and she lay there until 30 December, when *Peel Castle* received orders to proceed to Liverpool. She left Immingham on 31 December 1918, finally headed back to peace and home. And the last convoy out of Norway had sailed on 21 November, with the final Methil-Norway convoy on the 23rd.

Things took time to return to peacetime conditions. Many ships had, like SS *Peel Castle*, been requisitioned for wartime use, and in January 1919 the Norwegian and British-based Christian Salvesen Company applied for the release of their ships back to them. The office of the Director of Commercial Services at the Ministry of Shipping wrote back, claiming that the matter 'will in due course receive consideration', but 'no immediate action can be taken in so far as release is concerned'.[42]

In Shetland, the balloon and seaplane stations were closed soon after the Armistice, but the naval bases remained operational. Many of the RNR men based at Lerwick were demobilised early in 1919, and all the rest applied for the same treatment. There was still active naval work to be done, though, for the Northern Mine Barrage, which had cost Beatty so much of his patience and the Americans so much treasure, now needed to be cleared. Volunteers were sought and permission was given to enrol up to thirty recruits for a period of six months. The minesweeping vessels were stationed at Lerwick and Kirkwall. The USS *Black Hawk* was now based at the latter port, her force now dedicated to removing the mines they had so recently laid.

The war against the Bolsheviks in Russia caused troops and supplies to be sent there, and these were transported via Lerwick, later to return the same way, together with many Russian refugees. The Lerwick naval base was not finally closed until 13 December 1919.

PART THREE

'A grey-green expanse of smudgy waters grinning angrily at one with foam-ridges and over all a cheerless unglowing canopy, apparently made of wet blotting paper.'

Joseph Conrad, <i>Notes on Life and Letters</i> (1921)

republished by Floating Press (2011), page 150.

CHAPTER 19

A Hard Duty

If this story has heroes, it is the destroyers and men that protected the Scandinavian trade. *Mary Rose, Strongbow, Partridge, Opal, Narborough, Falcon* and all the others were the most visible fighting presence of Royal Navy in northern waters.

They were, by modern standards, tiny ships. The 'River'-class vessels displaced just 535 long tons; the 'M'-class, 994 long tons. Compare that with the modern 'River'-class offshore patrol vessels, built in the twenty-first century and in service now; they displace 1,700–2,000 long tons.

The weather, the sea and the enemy all conspired to make the northern North Sea a difficult and dangerous place in which to serve. No more was this so than on the destroyers, the workhorses of the trade protection and submarine hunting forces. Indeed, as the 'Official History' noted: 'Destroyers were run off their legs and no praise can be too high for the men who endured the strain, or for those who built the no less sorely tried hulls and engines.'[1]

In a similar vein, a postwar writer in the Royal Navy Historical Section noted: 'At times the strain on the personnel was very great, particularly the "30-knotters" and the whalers.'[2]

It was not a job for those who liked their creature comforts. As a contemporary writer wrote: 'The commanding officer, who came aboard in immaculate gold lace and spick and span uniform climbs the bridge, sea-booted and with a thick muffler round his throat, wearing a cap and jacket in which he would in no circumstances be seen ashore.'[3] All the rest of the crew followed their skipper's example, not only to protect their expensive naval uniforms, but also because 'destroyer work tells heavily upon clothes as well as upon the men who wear them'.[4]

A destroyer's bridge was reached by steep iron ladders, leading to a high-perched circular, canvas-screened structure in which were crowded several ratings, a gun, a chart table, wheel, helmsman and navigating officer. In any sort of sea the ship rocked giddily to and fro such that descending the bridge ladders became fraught with danger. Progress along the decks was risky, and hanging on to the lifelines essential. Spray and waves regularly soaked everybody on deck, including the occupants of the bridge.

Henry Taprell Dorling, a lieutenant commander on various North Sea destroyers during the war, later wrote that 'Going along the upper deck, which was constantly swept by the seas, was an undertaking of no little danger'.[5] Additionally, he said that 'the green seas came over everywhere while the ship lurched and tumbled, pitched and rolled, wallowed and buried herself without ceasing. The water found its way through our oilskins and down into our sea-boots within a quarter of an hour of leaving harbour. One remained wet … for four or five days on end.'[6] Eating properly was impossible; the staple diet whilst at sea was 'corned beef sandwiches and cocoa'.[7]

Brian de Courcy-Ireland remembered being on the bridge of *Relentless* continuously for forty-eight hours, taking time and time about on watch with his captain. The weather was too bad to risk going aft or for'ard, and he '… went fourteen days once without taking off any clothes and wet through several times'.[8] And Herbert Williams recalled his first passage to Scapa with *Nonpareil* in October 1917 as 'very dirty'. 'My cabin leaked after the dockyard had finished with it and it was rather like a snipe marsh. [I] was seasick all of one day but after that I got my eye in.'[9]

It seemed always to be cold. Surgeon Probationer Percy Story was on the destroyer HMS *Opal* in January 1918. On return from three days' escort duty with the Scandinavian convoys he described conditions in a letter to his parents:

> To begin with it was as rough as we have ever had it; sea breaking over us, and then, to put the finishing touches, it was snowing and hailing like mad and freezing so hard that the spray turned to ice as it came over us. The decks, masts and rigging were sheeted with ice and it was dangerous trying to get forrards with the slippery deck and heavy rolling.
>
> One came down from watch like a petrified iceberg and

nearly wept as one's fingers thawed out. It was impossible to keep even lukewarm – even in bed; and then you sat in a chair propped into position so that the roll could not fling it about in a white mist of your own breath, with hands and feet absolutely numb and cold. We could not get any hot water, could not eat our (wretched) meals that had to be eaten cold, as everything was off the table by rolling – in fact we had a regular little picnic. I can assure you that we were not sorry to get back into harbour. We looked as if we had arrived from the North Pole.[10]

Three days after Story wrote this description the weather killed him. His father sent his son's last letter to the *Daily Mail*, to refute another writer's claim that the Royal Navy was doing nothing and having an easy time of it.

Neither were destroyers forgiving ships for a commander. 'Being long and narrow, of light draught and easily influenced by every wind that blows,' Taprell Dorling noted, 'destroyers are tricky craft to handle.'[11] But there were compensations. Under an arcane edict of William IV (the 'Sailor King'), on appointment to a destroyer the ship's new commander was allowed to draw a cask of pickled tongues, and another when moved to his next commission.

Conditions on the armed trawlers were, if anything, even worse than for the destroyer men. At least the destroyers were designed to be fighting ships. Trawlers were peaceful fishing craft, rudely dragged from their occupation, fitted with one or two small guns and sent off to war. They hunted mines and submarines, as well as serving as convoy escorts and – all too often – rescue vessels too. Their crews were mainly the same fishermen who had sailed them in civilian life, but who were now serving as Royal Naval reservists, temporarily inducted into sea warfare. For example, some two-thirds of all the fishermen in Scotland volunteered for the RNR.

One of the Granton escort trawlers was a 110-ton Grimsby fishing vessel. In January 1918 her crew saw Force Eight, Nine and Ten gales, with waves anything up to 40 feet high. The Q-trawlers based on Granton suffered badly owing to the overcrowding caused by the extra gunnery ratings required. The *W S Bailey* was a 200-ton ex-Grimsby trawler fitted with three hidden 3in guns. She carried a crew of thirty, all of whom lived in a large cabin filled with sleeping bunks. In the cabin's centre stood an iron stove, always red-hot, on which men cooked their food as they came off watch. As part of her disguise she had to trawl for real, and the crew ate fish for breakfast, lunch and dinner, the cooking smells of which filled the room. Signalman Chadwick-Smith recalled that the 'atmosphere was hot and fuggy and saturated with the smell of cooking fat. Most of the bunks were tenanted by loathsome bed-bugs and then jumping fleas.'[12] Ventilation was provided by a small yard-square opening in the ceiling, against which rested a ladder, the only means of entrance or exit.

Nor did the light cruisers have it much better. Lieutenant Stephen King-Hall on HMS *Southampton*, patrolling off Norway and around Scotland, wrote:

> We experienced some terrific weather when cruising between the Orkneys and Shetland or off the Norwegian coast, and the seas breaking over our forecastle would come flying over the open bridge in sheets of icy spray. ... The only protection on the monkey island was a three-foot canvas screen ... frozen and numb, soaked to the skin, one would grope one's way underneath the hammocks in the stinking mess deck ... and fall into one's bunk in a tiny cabin with seas crashing down overhead, a cabin in which everything moveable had taken to the deck.[13]

It was not just surface vessels which suffered at the hands of the weather. Airships were particularly vulnerable. In December 1917 two airships and all their crews were lost in a storm.[14]

The receipt of mail from home (and the accurate sending of it to friends) was a source of much concern. Percy Story was an assiduous letter-writer to his father, but pined when there was no mail for him. 'We found no mail waiting for us this morning although we had been at sea for nearly four days', he complained, adding: 'There was some mess-up at the Mail Office ashore and we will have to make enquiries.'[15] Sometimes weather and mail became the problem. Story was able to complain about both in January. 'The mails are stopped here just at present on account of the weather, so perhaps I shall hear by the next arrival', he wrote.[16] For those based on or around Lerwick, mail could be expected only infrequently. Contact between Longhope and Shetland was maintained by the despatch vessel HMS *Vienna*, which made the journey at night (to avoid U-boats) twice weekly, weather permitting. She carried the sailors' mail, but these were not allowed to go to the civilian sorting office at Lerwick and were managed instead by the staff at the base. A mail service to and from Norway was established by the Norwegian government during 1917. The steamer *Gama* peddled between Scandinavia and Lerwick, and in 1918 provided a regular service for passengers as well, based at Bergen.

Apart from weather and mail, the other source of potential complaint was food. Naval photographer Arthur Willis thought that 'Their Lordships of the Admiralty were hard fathers to us in many respects but they took the view that, as it was the navy that enabled food to be brought into the country, it was only right that the sailor men should have a generous slice of it.'[17] But moaning soon started when it ran short. ERA Budden, on HMS *Yarmouth*, noted on 24 July 1918: 'No meat or spuds, corned beef, peas and rice instead.' Two days later 'still no spuds'; on the 27th, 28th and 29th, 'no spuds yet'. Then, glorious day, he was able to record on the 30th 'spuds at last, what a luxury'.[18] Lieutenant Williams of *Nonpareil* confided to his diary on 27 February 1918: 'Food is a serious problem now'.[19] He resolved the lack by going ashore with a rifle and shooting five rabbits and a brace of pheasants, thus 'doubling our meat ration'.[20] Another who took provisioning into his own hands was Lieutenant Commander Poignand of the destroyer *Menace*. He once caught 'sixty-eight pollock around the ship on a white fly'.[21]

Finally, it should be acknowledged that life on the merchant vessels was also harsh. Ordinarily a hard and dangerous existence, it became more so under wartime conditions. Hours were long and work exhausting. Although often not under military discipline, they operated under their own rules of teamwork and seamanship, although men frequently jumped ship when in a 'friendly' port. Some merchant sailors were sunk multiple times and, unlike in the Royal Navy, when a man's ship was sunk, his pay stopped.

When in port, life was characterised by heavy drinking and whoring, activities considered central to a seaman's life up to the time of the war. British merchant crews were generally cosmopolitan, with members coming from the British Empire, especially the 'lascars' – of Indian or South-east Asian heritage – or American, Scandinavian or European. There were also some 14,224 men of Chinese origin serving in British-registered ships by 1915.[22] Scandinavian crews tended to be more ethnically 'pure'.

In convoy, station and watchkeeping placed heavy demands on the masters and officers of merchant ships. Many of the prewar experienced officers had been called to serve in the RNR, on regular naval vessels. The remainder were either old or inexperienced, and often too few in number. The introduction of convoy 'pilots' was, among other factors, recognition of this.

Convoy Duty

Convoy escort was a tough and difficult job. Most of the sailors hated it.

The destroyer *Relentless* was a regular on the Scandinavian convoy run. 'It was a soul-destroying job', thought one of her officers, Sub-Lieutenant Brian de Courcy-Ireland.[23] 'The convoys were small, usually only half-a-dozen or so ships and the most antiquated collection of old crocks you ever saw. Worst of all was the "slow convoy", four knots in fine weather, almost nil in bad.'[24] Of course, canny shipowners were unlikely to operate their best vessels in such perilous conditions.

De Courcy-Ireland particularly hated the slowness of the convoys, dawdling along in dangerous waters. Serving on the destroyer HMS *Relentless*, he recalled:

> We were based on Lerwick in the Shetlands and we ran the convoys to Norway and back. We went from Lerwick to rather in the north, ... halfway up Norway. And we had these convoys to take over. Anything in numbers up to a dozen in the convoy and we took them over. They were awful old crocks. Every now and then – I think about once a month – we got what they call slow convoy. Well that was four knots in fine weather. We used to find that if you really wanted them to get a bit of a move on, we used to drop a depth charge which they thought was a submarine in the vicinity, you see, and up would go the smoke from their funnels and they'd belt on for a bit![25]

Maintaining convoy discipline was a nightmare for the escorts. 'Trying to keep that motley collection together was a continual headache', thought de Courcy-Ireland, 'as the faster ships tended to press on, particularly if there was a threatened U-boat attack. In these situations one of the two destroyer escorts would try to keep the U-boat down while the other herded the convoy away. Occasionally we lost a ship, in which case one of the two pick-up trawlers would be left behind... . It must have been hell to be a merchant seaman in one of those ships.'[26]

The round trip took about six-and-a-half days. Destroyers then had eighteen hours to fuel and provision and have a convoy conference with the masters of their next set of charges before setting out again.

In November 1917 Lieutenant Herbert Williams of HMS *Nonpareil* described a typical day. 'We have been covering the Norwegian convoy, a very elaborate business these days. We went over to the Norwegian coast and sighted the westbound convoy off Bergen at 1500, twenty-three ships, a fine haul for the Hun. We patrolled to the south of them, were with them again at dawn and at noon set out for home.'[27] Twenty days later he picked up another convoy off Norway at 1300 and set out for Lerwick against a big sea. 'What a hell of a life this is', he complained in his diary. 'Gales every day and we have been at sea almost continuously. Our motor boat has been stoved in beyond all repair by the sea and a trawler dragged into us this morning and ripped the bottom out of the whaler.'[28]

Sometimes the weather meant that the escorts simply could not do their job. HMS *Nonpareil* was with a convoy in April 1918. They ran into a north-east gale, became separated from their charges and spent the day and night off the Norwegian coast in very high seas. All the compasses were smashed, and the cabins and wardroom stores were flooded out. Williams's cabin sprang a leak and 'I lay on my bunk all the time I wasn't on watch and listened to the water swishing up and down'.[29]

Sometimes men broke under the strain. Lieutenant Commander Charles Astley Poignand had joined the 12th Destroyer Flotilla on 3 April 1916, commanding the new destroyer *Menace*, which he had commissioned. His first reaction was the same as most people on arrival at Scapa. 'Very cold up here, snow on the hills still.'[30] Poignand was a career Royal Navy man, having joined Royal Naval College *Britannia* aged twelve. He had been in destroyers since the start of the war, including being present in *Menace* at Jutland. By the end of 1916 the thirty-three-year-old commander estimated that he and his ship had steamed 27,800 miles since launch. He was an experienced and time-served destroyer captain.

However, 1917 did not start well for Poignand. On 14 January a heavy sea wrecked the after steering position, and the top of the wardroom hatch was smashed and jammed shut. Those inside could not get out for the next two hours. By May, *Menace* was part of the Scandinavian convoy escort group as well as conducting anti-submarine patrols. She was soon *hors de combat*, however, for on 2 June she collided with another destroyer, HMS *Marvel*, wrecking the bow. The subsequent court of enquiry found that the commanding officer of *Marvel* had made an error of judgement, and he was severely reprimanded.

Repaired and back on escort duty, by 1 September *Menace* was escorting an eastbound convoy and picked up the returning ships, eight in total, which were led out of the fjords by a Norwegian torpedo boat captained by a man who had been on Amundsen's South Pole expedition.

The stress of constant duty was beginning to tell on Poignand. On 5 September he wrote in his diary: 'This life is a bit too strenuous as one never has a minute's peace. As soon as you come in there is so much correspondence to attend to. The next morning you have to go to sea and [find out] what your eastbound convoy consists of and interview all the masters – almost as soon as that is done you have to sail.'[31] That same day he took out another convoy. 'Looks like blowing a gale so sent [back] separately the four tugs and their tows, also the Danish motor ship *Samso* under the charge of the yacht *Calista* and three armed trawlers.'[32]

The following day he noted that it was gale force from the SSE. The convoy could only make 4 knots, and even his vessel could only manage 7. By 0930 the convoy was unable to keep together, and Poignand ordered them to separate and proceed as best they could independently. The visibility was bad, not aided by a high sea. He returned to Lerwick in company with the SS *Prince*, arriving at 1600, oiled and sailed again to try to make contact with the incoming westbound convoy.

At 0430 on the 7th *Menace* arrived at the rendezvous point, but they could discover no trace of the merchant vessels. Poignand ordered a twenty-mile-radius search, without success, and then returned once more to Lerwick.

Once there, and at his own request, he met with the doctor from the depot ship, *Leander*. Poignand told him that '… he felt unable to compete with the continuous strain'.[33] In the army this might have earned him a firing squad, but the navy was more sympathetic.

Poignand was removed from duty, sent to the hospital ship *Berbice* and, from there, via a number of staging hospitals, to the Royal Navy medical facility at Haslar, Gosport. He was released from their care on 1 October and given four weeks' sick leave, with orders to report for duty on the 30th. On his return Charles Poignand was deemed fit only for shore duty and never commanded at sea again during the war.

When told of the loss of *Mary Rose* and *Strongbow*, sister 12th Destroyer Flotilla vessels, Poignand may well have thought 'There but for the grace of God go I', for he commented in his diary: 'I always thought something of that kind was bound to happen sooner or later.'[34]

*　　*　　*

Inevitably, the attitudes of the Scandinavian people had an impact on the sailors who had to work and fight in the North Sea. 'The Swedes are hostile to us', thought Commander George Plunkett England,[35] serving with the Northern Patrol on blockade duty. And many of them were, given their German leanings. Not so the Norwegians. 'The friendliness of the Norwegian people towards the Allies, and particularly the British, was an appreciable asset to the naval staff at Bergen and resulted in very close co-operation on the part of the Norwegian navy, who rendered invaluable assistance at all times (often overstepping the lines of neutrality)', wrote an anonymous naval officer in 1919.[36] After the *Pellew* affair, Captain Molteno of the *Shannon* wrote to the Admiralty to state: 'I would submit that the friendly service rendered by the Norwegian torpedo boat *Hvas* should not be allowed to pass unnoticed.'[37]

The relative warmth shown by Norwegians compared with that of Swedes was perhaps inevitable. Both Norway and, to a lesser extent, Sweden, were determined to stay neutral. Initially both were prisoners of geography and economics. If push came to shove, Norway would have to choose the Allies and Sweden, Germany. Sweden's economy was closely linked to Germany's at the start of the war, but her geographic position was also important. Only the Baltic Sea separates the two countries, and during much of the war the western Baltic was almost completely under the aegis of Germany. Norway, however, would have, *in extremis*, to turn to Britain, as the Norwegian economy faced westward and the Royal Navy controlled her supply routes.

CHAPTER 20

Death and Memorials

Being neutral did not mean being immune from the loss of property and life. Of the three Scandinavian countries, Norway suffered most from the war for trade. She lost 831 ships, a total of 1,535,275grt, nearly half her pre-war fleet[1]. Norway also lost almost 2,000 men. To these totals should be added sixty-seven ships and 943 men which just 'disappeared.'[2]

The Norwegians were the first of the three countries to honour their lost sailors officially. A monument was built near Stavern and dedicated on 1 August 1926. This *Minnehallen* contains eleven plaques in the crypt inscribed with 1,892 names of the dead.[*]

The Danes followed in May 1928 with a *Søfartsmonumentet* in Copenhagen, not without a heated public debate as to whether or not the money would be better spent on food and benefits for the widowed and their families. They had lost 249 ships of 253,622grt and 650 men.

Sweden was late in honouring its war dead; perhaps a function of the nation's conflicted loyalties during the war. It was not until 14 July 1933 that a *Sjomanstornet* (seaman's tower) was erected in Gothenburg. It depicted a sailor's wife at its apex, looking out to sea for a ship which will never appear. Two hundred and sixty Swedish vessels were sunk during the war, and the memorial records 684 Swedish dead, a total which includes thirty-six women.

British sailors washed up on the shores of Scandinavia throughout the war. After the Battle of Jutland on 31 May 1916, eighteen dead Royal Navy seamen were found on the beaches of Norway, only seven of whom could be identified by name. The Norwegians buried them

---

[*] The dead of World War Two were added later.

at Fredrikstad Military Cemetery, approximately fifty miles south of present-day Olso, and erected a granite memorial there. In 1961 a number of graves were brought into the cemetery from other small burial grounds all over Norway. These included men from HMS *Strongbow* and *Mary Rose*, *Marmion* and *Partridge*. The cemetery now contains a total of eighty-two Commonwealth burials of the First World War, fifty-one of them unidentified.

Britain's Merchant Marine has its own memorial, at Tower Hill, London, dedicated on 12 December 1928 and designed by Sir Edwin Lutyens, with sculpture by Sir William Reid-Dick. The memorial had originally been planned by its designer to be sited on the banks of the River Thames at Temple Gardens. This laudable ambition was thwarted by the Royal Fine Arts Commission, which ruled that such a site would interfere with Sir Joseph Bazalgette's scheme of decoration along the Embankment. Instead, the Commission suggested Tower Hill on the basis that it was an area long associated with seafaring occupations. Luytens was furious at what he saw as disrespect to the memory of Britain's seafarers, in denying them a more prominent position. Nonetheless, it commemorates the almost 12,000 Merchant Marine casualties who have no grave but the sea. In total Britain lost 17,000 merchant sailors and 3,305 merchant ships between 1914 and 1918. Many of these died in the North Sea, or off the coast of Scandinavia, keeping the Scandinavian trade running.

On 7 November 1929 fifty flag officers swelled the congregation of Portsmouth Cathedral* for a service of remembrance for the dead of the action of 17 October 1917. Admiral of the Fleet Sir John Jellicoe and Admiral Roger Keyes helped place into position a model of a previous HMS *Mary Rose*, one launched in 1654. She had been engaged in the Anglo-Dutch Wars and the War of the Grand Alliance before she fought off an attack by seven Algerine corsairs in 1669 under the command of Sir John Kempthorne, thus achieving lasting fame. The model had been built in Australia by a native of Portsmouth and donated to the Cathedral.

Mrs Hilda Cleghorn, widow of Engineer Lieutenant Commander Cleghorn, presented an ensign from her husband's *Mary Rose*, which was placed with the model by Jellicoe and Keyes.** Lieutenant Commander Fox's wife also attended, with her two

---

* Until 1927, the parish church of St Thomas of Canterbury.

** Which, by the 1950s, had gone missing, presumed lost.

children, Anthony and Elaine, teenagers now, but having grown up without their father.

The dead from the action of 12 December 1917 received less attention. The youngest man to die from HMS *Partridge* was seventeen-year-old Sub-Lieutenant Robert England Ferrier, son of Richard and Madeline Ferrier of Hemsby Hall, Hemsby, Norfolk. He has his memorial in the village church of St Mary the Virgin:

> To the Glory of God
> And in memory of the members of the
> Family of Ferrier who for over
> Three hundred years
> Worshipped in this Church
> Particularly of
> RICHARD F E FERRIER
> FSA JP Lord of the Manor
> Patron of the Living
> Born 1863 – died 1933
> And his wife
> MADELINE LUCY
> Born 1865 – died 1955
> And of their son
> ROBERT ENGLAND FERRIER
> Sub-Lieutenant R.N.
> Born 1899 killed in action 1917

Chief Petty Officer Arthur James Alden is remembered by a plaque in the lych-gate of St Mary's Church, South Benfleet, Essex; and five of *Partridge's* dead lie at Fredrikstad.

The bodies of ten men from *Opal* and *Narborough* were recovered after the disaster and are buried at Lyness Royal Naval Cemetery, Orkney. One of them was ERA Wesley Bramhall Bennett of the latter ship. His father in Leeds wrote to the Admiralty to ask if there was any money on the body, as 'in his last letter he said he hoped to send some money for me to bank for him'.[3] It is strange what people think of in the midst of tragedy. One of *Opal's* 4in guns and a Kisbee ring were eventually salvaged and donated to the Lyness Museum (Scapa Flow Visitor Centre and Museum). And all the dead of *Opal* and *Narborough* have a joint memorial above the cliffs near Hesta Rock. A metal plaque, let into stone, reads simply:

'In memory of the 188 men who perished here when HMS *Narborough* and HMS *Opal* were lost on the rocks of Hesta during the snowstorm of 12 January 1918.'

Lieutenant Commander Malan of HMS *Opal* is commemorated at St James Church, Albion Street, New Brighton, where an Astley family plaque records:

> To the glory of God
> And in ever loving memory of
> Christopher Basil Astley
> Lieut 10th (Scottish) the Kings Liverpool Regt
> Aged 22 youngest son of the Revd John Henry Astley MA
> (curate of this parish 1907-1919) and Sophia Ridgway his wife
> Who died at Rouen of wounds received in action
> July 27th 1918
> Also their son-in-law
> Charles Caesar de Merindol Malan
> Lieut-Commander Royal Navy, HMS 'Opal'
> Aged 31, drowned at sea on active service, Jan 12th 1918
> Called to higher service.

The commander of the *Narborough*, Lieutenant Edmond Mansel Bowly, has his memorial, too, in the precincts of Peterborough Cathedral.

Eight men from HMS *Marmion* were washed ashore on Norway's coast and are buried at Fredrikstad Military Cemetery. They include Engineer Lieutenant Donald Pearson, son of the Vicar of Seaford on the Sussex coast, and Surgeon Probationer G Brown from Cullen, Banffshire. Nearer home, at St Clements's Church, Leigh-On-Sea, Essex, there is a tablet on the altar dedicated to Stoker First Class Robert Louis Joslin:

> The altar in this chapel was given
> To the glory of God
> And in memory of Mabel Elizabeth
> Wife of Robert C Joslin
> Who died Sept 2nd 1917
> And of Robert Louis, son of the above
> Who was lost at sea
> In the sinking of HMS Marmion Oct 21st 1917.

Robert senior lost his wife and son in less than two months, yet still retained the faith to commemorate them.

Four men were lost when HMS *Tithonus* was sunk. One, Tom Westmoreland Walton, has a memorial grave in the tiny Teesdale village of Romaldkirk. It simply notes: 'Tom Westmoreland Walton engineer HMS *Tithonus* lost at sea 28 Mar 1918 aged 22 yrs'.

Commander Schafer, lost with the *Gaillardia*, was the elder son of the eminent physiologist and founder of endocrinology, Sir Edward Sharpey Schafer, KB, FRS, chair of physiology at the University of Edinburgh. Sir Edward gave both his sons to the war, for Commander Schafer's brother, Thomas Sydney, was killed at Loos on 26 September 1915, aged twenty-four. He had graduated in natural science from Cambridge in 1912, destined for a career in medicine. Both are remembered in a memorial at St Baldred's Church, North Berwick: '... their name liveth for evermore', 'sunset and evening star one clear call for me', *'par nobile fratres'.*

A memorial far afield recognises the seamen who died in the cause of the Scandinavian trade. In Mumbai, Adbul Muhammad and Abdur Rahim, seaman and fireman respectively who died with the SS *Destro*, are remembered on the Bombay 1914-1918 Memorial.

Battles, wrecks and U-boats claimed many victims, but sometimes death came in the most insidious ways. Lieutenant Commander Poignand heard that in November 1916 'six men were lost overboard and drowned from the various destroyers on the last trip'.[4] And Charles Budden of the *Yarmouth* noted that three doctors and a nurse from the hospital ship *China* at Scapa died in August 1918, while out fishing for their suppers. They caught a mine instead.[5]

Neutrals and combatants, all were united and equal in death. The battles they fought and the trade for which they died are long forgotten, but around Britain, in Scandinavia and across the continents there are still reminders of them. We should never forget.

---

* 'A pair of noble brothers'.

CHAPTER 21

Analysis and Conclusions

The Economic Consequences of Neutrality and Belligerence

'It can certainly be argued that Britain gained nothing and lost much as a result of the First World War. The principal results of the war were more than 700,000 young men dead, a similar number injured, many permanently, and a massive increase of national indebtedness.'[1] So thinks a modern Cambridge historian.

Financially, there is no doubt that the USA, neutral for so much of the war, was the only winner. At the war's end France owed the USA £550 million and Italy owed £300 million. As John Maynard Keynes noted: 'Europe was in complete dependence on the food supplies of the United States; financially, she was even more absolutely at their mercy. Europe not only already owed the United States more than she could pay; but only a measure of further assistance could save her from starvation.'[2]

As for Britain, she owed the USA £842 million.* The war had bankrupted her, not least because she gave so much of her precious treasure to her Allies to keep them in the war. There was no chance of getting back the £568 million owed by Russia, given the policies of the new government there**. France owed Britain £508 million which she was in no position to pay; Italy owed £467 million, Belgium £98 million. Some £20 million was due from Serbia and the countries that would become Yugoslavia, and £79 million elsewhere. In total, Britain was owed £1,740 million, possibly

---

*As early as 21 July 1917, Woodrow Wilson was recorded as saying that England and France would soon be 'financially in our hands', and that the beauty of having financial leverage over Britain and France was that 'when the war is over we can force them to our way of thinking'. See Ferguson N, *The Pity of War* (Penguin, 1999) pages 327 and 329.

** Russia had repudiated its foreign debts in February 1918.

£109,620,000,000 at today's values. As Winston Churchill put it, victory 'proved only less ruinous to the victor than to the vanquished'.[3] This change in the international order of things, with The USA emerging as top dog, had cost the USA only 53,400 men killed in combat,[*] with another 63,300 dead from all other causes, mainly influenza.

The Scandinavian neutrals also profited from their position, though not to the same extent as the USA. Due to the need to finance its rapid nineteenth-century industrialisation, Sweden had borrowed money internationally, and by 1910 was one of the most indebted countries in the world. But the war changed that. The demand for Swedish exports by the warring states, plus the inflation incurred in the combatant countries, meant that the price obtained for Swedish exports rose and allowed for a significant pay-down of outstanding overseas loans. This massive transfer of foreign money as payments for wartime Swedish exports meant that Sweden went from indebtedness to being a net creditor at the war's end.

But as an historian of the Scandinavian countries wrote: 'The war had been a shattering experience, psychologically if not physically, for all the neutral states.'[4] In Sweden, just two days after the Armistice, there were worker demonstrations in Stockholm calling for a general strike, the establishment of a socialist republic and the removal of the monarchy and the formation of workers' councils on the Russian model. The prosperity that war had brought to Swedish businesses had not filtered down to the working class, who had lived with shortages and rising prices for all sorts of commodities. There was widespread rioting and looting of stores; a very un-Swedish expression of anger. For a moment it looked as if revolution would come to Sweden, as well as to Russia and Germany.

The government reacted by introducing a proposal to grant universal suffrage, and this became law on 17 December 1918. Things settled down as food supplies picked up, and the potential for revolutionary upset faded into the background.

Throughout the 1920s 'developments in Sweden largely paralleled those in the United States. While the rest of Europe struggled with considerable hardships, Sweden experienced a real boom.'[5] Annual real wages between 1913 and 1929 increased by

---

[*] To be contrasted with the nearly 20,000 British soldiers killed on the first day of the Somme in 1916, and the 196,000 killed or wounded in the month of July of that year.

fifty-two per cent, despite a reduction in the statutory working week. Not until the Great Depression did the Swedish economy falter, and then only in the second half of the 1930s.

In Denmark, between 1914 and 1918, GDP declined by sixteen per cent. But this was a function of the disturbance of international trade rather than a structural change, and took only a minor toll on the assets and lives of the Danes themselves. This is amply demonstrated by the events of 1919 and afterwards, when GDP recovered strongly to reach higher than prewar levels by 1921.

The balance of payments positon was no cause for alarm either, external debt postwar being smaller than prewar, as a percentage of national income. Not everything in the garden was roses, however. In 1922 Denmark's largest bank* would have failed without government intervention and reconstruction.

For the Danes the war delivered a major prize; the reunification with Northern Schleswig, removed from Danish possession after the Second Schleswig War of 1864. This was granted as part of the Treaty of Versailles, which guaranteed a referendum on the issue. Given that the 165,000 people concerned (approximately 5 per cent of the entire Danish-speaking population) spoke Danish and thought they were Danish, the result was a forgone conclusion, and the territory was transferred from the defunct German Empire to the Kingdom of Denmark.

Norway also gained territorial advantage from the war. As part of the Versailles negotiations Norway acquired sovereignty over Svalbard in 1920 (finally enacted in 1925), an arctic archipelago called Spitsbergen at the time. Some of the population did well out of the war. Robert Bruce Lockhart, visiting in January 1918, noted that 'Christiania [*sic*], whose merchants had grown fat on supplying ships and fish to the Allies, was very expensive and almost gay. Champagne began to flow at 1100 in the morning and never ceased.'[6] Additionally, Britain, and especially the Royal Navy, was not unhappy at Norway's neutrality. Both Jellicoe and (eventually) Beatty had resisted attempts to persuade them that bases in Norway – with the concomitant need to man and protect them – would be an advantage, and the Norwegians generally recognised that, like it or not, they were in a British sphere of economic influence. Britain gained most of what it required from Norway with only the

---

* *Landmandsbank* (Farmer's Bank)

occasional need to deliver a sharp rebuke or punishment, and trade to Germany from Norway was gradually dried up.

Nonetheless, economically Norway entered the postwar period with a substantial national debt. Money had been spent, often inefficiently, and loans contracted to pay for it. The value of domestic production had increased through the war, but not its volume. Vast amounts of capital had been committed to the production of ersatz products which the end of the war made irrelevant, and little investment had been made in those industries which had prospered under war conditions. Norway emerged from neutrality somewhat enfeebled.

Naval Tactics

At the beginning of the war the Royal Navy had little idea how to stop U-boat attack. The prevailing tactic was to hunt them, the way one might hunt a fox or stalk a salmon or deer. Individual warships – destroyers, trawlers, drifters, and even light cruisers – would sail alone or in small groups and hope somehow to stumble across a U-boat, which would have the decency to stand and fight and not submerge and disappear.

This aggressive tactic was born of the navy's view of itself as a fighting force, one that should, in the best traditions of Vicwardian manliness, take the fight to the enemy. To stand on the defensive was somehow seen as rather shaming. As a whole, the Royal Navy looked forward to a climactic battle with the *Kaiserliche Marine* which would drive the Germans from the seas and win the war. To hide behind anti-submarine nets (as quickly became the norm), or later to sail in protected convoys, was somehow *infra dig.* Furthermore, the submarine itself was seen as an underhand weapon, not fit for a gentleman's war.

If one incident can be taken to represent the whole. This is Jellicoe's reply to an approach in November 1916 by Lloyd George, Secretary of State for War, and Andrew Bonar Law, Secretary of State for the Colonies. Asked by the two politicians why the navy would not introduce convoy to protect trade, First Sea Lord Jellicoe replied: 'The role of the Royal Navy was to search out and destroy, not provide passive protection.'[7]

Such behaviour had been laid down as close to the onset of war as 22 November 1913, in a document prepared jointly by the Director of the Operations Division (Captain George A Ballard) and the Chief of Staff (Vice Admiral Sir Henry Jackson), entitled 'Summary of Principles of Trade Protection and Organisation of Trade Branch'.

The authors adumbrated the precepts by which officers should act. 'It should be laid down as a fundamental principle', they asserted, 'that our first and most important duty is the location and destruction of all enemy cruisers and mercantile cruisers, both potential and actual. If, and when, circumstances permit, destruction of the enemy's trade should also be pressed, but not to the hindrance of the primary duty of destroying enemy war vessels.'[8]

With regard to convoy, Jackson and Ballard were curtly dismissive. 'Convoy and groups are not considered practicable chiefly due to difficulties with owners and in the case of convoy the removal of cruisers from their proper function of attacking the enemy.'[9]

As historian Richard Hough has written: 'In short, defence was an unacceptable principle, offence correct – right-minded, valorous, glorious and correct. To protect merchantmen, to scurry about them like a sheepdog was *defensive*. To send out hundreds of men o'war to hunt down and destroy commerce raiders was *offensive*. That such a policy was flying in the face of reason was considered by only a small minority of thinkers at the Admiralty.'[10]

These attacking instincts are seen clearly in the behaviours of the commanders of *Mary Rose*, *Strongbow*, *Partridge* and *Pellew*, when in both actions the destroyers might have better served their purpose by standing off the enemy; a less glorious but more pragmatic strategy.

The reasons for these beliefs are not hard to find. The officer class came from the public schools and from the navy's own Britannia Naval College, and the late Victorian public schools and colleges produced a breed of men who were 'devoid of guile ... conditioned to believe in romantic notions of honour, glory and sacrifice'.[11] These educational establishments raised boys to 'believe in chivalric values that were all the more potent because they had not been tested in the real world'.[12] As another historian has written: 'Every public schoolboy was familiar with the *Iliad* and the *Odyssey* and the poetry – with its emphasis on honour, discipline, athleticism and courage in the face of death – spoke across the ages about what it meant to be a gentleman and a scholar at the height of empire.'[13]

At Britannia boys were inducted into a club, the Royal Navy. Like most clubs it had rules about who could join. The aristocracy, the land-owning squirarchy, younger sons of the nobility – this was the officer group's core membership profile. Eldest sons of the aristocracy went to the army or Parliament before inheriting their father's estate and titles. Younger sons joined the Church or the navy. Once in the club it was important to follow the rules. If one did so, promotion would inevitably follow. If not, 'troublemaker' status would ensue and it was a long and lonely road to advancement. The Royal Navy that started the war was, in the main, a complacent, arrogant body, sure of its own authority and greatness, and in the merits of an aggressive fighting stance. The Admirals who commanded it had grown up in a world where, educated in the navy from the age of twelve years old, and frequently serving for long periods abroad, they had very little contact with modern thinking or culture. Succession to flag rank was generally by seniority, on the 'one-in-one-out' principle. Flag officers had usually reached their rank through adherence to the traditions and thinking of the past, not the future.[*]

So merchant ships sailed alone and U-boats were sought by single warships or massed random searches. The tactics were not successful, but they took a long time to die. As late as autumn 1917 Beatty was carrying out multi-ship sweeps for U-boats. Sweeps along the Scandinavian coast were still commonplace even after convoy had been introduced. Finally it was convoy that changed the rules.

Convoy and its Success

Few in high prewar naval circles had foreseen the impact that the submarine would have on the ability to maintain trade. As a result the Royal Navy was largely unprepared for the war that it eventually had to fight. There was no great decisive battle of dreadnoughts, and the risk to British supply lines from German surface raiders was ephemeral. Instead it was the U-boat which threatened Britain's trade and survival.

Convoy was eventually found to be the solution, but would the Scandinavian convoys have come about if it had not been for Beatty's badgering of the Admiralty and support of the plan developed by

---

[*] In modern management-speak this is the 'Peter Principle'; 'in a hierarchy everyone rises to their level of incompetence'.

Admiral Brock? Beatty was certainly advancing the arguments in favour with fervour, and apparently in the face of much opposition. 'Every proposal of Beatty's for convoy has been opposed', wrote Captain Herbert Richmond of HMS *Conqueror* (admittedly no fan of Jellicoe), who quoted Beatty as saying: 'It was impossible. Everything was impossible. It is like running your head against a brick wall – no, a wall of granite – to try to get your ideas through.'[14]

But the Admiralty were certainly on a journey towards the adoption of convoy, driven not least by the concerns vociferously voiced by Norwegian shipowners and government ministers, British Prime Minister Lloyd George and the US naval supremo in Britain, Vice Admiral William Sowden Sims. The French coal trade provided valuable lessons, and the work of a commander on the Admiralty staff proved that the prevailing wisdom concerning the number of ship movements that would have to be escorted was wildly overestimated. The first experimental non-Scandinavian-related convoy left Gibraltar on 10 May 1917 and arrived at the Downs on 22 May, just postdating the end of April commencement of Brock's operations.

However, the real concern of Lloyd George, the War Cabinet and Sims was to escort the US convoys bringing supplies and men across the Atlantic. It is entirely possible that the East Coast and Scandinavian trade might have been overlooked for longer than it was. Beatty's pressure, at least in the author's view, was necessary to get things started as early as they were. Otherwise it is probable that matters would have continued to languish until later in the year, with more men, *materiel* and ships lost as a result.

It is indisputable that the introduction of the Lerwick-Bergen (and *vice versa*) and east coast Immingham-Lerwick and back convoys was a success, as measured in terms of minimising the number of merchant vessels lost. From the introduction of full convoying on 28 April 1917 to the change of hub from Lerwick to Methil on 18 January 1918, 7,077 ships were conveyed with a loss rate of only 0.93 per cent (see Appendix 8).

During 1918 the loss rate was further reduced. Shipping losses on all of the East Coast sailings (i.e. including those operating south of the Humber) reduced to thirty-five out of 16,102 ships sailed (from 16 January).[15] There was an incidental benefit too. 'The development of the coastal convoy system forced the U-boats back in to the Western Approaches',[16] and thus away from easier prey.

On the east-west sailings, from 19 January 1918 to the end of the war, 4,230 ships were convoyed with only fifteen sunk,[17] a loss rate of just 0.35 per cent.

The pattern of forces deployed reflected the growing importance of convoy escort and the protection of Scandinavian trade. On 1 January 1916 the 7th Destroyer Flotilla of twenty old destroyers was based on the Humber. The same day a year later they were still there, with the addition of the old *Canopus*-class pre-dreadnought battleship *Albion* as guard ship and a P-boat. At these times the role of the destroyers was firmly coastal protection and U-boat hunting.

But by January 1918, following the eventual introduction of Scandinavian convoys, there were twenty-eight destroyers based at Immingham on the Humber, a mixture of 1897–8 vintage '30-knotters' and 1903–05 'River'-class. In addition there were now eight 'R'-class destroyers based at Lerwick. These were modern vessels, armed with three 4in and one 2pdr, four 21in torpedo tubes and capable of 36 knots. Their deployment there reflected the fact that the older vessels simply could not stand up to the weather encountered on the crossing to Norway.

Finally, by the time of the Armistice, even the nomenclature of the flotillas had changed to reflect the primacy of their escort duties. At Methil, the Methil Convoy Destroyer Flotilla comprised six 'L'-class ships, again of a modern type dating from 1913–14. On the Humber the 7th Destroyer Flotilla, now additionally entitled East Coast Convoys, boasted twenty-eight old vessels together with three torpedo boats. These were supported by the Southern Patrol, the 4th Sloop Flotilla at Granton and the Northern Patrol of three 'M'-class destroyers, built between 1914–16. The importance of protecting the Scandinavian trade was reflected in the resources devoted to it.[18]

Despite all this resource there never seemed to be enough escorts. Armed Boarding Steamers became convoy leaders, but were in short supply. Yachts had to take that duty on occasion. Destroyers had to be begged, borrowed and stolen from the Grand Fleet, which under successive CinCs hoarded them like a miser with gold. Trawlers were wanted everywhere, and again the Grand Fleet demanded many for minesweeping. That the Scandinavian and their East Coast extension convoys manged to muddle through at all is a testament to the many now forgotten and unknown staff officers at Longhope, Lerwick and Methil, who somehow cobbled together forces and convoys.

The demands made of such destroyers and smaller ships that

were available were amplified by the shortage of experienced officers to command them. The example of HMS *Narborough*, wrecked in a storm on 12 January 1918, illustrates just how little support there was for the captain of such a vessel. *Narborough* carried a complement of ninety-one, of whom five were officers, but this was a misleading command structure. Thirty-year-old Lieutenant Edmond Mansel Bowly, the captain, had served in command of destroyers throughout the war, but the remaining four officers were a lieutenant, a sub-lieutenant and two midshipmen RNVR; young volunteers. They were very young and hardly an experienced team whom Bowly could rely on the run the ship.

Lieutenant John Gould Nicolas, aged twenty-six when *Narborough* was wrecked, had won the DSC at Gallipoli two years previously while serving in HMS *Chelmer*, a 'River'-class destroyer. He 'was twice wounded during the landing operations of 6th and 7th August, but refused to give up his duty of directing gunfire until no longer able to stand', according to the citation.[*] Clearly he was a courageous officer and one with some experience. As for the other officers, Sub-Lieutenant Eric de Wet was not quite twenty years old but had already been mentioned in despatches and awarded the DSC for his actions, also at Gallipoli. He too was brave, but undoubtedly inexperienced. Midshipman Cecil G Kennedy RNVR was a volunteer aged nineteen who had joined up straight from the High School of Glasgow; and Midshipman Harry A Venables RNVR, from Cardiff, was eighteen years old. It is interesting, and noted without comment, that these five men required no fewer than three officers' stewards to attend them; one first class, one second and one third.

Such a wardroom was not unusual in these types of ships. There were not enough experienced men to go round, and there were many officers retained with the Grand Fleet. These young men had to fight the war for the Scandinavian trade.

Working under them on *Narborough* were three chiefs, the backbone of the ship. Forty-five seamen were led by Chief Petty Officer Walter Edward Cobb, and Chief Stoker John Marshall and Chief Engine Room Artificer James Till led the four artificers and twenty-six stokers. They would make the ship function, but the officers directed it, and on that day in January their judgement proved inadequate.

[*] *London Gazette* No 29507, 14 March 1916.

Diplomacy

The responsibility for dealing with the neutral states, Scandinavian and otherwise, lay with the Foreign Office and the Foreign Secretary. At the outbreak of war this was Sir Edward Grey, whose diplomatic focus was to try and maintain good relations with all the neutrals and especially with the USA. This led to constant tension with the Admiralty, who felt that their hands were being tied and that they were prevented from prosecuting the war in the most expeditious manner. Jellicoe's statement given at the beginning of Part One of this book shows that frustration.

However, Grey was more sinned against than sinning, for Britain needed vast amounts of supplies from the USA, as it did from Scandinavia. He had to 'hasten slowly' in trying to balance the needs of the country with the needs of war; and he was most concerned that Britain's Empire should not be threatened by American antagonism once war was over. In his autobiography he wrote that: 'In all this discussion of contraband with the United States we were like men who had to steer a ship through an uncharted seas, perilous with shoals and rocks and treacherous currents. We kept on our course and came safely through, but we had to feel our way and often go slow.'[19]

Gradually the power of the Foreign Office waned. Grey believed that wartime diplomacy should give way to military considerations; indeed, according to his biographer, 'he had no interest in military matters'.[20] The influence of the FO declined, perhaps as a result of the deterioration in Grey's health, and certainly from the advent of the Blockade Ministry headed by Lord Robert Cecil.

When Grey finally left office at the end of 1916 he was replaced by Arthur Balfour. It fell to Balfour to deal with the introduction of the USA into the war. Following the declaration of war by the USA on 6 April 1917, Balfour left for Washington five days later on what became known as the Balfour Mission. (One of his party was Rear Admiral Sir Dudley de Chair, last noted as an adviser to the Ministry of Blockade.)* Urbane, cultured and languidly polite, Balfour was the ideal person to treat with the philosopher-president, Woodrow Wilson, the world's self-appointed saviour. Arriving in Washington on the 22nd, via Halifax, where he had disembarked from RMS *Olympic* to be met by a special train, Balfour dined at the White

---

* De Chair had been British Naval Attaché in Washington between 1902 and 1905.

House on 30 April with Wilson and the president's confidante, Colonel House (Sancho Panza to Wilson's Don Quixote), and laid out the details of the secret treaties regarding Italy and the Near East to the President.

Balfour also addressed both houses of Congress – the House of Representatives on 4 May and the Senate on 8 May – becoming the first Englishman to do so.

The visit was a diplomatic success, and British ambassador Sir Cecil Spring-Rice stated that the mission had created an entirely new atmosphere in Anglo-American relations, adding: 'Mr Balfour's personal influence has been an asset of immense importance.'[21]

So diplomacy triumphed; but it was on the ground in Scandinavia that the practical contribution of the British diplomatic corps could be seen to best advantage. In Norway, Sir Mansfeldt de Cardonnel Findlay worked tirelessly to gain the maximum benefit for Britain from the Scandinavian trade. As his fellow diplomat Robert Bruce Lockhart described him, Findlay was 'one of the tallest Englishmen in the world and certainly the tallest man in diplomacy. He was a good organiser and, aided by Charles Brudenell-Bruce, ran his huge Legation (Christiania [sic], in peacetime a diplomatic backwater, had, owing to the blockade, the largest staff of any Legation or Embassy during the war with great efficiency.'[22])

The Times newspaper described his work in Findlay's obituary on 2 January 1933.

Christiania [sic], which up till 1914 was an extremely pleasant post for a Minister who happened to be fond of fishing, became on the outbreak of the War one of intense and arduous difficulty. The problem that increasingly dominated Findlay's work was the double problem of the blockade of Germany and the passage of goods in transit to Russia. The normal difficulties of exercising control over the imports into neutral countries so as to ensure that a surplus over and above their own needs did not go on to fatten Germany, a control that was resisted by all the neutrals and took years to perfect, were enormously increased in the Scandinavian countries by the fact, little realised by critics, that pressure by Great Britain was apt to provoke interference in the free transit to Russia of arms, munitions, and other essential war supplies. Findlay in Christiania [sic], like Howard in Stockholm, had to act with the greatest circumspection, and in his multifarious negotiations with the Norwegian Government, trade trusts, and individual firms, had to contrive to get the maximum harm done to German interests with the minimum harm to Russian and Allied interests.

The full effect of his work was understood by few people outside the Contraband Department of the Foreign Office. It was certainly not understood by the general public.[23]

Findlay's work was probably made more difficult by language difficulties. He spoke no Norwegian, and Foreign Minister Nils Claus Ihlen spoke no English. They communicated in the traditional language of diplomacy, French.

The work of the British Consul at Bergen, Captain Arthur Halsey, was also essential to the convoy system. As Admiral Jellicoe noted: 'The whole of the arrangements in regard to the working of the convoys, the issue of orders, etc, from the Norwegian side came under him and his staff … . The position was peculiar in that British naval officers were working in this manner in neutral country and it says much for the discretion of Captain Halsey and his staff that no difficulties occurred'.[24] A grateful nation awarded Halsey the CBE in 1919. He probably deserved more.

*　　*　　*

The management and protection of the Scandinavian trade turned out to be a multifaceted operation. Government, foreign relations, diplomacy and naval strategy had to move in close synchronisation, like a Swiss watch mechanism, to protect Britain's vital supply needs and deny them to Germany and her allies. It proved to be a long learning process, in which the bloody-minded perseverance of men such as Frederic Brock, David Beatty, Mansfeldt Findlay and, yes, Sir Edward Grey too, was necessary to see the game through.

In the end, however, it was mainly the British, Norwegian, Danish and Swedish sailors who made the sacrifices and provided the courage and bravery – or just quotidian stubbornness – that made the operation work. Whether Royal Navy or mercantile marine, theirs was the triumph and, if there was any, the glory.

CHAPTER 22

Envoi

Of course, 'The War To End All Wars' did not. The Treaty of Versailles left too many ends untied, and the reparations meant Germany had an unbearable and unpayable debt. By 1939 the world was at war once again.

History did not quite repeat itself. The Great Neutral, the USA, once again tried to sit out the fight, until Japan precipitated her into the war in December 1941, not before she had once again profited from others' misfortunes.

The Northern Neutrals also attempted to remain a dignified distance from the battle. Sweden succeeded, but not without compromising her principles to a degree unseen in the First World War.

The Swedish Government made concessions to both sides, and definitely breached the nation's neutrality in favour of both Germany and the Allies. As Patrick Salmon noted: 'Swedish neutrality was preserved largely by default'.[1] During the German invasion of the Soviet Union, Sweden allowed the Wehrmacht to use Swedish railways to transport the German 163rd Infantry Division, along with howitzers, tanks and anti-aircraft weapons and its associated ammunition, from Norway to Finland. German soldiers travelling on leave between Norway and Germany were allowed passage through Sweden; the so-called *permittenttrafik*. Iron ore was once again sold to Germany throughout the war. In an attempt at evenhandedness, Sweden shared military intelligence with the Allies and helped to train refugees from Denmark and Norway to fight in the liberation of their homelands. She also allowed the United States Army Air Force to use Swedish air bases between 1944 and 1945 for the repatriation of downed American and British airmen and the transfer to safe havens of Norwegian refugees. Other covert missions included delivering resistance fighters and OSS operatives.

Once again Sweden suffered from a Royal Navy blockade. Between 1938 and 1944 the Swedish imports of petroleum products and coal decreased by eighty-eight per cent and fifty-three per cent respectively. There were persistent shortages of food, and fuel and rationing was both widespread and punitive. Iron ore was once again exported to Germany and precision ball-bearings, critical for, *inter alia,* the aircraft industry, sold to both sides. It all seemed so familiar.

Norway was threatened from the start and did not manage to preserve her freedom. At the outbreak of war France and Britain developed a plan to cut off German supplies of Scandinavian iron ore. Churchill, back at the Admiralty as First Lord, was enthusiastic; 'nothing would be more deadly ... than to stop for three or even six months this export', he wrote, urging that Britain should 'violate Norwegian neutrality' and mine Norwegian waters.[2] Of course, as it transpired, the Germans got there first. Germany launched an invasion in April 1940 and controlled the country from then until the end of the war. Government was assumed by the *Reichskommissariat Norwegen*, which acted in concert with a pro-German puppet government, while the Norwegian King[*] and pre-war government escaped to London and formed a government in exile.

The economic impact of the occupation was harsh. Norway lost all its major trading partners except Germany. Production capacity largely remained intact, but the Germans appropriated and repatriated most of the output, less than half remaining for domestic consumption. This led to shortages of basic commodities and a risk of famine. Many Norwegians started growing their own crops and keeping their own livestock. City parks were divided among inhabitants, who grew potatoes, cabbage and other hardy vegetables. People kept small livestock in their houses and outhouses. Foraging and fishing were widespread. Black markets flourished, as did the production of ersatz substitutes.

Denmark also lost its independence, becoming first an associated and then an occupied territory under Germany. On 9 April 1940 Germany invaded Denmark in Operation *Weserübung* and established a *de facto* protectorate over the country. After an uneasy

[*] Still Haakon VII.

co-operation, on 29 August 1943 Germany imposed military occupation and rule, after the Danish government stepped down in a protest against German demands to institute the death penalty for sabotage together with other totalitarian measures.

Denmark lost its main trading partner, Britain, and the Danish economy was refocused on meeting German demands, for German domestic consumption. The Danish authorities took an active part in the development of, and even initiated negotiations on, a customs union. The blockade against Germany affected Denmark too, and rationing was widespread. Once again profiteers emerged; the renaissance of the 'Goulash Barons'.

Overall, as in the First World War, a declaration of individual or collective neutrality had failed both as a defensive or, indeed, offensive stance. To try to tackle this problem, in 1948 Sweden proposed a Scandinavian defence alliance, but the idea of a neutral Scandinavian bloc was, in reality, impractical from the start. There could be no doubt that the enemy Sweden wished to defend itself against was Soviet Russia, and none of the countries involved had sufficient military weight to withstand an attack from the East for very long. Such a grouping's sole function could only be to hold out long enough for Western support to arrive, and thus the association could not be neutral; it had to lean to the West. In a divided world, smaller countries must cleave to one power block or another. Thus Denmark and Norway preferred NATO's embrace to Swedish tutelage.

Neutrality was over. One cannot be friends to all without becoming friends to none.

APPENDIX 1

Gross Domestic Product and Trade

UK, Real GDP and GDP per head

	Real GDP at market prices £M	Real GDP per head at market prices £K
1815	36,630	1,954
1870	108,288	3,557
1900	188,105	4,715
1913	231,907	5,240

(Source: Bank of England 'Three Centuries Macroeconomic Dataset', v2.3, 30 June 2016)

Exports + Imports as a Percentage of GDP

	1870	1913
UK	43.6%	51.2%
France	23.6%	30.8%
Germany	36.8%	37.3%

(Source: Daudin G, Morys M, O'Rourke K, 'Globalisation 1870-1914', paper, University of Oxford, 2008)

APPENDIX 2

Absolute and Conditional Contraband Items as per the Treaty of London, 1909

Absolute Contraband

Art. 22. The following articles may, without notice, be treated as contraband of war, under the name of absolute contraband:

(1) Arms of all kinds, including arms for sporting purposes, and their distinctive component parts.

(2) Projectiles, charges, and cartridges of all kinds, and their distinctive component parts.

(3) Powder and explosives specially prepared for use in war.

(4) Gun-mountings, limber boxes, limbers, military waggons, field forges, and their distinctive component parts.

(5) Clothing and equipment of a distinctively military character.

(6) All kinds of harness of a distinctively military character.

(7) Saddle, draught, and pack animals suitable for use in war.

(8) Articles of camp equipment, and their distinctive component parts.

(9) Armour plates.

(10) Warships, including boats, and their distinctive component parts of such a nature that they can only be used on a vessel of war.

(11) Implements and apparatus designed exclusively for the manufacture of munitions of war, for the manufacture or repair of arms, or war material for use on land or sea.

Conditional Contraband

Art. 24. The following articles, susceptible of use in war as well as for purposes of peace, may, without notice, be treated as contraband of war, under the name of conditional contraband:

(1) Foodstuffs.

(2) Forage and grain, suitable for feeding animals.

(3) Clothing, fabrics for clothing, and boots and shoes, suitable for use in war.

(4) Gold and silver in coin or bullion; paper money.

(5) Vehicles of all kinds available for use in war, and their component parts.

(6) Vessels, craft, and boats of all kinds; floating docks, parts of docks and their component parts.

(7) Railway material, both fixed and rolling-stock, and material for telegraphs, wireless telegraphs, and telephones.

(8) Balloons and flying machines and their distinctive component parts, together with accessories and articles recognisable as intended for use in connection with balloons and flying machines.

(9) Fuel; lubricants.

(10) Powder and explosives not specially prepared for use in war.

(11) Barbed wire and implements for fixing and cutting the same.

(12) Horseshoes and shoeing materials.

(13) Harness and saddlery.

(14) Field glasses, telescopes, chronometers, and all kinds of nautical instruments.

Source: The International Committee of the Red Cross

Steam and Motor Merchant Tonnage owned by Selected Maritime Powers, 1914

Powers 1914, Gross Register Tons (GRT)

Country	Tonnage '000
Britain (inc. Dominions and Colonies)	20,524
Germany	5,135
USA (excl. Great Lakes)	2,070
France	1,922
Scandinavia	
Norway	1,957
Sweden	1,015
Denmark	770

Source: Fayle, *Seaborne Trade*, vol III p.469

Tonnage Losses to U-boats and Mines, Autumn 1916

Month	GRT
July	110,757
August	160,077
September	229,687
October	352,902
November	327,245

(Source: Jellicoe, *The Crisis of the Naval War*, p.4)

APPENDIX 5

Neutral Ships Lost in the Action of 17 October 1917

Ship	GRT	Cargo (where known)
Danish		
Margrethe	1,245	In ballast
Norwegian		
Dagbjorg	787	Pit props
Habil	636	Iron ore
Silja	1,231	Pit props
Sorhaug	1,007	General merchandise
Kristine	568	Wood pulp
Swedish		
Visbur	962	General merchandise
H Wicander	1,256	n/a
Stella	836	Iron ore and paper pulp

The British ships present were the SS *City of Cork* and SS *Ben Cleugh*, and the Belgian vessel was SS *Londonier*.

APPENDIX 6

Merchant Vessels Sunk in the *Pellew* and *Partridge* Action of 12 December 1917

Ship	GRT	Cargo (where known)
British *Cordova*	2,284	
Danish *Maracaibo*	526	
Norwegian *Bollsta* *Kong Magnus*	1,701 1,101	Probably salt meat
Swedish *Torlief* *Bothnia*	832 1,723	1,000 tons coal for Gothenburg

APPENDIX 7

US Navy Planning Section View of Aerial Escort

In early 1918 Admiral William Sowden Sims, in charge of all US naval forces in Europe, asked his Planning Section to study the use of aircraft as convoy escorts. The American planners worked closely with the Admiralty Plans Division and used much of its data. In a report dated 15 February, the Planning Section reported back and drew some important conclusions.

They deduced that, since the speed of a convoy rarely if ever exceeded 10 knots, and the speed of an aircraft was over four times as great, the efficient range of an aircraft for escort was only thirty miles for a slow convoy and fifty miles for a fast one, and, as they could not fly in poor weather, the use of aircraft was a poor method of protection.

The lower speeds of dirigibles made them superficially more attractive. However, the fact that they were less manoeuvrable, more vulnerable and less well suited to attack than aeroplanes, led them to rule out airships too.

As a result the planners stated: 'Neither dirigibles nor heavier-than-air machines should be designated for this duty [convoy escort], although they may be employed as escorts on special occasions.'[1]

However, they came down heavily in favour of kite balloons. Their advantages included the facts that 'the distance patrolled equals the distance advanced by the convoy during daylight hours – fog neglected', and 'a surface vessel can be directed with precision towards any object sighted'. Analysis demonstrated that 'vessels in a convoy escorted by two kite balloon vessels were three times as safe from attack as when they are not so escorted'. As a consequence it was recommended 'to use kite balloons for escort and patrol duty where practicable'.[2]

The Admiralty, in the use of *Peel Castle* and other such ships, was therefore in line with best practice as identified by the USN.

APPENDIX 8

Scandinavian Convoys
28 April 1917 to 18 January 1918

Eastbound, westbound and coastal convoys until the transfer of the western hub to Methil.

Convoy	Ship numbers
Eastbound Conveyed Sunk Damaged	1,617 17 0
Westbound Conveyed Sunk Damaged	1,806 23 2
East Coast Northbound Conveyed Sunk Damaged	2,179 15 3
Southbound Conveyed Sunk Damaged	1,475 19 1

(Source; ADM 137/2660, National Archives)

Author's Notes

So the story ends. This is my seventh book on the Royal Navy of World War One, and I am still amazed by the quotidian bravery and commitment shown by the officers and men who served through the conflict. We continue to owe them a debt of gratitude which can never be repaid. Some of them, of course, had to do it all over again as Britain failed to learn the lessons that should have been etched on to politicians' and the public's minds alike. The Great War Royal Navy never lost command of the sea, although it was a close-run thing on occasion. And command of the sea gave Britain dominion over its own, and the enemy's, supply lines. Germany was slowly strangled into submission as a result.

Admiral David Beatty emerges from this story with credit. In the unending Jellicoe vs Beatty debate I had always been a Jellicoe man, but writing this book showed me that there was more to Beatty than is often acknowledged. It is clear that without his support and drive the Scandinavian convoys would conceivably never have come about or, at least, would have happened later and with less impact than they did.

The timescale covered by this book is more than 100 years away from the contemporary reader. It is sometimes difficult to get a 'flavour' of the times and the social structure. During the narrative I have tried to give people their full names; firstly because they deserve it, and secondly because there is a euphony to them, especially those which have now passed out of fashion. But also because I think it gives a better feel for the period, and emphasises how many of the Royal Navy's officer class came from the aristocracy or gentry; the profusion of double or triple family-derived namings illustrates this well.

The story has been told from a largely British prospective and mainly (but not solely, see bibliography) using Anglophone sources. However, it is informed by wide reading of academic books on Scandinavia in the period, and the work of Patrick Salmon (now the Chief Historian at the Foreign and Commonwealth Office but previously Professor of International History at the University of Newcastle) proved particularly useful.

As a writer of historical works in the UK, one is helped immensely both by the quality and the availability of archives and by the skill of the archivists who manage them. To the staff and trustees of the following institutions I owe a debt of thanks. The National Archives, Kew; the Imperial War Museum, London; the British Library, London; the Churchill Archive, Churchill College, Cambridge; the National Maritime Museum, Greenwich; the University of Edinburgh; and the Liddle Collection, Leeds University Library (Special Collections). In addition, those who maintain on-line resources, such as the incomparable http://www.naval-history.net deserve my gratitude. A special word of thanks is merited for the tribe of secondhand book sellers who provide out-of-print editions of all sorts of valuable source volumes.

Dr Ian Tait, Curator of the Shetland Museum and Archive, was kind enough to find some first-hand accounts of the travails of merchant ships around Lerwick for me, and relevant pictures from their photographic collection. It is not the first time that Ian has been of assistance, and I thank him. David MacKie, Senior Archivist at Orkney Library and Archive,was also helpful in tracking down rare photographs.

This is my fourth book published by Seaforth Publishing, and I thank Julian Mannering of that esteemed house for his continued support and sage advice. The index was once again prepared by the indefatigable Dave Cradduck, with his usual skill and promptitude.

Most books contain errors of commission or omission. If there are errors or solecisms in this volume the fault is mine, and I should like to hear of them. To err is human.

My friends in both Britain and France are by now inured to my peculiar passion for the Royal Navy in World War One, and thankfully bear my enthusiasms stoically. Finally, very many thanks to Vivienne for her help, support and belief, without which this book – or, indeed, any of my others – would not have been completed.

Steve R Dunn
Worcestershire

Notes

Sources
The following abbreviations will be used for brevity:

Institutions
BL: British Library, London.
CAC: Churchill Archive, Churchill College, Cambridge.
IWM: Imperial War Museum, London.
LC: Liddle Collection, Brotherton Library, University of Leeds.
NA: National Archives, Kew.
NMM: National Maritime Museum, Greenwich.

Books
FTDTSF: Marder, *From the Dreadnought to Scapa Flow* vols I–V.
FTGWAS: Friedman, *Fighting the Great War at Sea*.
NO: *Naval Operations, The History of the Great War based on Official Documents,* vols I–V.
SATGP: Salmon, *Scandinavia and the Great Powers.*
SITFWW: Ahlund, *Scandinavia in the First World War.*

It is the convention that page numbers be given for citations. This is not always possible in the modern world. Some digitised documents lack page numbering and some archives hold unnumbered single or multiple sheets in bundles under one reference or none at all. Thus, page numbers will be given where possible, but the reader will understand that they are not always available or, indeed, necessary.

Chapter 1
1. Clarke, *Locomotive of War*, p.9.
2. Friedman *FTGWAT,* p.12.
3. Winchester, *Atlantic*, p.245.

Chapter 2
1. Knutsen, *Norway in the First World War,* p.44.
2. Ahlund, SITFFW p.201.

3. Ibid, p.209).
4. Bruce-Lockhart, *Memoirs of a British Agent*, p.216.
5. Salmon, *SATGP*, p.59.
6. ADM 137/500/1, NA.
7. Ibid.
8. Ibid.
9. Ibid.

Chapter 3
1. NO, vol 1, p.39.
2. CHAR 13/36/49, CAC.
3. Ibid.
4. Diary 15 Sep 1914, docs 12222, IWM.
5. Salmon, *SATGP*, p.123.
6. www.navalhistory.dk/English/History/ 1914_1918/TheNavy_1914_18.htm.
7. Salmon, *SATGP*, p.124.
8. CHAR 13/40/55, CAC.
9. CHAR 13/42/115, CAC.
10. *Daily Telegraph*, 6 Oct 1914.
11. Newspaper cutting 5 Jan 1915, Salvesen Archive Coll-36 1st tranche, News-cutting Album, H27. Univ of Edinburgh.
12. Salmon, *SATGP*, p.129.
13. ADM 137/500/1 15 Mar 1915, NA.
14. Ibid, 25 Mar 1915, NA.

Chapter 4
1. King-Hall, *My Naval Life*, p.98.
2. Marder, *Fear God and Dread Nought*, vol 2, p.505).
3. Churchill, *The World Crisis*, vol 2, p.280.
4. Diary 16 Oct 1914, docs 12165, IWM.
5. Naval Monograph XIII, p.29.
6. CHAR 13/61/56, CAC.
7. NO vol 2 p.404.
8. CHAR 13/64/49, CAC.
9. CAB 37/124/39, letter 20 Feb 1915, NA.
10. Ibid.
11. ADM 196/46/130, NA.
12. CHAR 13/61/76, CAC.
13. ADM 137/3603, NA.
14. Ibid.
15. Ibid.
16. Ibid.
17. NO vol 3, p.143.

Chapter 5

1. Docs 22, box 3, IWM.
2. Salmon, *SATGP*, p.135.
3. Grey to Louise Creighton, 9 Aug 1914, MS Eng.lett.e.73, Bodleian Library.
4. Bruce-Lockhart, *Memoirs of a British Agent*, p.47.
5. Marder, *FDTSF* vol 2, p.375.
6. Lambert, *Admirals*, p.349.
7. Marder, *Portrait of an Admiral*, p.198.
8. De Chair, *The Sea is Strong*, p.206.
9. Kipling, *Sea Warfare*, p.66.
10. *Spectator*, 25 May 1923.
11. Grey to Lansing, 24 Apr 1916, https://history.state.gov/historicaldocuments/frus1916Supp/d481.
12. https://history.state.gov/historicaldocuments/frus1916Supp/d451.

Chapter 6

1. Consett, *The Triumph of Unarmed Forces*, p.viii.
2. Ibid, p.80.
3. *Morning Post*, 19 Jan 1916.
4. Ibid.
5. *Hansard*, HL Deb 26 Jan 1916 vol 20 cc1025-36.
6. Ibid.
7. Ibid.
8. Ibid.
9. *Indianapolis News*, 26 Jan 1916.
10. Ibid.
11. Philpott, *Attrition*, p.200.
12. https://history.state.gov/historicaldocuments/frus1916Supp/d452.

Chapter 7

1. *Shetland Times*, 1 Mar 1919.
2. Keilhau, *Norway and the World War*, p.335.
3. Consett, *The Triumph of Unarmed Forces*, p.114.
4. Ibid, p.113.
5. Greenhalgh, *Victory thro Coalition*, p.109.
6. 29 Sep 1914, docs 7907, IWM.
7. Ibid, 2 Oct 1914.
8. Ibid, 6 Oct 1914.
9. Ibid.
10. Ibid, 2 Oct 1914.
11. Ibid, 13 Oct 1914.
12. Jellicoe, *The Crisis of the Naval War*, p.190.
13. Hepper, *British Warship Losses*, p.56.

14. https://southamptoncenotaph.com/william-henry-john-chaplow/.
15. Lambert, *Admirals*, p.327.
16. Ibid, p.322.
17. Halpern, *A Naval History*, p.103.
18. Avedian, *The Armenian Genocide 1915 From a Neutral Small State's Perspective*, p.21.
19. King-Hall diary, 4 Sep 1916.
20. Ibid, 14 Feb 1917.

Chapter 8

1. ADM 137/2660, NA.
2. Jellicoe, *The Crisis of the Naval War*, p.120.
3. *Tidens Tegn*, 10 Oct 1916.
4. Riste, *The Neutral Ally*, p.139.
5. ADM 137/500/1, NA.
6. Naval Monograph vol XVII Part VII p.191.
7. Naval Monograph vol XVII Part VI p.159.
8. Halpern, *A Naval History*, p.352.
9. Naval Monograph vol XVII Part VI p.159.
10. Roskill, *The Naval Air Service*, p.xiv.
11. Cameron, *1916*, p.96.
12. Roskill, *The Naval Air Service*, p.xiii.
13. King-Hall, *My Naval Life*, p.222.
14. ADM 203/99, ADM 203/100, NA.
15. Letter 20 Nov 1916, Add. Mss. 49692. ff. 175-178, BL.
16. Salmon, *SATGP*, p.141.
17. Cameron, *1916*, p.163.

Chapter 9

1. CAB 1/22 fl1-2, NA.
2. von Bernstorff to Robert Lansing, 31 January 1917, www.firstworldwar.com.
3. Diary 1 Feb 1917, docs 4643, IWM.
4. *Hansard,* HC Deb 01 Mar 1917 vol 90 cc2118-9.
5. *Daily Telegraph*, 24 Feb 1917.
6. *Hansard*, HC Deb 30 Mar 1917 vol 92 c755.

Chapter 10

1. ADM 137/1322, NA.
2. Ibid.
3. Ibid.
4. Ibid.
5. Ibid.
6. Ibid.
7. Ibid.

8. ADM 137/2660 22 Jan 1919, NA.
9. Jellicoe, *The Crisis of the Naval War*, p.121.
10. ADM 196/87/55, NA.
11. Diary 10 Jun 1916, DFF/15, NMM.
12. Jellicoe, *The Crisis of the Naval War*, p.23.
13. Marder, *FTDTSF*, vol IV, p.141.
14. ADM 137/2660, 22 Jan 1919, NA.
15. ADM 137/1322, NA.
16. ADM 137/1322, 14 Apr 1917, NA.
17. Marder, *FTDTSF*, vol IV p.143.
18. Monographs XVII, part VII, p.374.
19. Winton, *Jellicoe*, p.247.
20. Jellicoe, *The Crisis of the Naval War*, p.22.
21. Ibid, p.122.
22. ADM 137/3704, NA.
23. ADM 137/1322, NA.
24. Marder, *FTDTSF*, vol IV, p.144.
25. Jellicoe, *The Crisis of the Naval War*, p.110.
26. ADM 137/1322, NA.
27. ADM 137/2660, NA.
28. Jellicoe, *The Crisis of the Naval War*, p.123.
29. Monographs XIX part IX, p.112.
30. ADM 137/1322, NA.
31. Ibid.
32. 'Taffrail', *Endless Story*, p.270.
33. *The First World War in Shetland.*
34. ADM 203/99, NA.
35. Jellicoe, *The Crisis of the Naval War*, p.191.
36. ADM 196/50/214, NA.

Chapter 11
1. Fayle, *Seaborne Trade*, vol III, p.467.
2. NO, vol V, pp.21–4.
3. Fayle, *Seaborne Trade*, vol III p.467.
4. Knutsen, *Norway in the First World War*, p.55.
5. AMER1/3/50, CAC.
6. Ibid.
7. Marder, *Portrait of an Admiral*, p.264.
8. Marder, *FTDTSF*, vol IV p.252.
9. Ibid, p.253.
10. Ahlund, *SITFWW*, p.33.
11. ADM 137/500/1, NA.
12. Ibid, 11 Oct 1916, NA.
13. *Daily Telegraph*, 29 Aug 1917.
14. Ibid 28 Aug 1917.
15. Salmon, *SATGP*, p.144.

16. Ibid, p.145.

Chapter 12
1. ADM 137/3675, NA.
2. Monographs XIX, p.270.
3. Halpern, *A Naval History of World War 1*, p.367.
4. Ibid, p.368.
5. Diary 31 May 1917, docs 12165, IWM.
6. Ibid 1 Jun 1917.
7. Ibid 19 Jun 1917.
8. Ibid 23 Jul 1917.
9. Ibid.
10. *Daily Telegraph*, 25 Jun 1917.
11. ADM 137/2660, NA.
12. *Shetland Times*, 7 Jun 1919.
13. ADM 137/3709, NA.
14. Ibid.
15. ADM 137/1322, NA.
16. Docs 24346, p11, IWM.
17. Mouat, 'With the WRNS 1914–18', *New Shetlander*, 107, (1974), pp.23–5.
18. Docs 24346, p.11, IWM.

Chapter 13
1. Ramsay, *Blinker Hall*, p.237.
2. ADM 196/49/48, NA.
3. *The Times*, 14 Feb 1918.
4. Ibid.
5. *The Scotsman*, 22 Oct 1917.
6. Ibid.
7. Marder, *FTDTSF*, vol IV, p.298.
8. *The Scotsman*, 22 Oct 1917.
9. Diary 26 Oct 1917, docs 12735, IWM.
10. *The Scotsman*, 22 Oct 1917.
11. Letter 2 Nov 1917, docs 753, IWM.
12. Letter 7 Nov 1917, Ibid.
13. ADM 137/3723, NA.
14. Ibid.
15. Ibid.
16. Ibid.
17. Ibid.
18. Ibid.
19. Marder, *FTDTSF*, vol IV p.297.
20. ADM 137/3723, NA.
21. Marder, *FTDTSF*, vol IV p.334.
22. *Daily Telegraph*, 2 Nov 1917.
23. Ibid.
24. Ibid.
25. *Evening Standard*, 21 Apr 1920.
26. *The Queenslander*, 10 Nov 1917.
27. NO, vol V p.155.
28. Roskill, *Earl Beatty*, p.234.

29. Ibid p.235.
30. NO, vol V, p.184.

Chapter 14
1. ADM 137/3303, NA.
2. CAB 23/4/28, NA.
3. ADM 137/3303, NA.
4. Ibid.
5. Ibid.
6. Ibid.
7. Private collection.
8. NO, vol V p.159.
9. NO, vol V p.185.
10. NO, vol V p.187.
11. de Courcy-Ireland, *A Naval Life*, p.49.
12. *Stoke Sentinel*, 20 Apr 2015.
13. Diary 17 Dec 1917, docs 12735, IWM.
14. ADM 137/3744, NA.
15. CAB 23/4/72, NA.
16. CAB 23/5/11, NA.
17. Winton, *Jellicoe*, p.256.
18. 18 Dec 1917, ADM 137/3744, NA.
19. Ibid.
20. 21 Dec 1917, Ibid.
21. Letter 25 Dec 1917, JJ to Bacon, held in private collection.

Chapter 15
1. Fayle, *Seaborne Trade*, vol 3, p.253.
2. ADM 137/2752, NA.
3. ADM 137/2637, NA.
4. Ibid.
5. ADM 137/3726, NA.
6. Docs 12735, p.173, IWM.
7. Letter 31 Dec 1917, docs 26101, IWM.
8. ADM 137/3726, NA.
9. Bruce-Lockhart, *Memoirs of a British Agent*, p.201.
10. Milton, *Russian Roulette*, p.70.
11. Diary 16 Jan 1918, docs 12137, IWM.
12. ADM 137/1894, 97-99, NA.
13. Ibid.
14. Ibid, 100.
15. Ibid, 103.
16. ADM 1/8522/112, NA.

Chapter 16
1. Roskill, *Earl Beatty*, p.257.
2. Ibid, p.259.
3. Marder, *FTDTSF*, vol V p.150.
4. Halpern P, *Relevance*, Spring 2004, Volume Thirteen, Number Two.

Chapter 17
1. 'Taffrail', *Endless Story*, p.278.
2. *The Times*, 17 Dec 1919.
3. LIDDLE/WW1/RNMN/REC/015, LC.
4. Furbringer, *Fips – Legendary U-boat Commander*, pp.118–121.
5. Diary 24/25 Aug 1914, docs 1222, IWM.
6. Diary 6 Jul 1916, docs 4643, IWM.
7. Taylor, *Dazzle*, p.27.
8. ADM 137/2660, NA.
9. Abbatiello, *Anti-Submarine Warfare*, p.15.
10. Roskill, *The Naval Air Service*, p.545.
11. Docs 24346, p.15, IWM.
12. Ibid.
13. Abbatiello, *Anti-Submarine Warfare*, p.116.
14. Turpin, *Coastal Patrol*, p.257.
15. http://www.isle-of-man.com/manxnotebook/fulltext/mf1923/p18.htm.

Chapter 18
1. Rockhoff H, EH.net.
2. Ibid.
3. *Chicago Tribune*, 9 Sep 1917.
4. Ibid.
5. Ibid.
6. Ibid.
7. Ibid.
8. Ahlund, *SITFWW*, p.39.
9. Salmon, *SATGP*, p.144.
10. Freidman, *FGWAS*, p.343.
11. Add. Mss.49714, BL.
12. ADM 116/1616, NA.
13. ADM 137/3737, NA.
14. ADM 116/1616, NA.
15. ADM 137/3737, NA.
16. Ibid.
17. 13 Jun 1918, docs 12735, IWM.
18. de Courcy-Ireland, *A Naval Life*, p.50.
19. Ibid.
20. Ibid, p.52.
21. Marder, *FTDTSF*, vol V p.67.
22. 11 Feb 1918, ADM 137/2707, NA.
23. Marder, *FTDTSF*, vol V p.71.
24. Ibid.
25. Ibid, p.72.
26. 20 Aug 1918, ADM 137/2752, NA.
27. Halpern, *A Naval History of World War I*, p.424.
28. Diary entries, docs 12137, IWM.
29. Ibid.

30. ADM 196/154/23, NA.
31. Roskill, *Earl Beatty*, p.272.
32. *Stornaway Gazette* at https://lewis-lost-ww1.blogspot.co.uk/2012/07/donald-macdonald-10-holm.html.
33. Hattersley, *David Lloyd George*, p.475.
34. *Shetland Times*, 16 Nov 1918.
35. Roskill, *Earl Beatty*, p.275.
36. Ibid.
37. Diary 11 Nov 1918, docs 12137, IWM.
38. de Courcy-Ireland, *A Naval Life*, p.54.
39. LIDDLE/WW1/RNMN/REC/015, LC.
40. Ibid.
41. Armistice terms, part V, clause 32.
42. Letter 9 Jan 1919, Salvesen Archive. Coll-36 1st tranche, letter book, A77, Univ of Edinburgh.

Chapter 19
1. NO, vol 2 p.403.
2. 22 Jan 1919, ADM 137/2660, NA.
3. Jackstaff, *The Dover Patrol*, p.180.
4. Ibid.
5. 'Taffrail', *Endless Story*, p.263.
6. Ibid, p.12.
7. Ibid, p.263.
8. de Courcy-Ireland, *A Naval Life*, p.48.
9. 12 Oct 1917, docs 12735, IWM.
10. Letter 9 Jan 1918, docs 26101, IWM.
11. 'Taffrail', *Endless Story*, p.15.
12. LIDDLE/WW1/RNMN/REC/015, LC.
13. King-Hall, *My Naval Life*, p.108.
14. Brock to Beatty 23 Jan 1918, ADM 137/1448, NA.
15. Letter 11 Sep 1917, docs 261010, IWM.
16. Letter 9 Jan 1918, docs 26101, IWM.
17. Turpin, *Coastal Patrol*, p.63.
18. Diary entries, docs 12137, IWM.
19. 27 Feb 1918, docs 12735, IWM.
20. Ibid.
21. Diary 16 Sep 1916, docs 4643, IWM.
22. White, *Zeppelin Nights*, p.82.
23. de Courcy-Ireland, *A Naval Life*, p.47.
24. Ibid.
25. Oral History 12243, IWM.
26. de Courcy-Ireland, *A Naval Life*, p.48.
27. Diary 10 Nov 1917, docs 12735, IWM.
28. Ibid, 30 Nov 1917.
29. Ibid, 23 Apr 1918.
30. Docs 4643, IWM.
31. Ibid.
32. Ibid.

33. Ibid, 7 Sep 1918.
34. Ibid, 27-31 Oct 1918.
35. Diary 14 Mar 1917, docs16886, IWM.
36. ADM 137/2660, 22 Jan 1919, NA.
37. ADM 137/3744, NA.

Chapter 20
1. Ahlund, *SITFWW*, p.11.
2. Ibid, p.329.
3. ADM 1/8510/13, NA.
4. Diary 27 Nov 1916, docs 4643, IWM.
5. Diary 10 Aug 1918, docs 12137, IWM.

Chapter 21
1. Gregory, *The Last Great War*, Introduction.
2. Keynes, *Essays in Biography*, p.12.
3. Churchill, *World Crisis*, vol 1 p.929.
4. Scott, *Sweden, the Nation's History*, p.477.
5. Heckscher, *Economic History of Sweden*, p.273.
6. Bruce-Lockhart, *Memoirs of a British Agent*, p.212.
7. Hattersley, *David Lloyd George*, p.434.
8. ADM 137/2864, NA.
9. Ibid.
10. Hough, *The Great War at Sea*, p.306.
11. de Groot, *Back to Blighty*, p.61.
12. Ibid.
13. Crawford, *Fallen Glory*, p.84.
14. Diary 15 May 1917, RIC/1/15, NMM.
15. Marder, *FTDTSF*, vol V, p.85.
16. Ibid.
17. Ibid, p.86.
18. From Admiralty 'Pink Lists'.
19. Waterhouse, *Edwardian Requiem*, p.370.
20. Ibid, p.354.
21. Egremont, *Balfour*, p.289.
22. Bruce-Lockhart, *Memoirs of a British Agent*, p.212.
23. *The Times*, 2 Jan 1933.
24. Jellicoe, *The Crisis of the Naval War*, pp.124–5.

Chapter 22
1. Salmon, *SATGP*, p.362.
2. ADM 205/2 17 Nov 1939, NA.

Appendix 7
1. *Naval Air Service*, p.630.
2. Ibid, pp.631–2.

Bibliography

The following books have been cited in the main text. The place of publication is London unless otherwise stated.

Abbatiello, J, *Anti-Submarine Warfare in World War 1*, Routledge (2006)

Ahlund, C (ed), *Scandinavia in the First World War*, Nordic Academic Press (Lund, 2012)

Bruce-Lockhart, R, *Memoirs of a British Agent*, Putnam (1932)

Cameron, J, *1916, Year of Decision*, Oldbourne (1962)

Churchill, W, *The World Crisis vol 1 & 2*, Thornton Butterworth (1923)

Clarke, P, *The Locomotive of War*, Bloomsbury (2017)

Consett, M, *The Triumph of Unarmed Forces*, Williams and Norgate (1923)

Conrad, J, *Notes on Life and Letters* (1921), republished Floating Press (2011)

Corbett, J and Newbolt, H, *Naval Operations, The History of the Great War based on Official Documents, vols I–V*, republished Naval and Military Press and Imperial War Museum (2014)

Crawford, J, *Fallen Glory*, Old St Publishing (2016)

De Chair, D, *The Sea is Strong*, George G Harrap and Co (1961)

De Courcy-Ireland, S B, *A Naval Life*, Englang Publishing (1990)

De Groot, G, *Back in Blighty*, Vintage (2014)

Egremont, M, *Balfour,* Phoenix (1998), originally published 1980

Evans, R, *The Pursuit of Power*, Allan Lane (2016)

Fayle, C E, *Seaborne Trade*, vols I-III, John Murray (1924), republished Naval and Military Press (Sussex, undated)

Friedman, N, *Fighting the Great War at Sea*, Seaforth Publishing (Barnsley, 2014)

Fürbringer, W, trans Brooks, G, *Fips – Legendary U-boat Commander*, United States Naval Inst (Annapolis, 2000).

Greenhalgh, E, *Victory through Coalition*, Cambridge University Press (Cambridge, 2005)

Gregory, A, *The Last Great War*, Cambridge University Press (Cambridge, 2008)

Halpern, P, *A Naval History of World War 1*, UCL Press Ltd (1994)

Hattersley, R, *David Lloyd George*, Abacus (2012)

Heckscher, E, *An Economic History of Sweden*, Harvard University Press (Cambridge, Mass, 1954)

Hepper, D, *British Warship Losses in the Ironclad Era*, Chatham Publishing (2006)

Hough, R, *The Great War at Sea*, OUP (Oxford, 1986)

'Jackstaff', *The Dover Patrol,* Grant Richards (1919)

Jellicoe, J, *The Crisis of the Naval War*, George H Doran Company (New York, 1920)

Keilhau, W, 'Norway and the World War', in Heckscher, E (ed) *Sweden, Norway Denmark and Iceland in the World War*, Yale University Press

(New Haven, 1930)

Keynes, J M, *Essays in Biography*, Harcourt, Brace and Company (New York, 1933)

King-Hall, S, *My Naval Life*, Faber and Faber (1951)

Kipling, R, *Sea Warfare*, Uniform Press (2015), original edition published 1915

Lambert, A, *Admirals*, Faber and Faber (2008)

Marder, A, *Fear God and Dread Nought*, vol II, Jonathan Cape (1952)

Marder, A, *From the Dreadnought to Scapa Flow*, vol II, OUP (1965), vol IV, V, Seaforth Publishing (Barnsley, 2014)

Marder, A, *Portrait of an Admiral*, Harvard University Press (Cambridge, Mass, 1952)

Maynard, C, *The Murmansk Venture*, Hodder and Stoughton (1928)

Milton, G, *Russian Roulette*, Sceptre (2013)

Philpott, W, *Attrition*, Abacus (2014)

Ramsay, D, *'Blinker' Hall, Spymaster*, Spellmount Ltd (Stroud, 2008)

Riste, O, *The Neutral Ally. Norway's relations with belligerent powers in the First World War*, Universitetsforlaget (Oslo, 1965)

Roskill, S, *Earl Beatty*, Collins (1980)

Roskill, S (ed), *The Naval Air Service, volume 1, 1908-1918*, Navy Records Society (1969)

Salmon, P, *Scandinavia and the Great Powers*, Cambridge University Press, (Cambridge, 1997)

Scott, F, *Sweden, the Nation's History*, SIU Press (Illinois,1988)

'Taffrail', *Endless Story*, Hodder & Stoughton (1938)

Taylor, J, *Dazzle*, Pool of London Press (2016)

Turpin, B, *Coastal Patrol*, Fonthill Media (2016)

Waterhouse, M, *Edwardian Requiem*, Biteback Publishing Ltd (2013)

White, J, *Zeppelin Nights*, Vintage (2015)

Winchester, S, *Atlantic*, Harper Press (2011)

Winton, J, *Jellicoe*, Michael Joseph (1981)

Archival Documents

Churchill Archive, Char 13, Churchill College, Cambridge

Private papers of Leopold Amery, AMEL 1/3/50, Churchill Archive, Churchill College

Hampshire papers, Docs 22, Imperial War Museum, London

Private papers of L Story, Docs 26101, Imperial War Museum

Private papers of C Budden, Docs 12137, Imperial War Museum

Private papers of Captain C de Burgh, Docs 12165, Imperial War Museum

Private papers of Admiral A Paget, Docs 7907, Imperial War Museum

Private papers of Lieutenant Commander (E) W Cleghorn, Docs 752, Imperial War Museum

Private papers of Commander K R Walker RNVR, Docs 13075, Imperial War Museum

Private papers of Commander George Plunkett England, Docs 16886, Imperial War Museum

Private papers of Captain H W Williams, Docs 12735, Imperial War Museum

Private Papers of Captain Charles Poignand, Docs 4643, Imperial war Museum

History of Lerwick base, Docs 24346, Imperial War Museum
Oral History 12243, Imperial War Museum
MS Eng.lett.e.73, Bodleian Library, Oxford
Balfour Papers, Add. MSS. 49692, 49714, British Library, London
Salvesen Archive, Coll-36, University of Edinburgh
Richmond MSS, RIC/1/15, National Maritime Museum, Greenwich
Duff Papers, DFF/15, National Maritime Museum
Oral History, Harry Chadwick-Smith, Liddle Collection, Brotherton Library, University of Leeds
Various files in the ADM and CAB series, The National Archives, Kew

Newspapers and Magazines
Chicago Tribune
Daily Telegraph
Evening Standard
Flight
Hansard
Indianapolis News
London Gazette
Morning Post
New Shetlander
Relevance, the Quarterly Journal of the Great War Society
Scotsman
Shetland Times
Shetland News
Spectator
Stoke Sentinel
Stornaway Gazette
The Queenslander (Brisbane)
The Times
Tidens Tegn (Norway)

On-line Resources
http://www.kinghallconnections.com/
Economic History Association online, USA.
Manx Notebook

Royal Navy Historical Section
Naval Staff Monographs volume XIII, part IV (October 1925)
Naval Staff Monographs volume XVII, part VII (October 1927)
Naval Staff Monographs volume XIX part IX (August 1939)

Other
The Armenian Genocide 1915 From a Neutral Small State's Perspective: PhD thesis by Vahagn Avedian, University of Uppsala, Sweden, 2008
The First World War in Shetland, Shetland Libraries, 2014
Daudin, G, Morys M, O'Rourke, K, *Globalisation 1870-1914*, paper, University of Oxford, 2008
Knutsen, J N, 'Norway in the First World War', published in *Folia Scandinavica*, vol 5, Poznan 1999

Index